Following Dignity

7 Guiding Principles of Short-Term Missions

Terri Taylor & Stephen Sickel

Copyright © 2025 by The Foundry Publishing

The Foundry Publishing®
PO Box 419527
Kansas City, MO 64141
thefoundrypublishing.com

978-0-8341-4389-0

All rights reserved. No part of this publication may be reproduced, stored in a retrieval system, or transmitted in any form or by any means—for example, electronic, photocopy, recording—without the prior written permission of the publisher. The only exception is brief quotations in printed reviews.

Interior design: Sharon Page

All Scripture quotations, unless indicated, are taken from THE HOLY BIBLE, NEW INTERNATIONAL VERSION®, NIV®. Copyright © 1973, 1978, 1984, 2011 by Biblica, Inc.® Used by permission. All rights reserved worldwide.

Scripture quotations marked (NLT) are from the *Holy Bible*, New Living Translation (NLT), copyright © 1996, 2004, 2015. Used by permission of Tyndale House Publishers, Inc., Wheaton, Illinois 60189. All rights reserved.

Scripture quotations marked (NKJV) are from the *New King James Version* (NKJV). Copyright © 1979, 1980, 1982, Thomas Nelson, Inc. Used by permission. All rights reserved.

Published in cooperation with Nazarene Missions Teams.

The internet addresses, email addresses, and phone numbers in this book are accurate at the time of publication. They are provided as a resource. The Foundry Publishing does not endorse them or vouch for their content or permanence.

Connecting the church by laying down self to build transformational relationships

Your ordinary acts of love and hope
point to the extraordinary promise
that every human life is of
inestimable value.
—Desmond Tutu

Contents

Preface	7
The Seven Principles	11
Our Call to Follow Dignity	15
How to Use This Book	19
The Journey	23
Principle 1: Dignity	29
Principle 2: Hospitality	51
Principle 3: Culture	73
Principle 4: Learning Posture	115
Principle 5: Relationship	139
Principle 6: Expectations	191
Principle 7: Spirituality	229
Conclusion: Following the Call to Dignity	271
Defining Terms	273
About the Authors	285

Preface

*So in Christ we, though many,
form one body, and each member
belongs to all the others.*
—Romans 12:5

This book, as is true with so many good things, grew out of years' worth of Spirit-led conversations in multiple countries. The idea of healthy short-term missions that help propel the kingdom of God forward was a theme that seemed to reemerge every time our missions-minded friends and colleagues got together over a cup of coffee.

Terri and I (Stephen) served in similar roles on different continents, coordinating short-term teams to join with established churches and districts to advance the vision God had given them for their communities. Terri and her husband, Greg, served as missionaries in Guatemala and in the Asia-Pacific Region while my family served in Central America and Mexico. When we had a chance to be together at various missions-oriented events, I noticed and appreciated the markedly respectful way Terri and Greg spoke about the people they served alongside.

As missionaries do, we also shared stories about the teams we had hosted over the years. There are teams that make you smile, some that are more of a learning experience, and some with great intentions who have perhaps not received much preparation.

Recognizing that short-term missions often serves as a launching point into a lifetime of ministry—not only for missionaries but also for pastors and missions-minded laypeople—two important thoughts came out of one late-night conversation in Terri and

Greg's kitchen: (1) the need to offer teams more than an opportunity to serve, but to train team members in healthy missiological principles right from the start—on their very first mission trip—by providing practical tools that they can use in any future avenue of Christian service, and (2) even more importantly, for those with a strong desire to serve in missions but with little experience, short-term missions could very well serve as a true first-steps training ground for those who are feeling called.

Fast-forward a few years to when Terri and I had both shifted to roles that brought our families to the U.S.—I was leading the Nazarene short-term missions program, Nazarene Missions Teams, and Terri was a key trainer for Nazarene missionary candidates. We went back to that long-ago conversation and realized we had a chance to help missionary candidates, teams, local churches, and districts think differently about how the church works together in short-term missions. We talked weekly—sometimes several times a week—for more than three years, refining ideas and working to explain what we had seen lived out in ministry. We noticed from our own experiences, and had it confirmed when we checked in with many other colleagues, that some teams just seem to get it, and other teams need more guidance getting it. What we weren't sure of, initially, was just exactly what "it" was.

Through the years of conversation, prayer, and discussion with other leaders in short-term missions, we kept returning to the idea of dignity. It seemed to be a unifying thread, but defining how it worked proved difficult to articulate. Then we realized something important: when a visiting team and a host church successfully connect and the trip goes well, it is because the dignity of each party was respected. On the other side, when a trip deteriorates and things do not go well, it is because people were not treated with dignity. As it turns out, we discovered the "it" to be dignity, and it wasn't just *a* unifying thread—it was *the* unifying thread.

This book is us pinning down the most key aspects of this dignity thread. It helps us to identify when we are honoring and recognizing the innate value of other people, acknowledging that the people we serve and whom we serve with have value because they too were made in the image of God. This material applies this universal idea to short-term missions in particular in practical ways.

I have hosted and led a lot of teams. I wish I'd had this book when I began to prepare myself, the churches hosting the teams, the volunteers I worked with, and the teams that came. These ideas and guidelines represent many lessons learned—often the hard way. I appreciate the brothers and sisters God put in my path to teach me along the way. There are incredible people around the world who show us God because they too bear his image. We have the privilege to listen to and learn from them.

Terri and I have read more than a few books and resources that point out the shortcomings of short-term missions. Some even conclude that it is better to send money and not take the risk to build relationships with our brothers and sisters around the world. Maybe this is giving away the ending, but after so many hours of talking, we have never reached that conclusion. The risk we take to know one another, serve together, and learn from each other is well worth it. Let's learn to engage in short-term missions with dignity. By, as Paul tells us in Ephesians, submitting "to one another out of reverence for Christ" (5:21), we can see more broadly the beauty of Christ's bride, the church.

Imagine yourself sitting at Terri's kitchen table a little later than you were planning to be awake, and join us in the holy work of reflecting God to the world.

It would not be possible to thank by name all the people who helped shape these ideas. I am thankful to all those who have answered God's call to serve as pastors, missionaries, and lay leaders. I am thankful for those who have hosted short-term missions teams and have offered hospitality, no matter how it was received. I am thankful for those who have taken a step of faith for any amount of time to go where God calls them.

Stephen Sickel
Coordinator of Missions and Partnerships
Global Missions, Church of the Nazarene

Terri Taylor
Global Missionary and Training Specialist
Global Missions, Church of the Nazarene

The Seven Principles

1. Dignity

Everyone is created in the image and likeness of God. All people possess inherent value and are worthy of dignity. Dignity is foundational in the ministry of Jesus. In missions, dignity is the thread that binds everything together. Missional success depends on dignity's presence in all interactions.

2. Hospitality

Hospitality is a key theme throughout Scripture. When the spirit of hospitality is present, the deep fellowship of *koinonia* is shared. Every culture expresses hospitality differently. Learning what it means to be a good guest is essential to the success of all cross-cultural ministry projects.

3. Culture

God is alive and present in all cultures throughout the world. Culture should not be viewed as right or wrong, but as diverse and different. When entering another culture, it's important to set aside our own cultural comforts and be open to new and unexpected ways of doing things.

4. Learning Posture

Taking on the posture of a learner, rather than a teacher or expert, goes a long way toward developing the relationships necessary for missions. When encountering differences, those who let go of judgment and maintain a learning mindset are ready to see God at work in new ways.

5. Relationship

The project may be the conduit that brings people together, but the relationship is what it's all about. Cross-cultural projects are more than transactional. The deeper value comes when trusting relationships with brothers and sisters in Christ are formed. The relationships are what will be remembered long after the team goes home.

6. Expectations

"Clear is kind" is a phrase that is often expressed when working cross culturally. People from different cultures have a broad range of assumptions and methods. Missional success relies on excellent planning and clear communication from the start of the project through its completion.

7. Spirituality

Hearts that are centered on God and what he is doing are paramount for everyone participating in a short-term missions project. God is at work. When people participate in kingdom building, focusing on God while loving one another gives them the strength to accomplish their tasks with dignity and flexibility.

Following Dignity Leads Us to Jesus

We start with **dignity**. Recognizing the worth and value that all people have is our foundation. We are all image bearers of God. With our ability to recognize the innate beauty of each person, we gain a better understanding of who God is.

As we consider the inherent worth and value of each person, we come to appreciate the spirit of **hospitality** in a new light—a heartfelt gift from those who bear God's image. And with this perspective, hospitality takes on profound significance.

Through the spirit of hospitality, we are better able to understand **culture**. As we sit with, share meals with, and join in the daily lives of others, we learn new perspectives, allowing us to see the reflection of God's beauty displayed throughout the diversity and vastness of our world's cultures.

By integrating these insights, our curiosity grows. We want to learn more about who God is and how he expresses himself through other people and their cultures. We are ready to engage a **learning posture**, delving deeper to absorb and discover more.

As these pieces build on each other, we arrive at **relationship**. Through receiving hospitality and participating in culture with a genuine desire learn about another's way of life, sincere connections are formed. Genuine relationships are not rooted in transactions but in honoring each person's intrinsic value and worth, where mutual understanding is cultivated as Christ's love is reflected to one another.

Honoring and cultivating relationships resets our **expectations**, clearing away any preconceived notions we may hold about what to anticipate from a mission trip—from ourselves, from other people, or even from the church. By considering the dignity of everyone, we are freed from the mental hierarchies we may have constructed, and we can reset our expectations so they align more closely with how God views his people: with immense and infinite value.

Finally, **spirituality** is where everything comes together to enrich our experience of God. As we embrace the principle of spirituality, we see God's people with eyes of appreciation and love, just as he does. Spirituality is not just the final principle but also the most profound one, where the paths of dignity, hospitality, culture, learning, expectations, and relationship come to rest—the place where we see others as God does, recognizing the intrinsic value and worth of all people. In doing so, we find everyone to be reflections of God's very essence.

Our Call to Follow Dignity

There is neither Jew nor Gentile, neither slave nor free, nor is there male and female, for you are all one in Christ Jesus.
—Galatians 3:28

Dignity is woven into the very fabric of every human heart. It is a sacred reflection of Christ's image within us, a gentle reminder that we are all lovingly created in God's likeness. This divine imprint speaks to the immeasurable worth of every life, no matter one's background, status, or circumstances. The image of God in us invites us to truly see one another, to recognize the beauty of our shared humanity, and to honor it with compassion, kindness, and fairness. When we embrace this truth, we open our hearts to extend love and inclusion, cherishing each person as a living expression of God's boundless grace.

Donna Hicks, PhD, a renowned expert on dignity and conflict resolution, has shaped global conversations in some of the world's most complex arenas. She defines dignity as "an attribute that we are born with—it is our inherent value and worth."[1] Hicks emphasizes that humans are not only valuable but *invaluable*, priceless, and irreplaceable. Yet she also highlights our shared vulnerability to being hurt, shamed, or devalued. Dignity, she explains, balances the truths that we are both infinitely valuable and deeply vulnerable. To

---

1. Donna Hicks, *Leading with Dignity: How to Create a Culture That Brings Out the Best in People* (New Haven, CT: Yale University Press, 2018), 2.

treat someone with dignity is to honor their humanity—recognizing both their worth and their fragility.[2]

Dignity also transcends the individual and moves into the neighborhood, shaping how we engage with the vibrant cultures that color our world. Each culture carries its own beauty and significance, shaped by history, traditions, and the lived experiences of its people. Honoring dignity means embracing this richness, recognizing the diversity God has intricately woven into creation. By respecting the cultural expressions, values, and practices of others, we affirm their worth and honor the sacredness of their identity—just as we would our own.

Our respect for dignity shapes every relationship we have. When it's overlooked, we risk wounding hearts—both within our missions teams and among those we serve. Neglecting dignity can create misunderstanding and resentment, pushing people apart instead of drawing them together. But when we honor dignity, trust takes root, paving the way for deep, lasting connections that reflect Christ's love. In every interaction, embracing dignity invites us into God's transformative work, allowing his love to flow through each person, conversation, and act of service.

Our call to dignity compels us to act with humility. It invites us to listen more than we speak, and to learn from others and from the world around us. Our words, actions, and attitudes must reflect the recognition of each person's intrinsic worth, never diminishing or belittling their humanity. When we embrace dignity in our words and deeds, we cultivate a world where people feel seen, heard, and loved just as they are.

Following dignity helps us respond faithfully to the call to honor the inherent worth of every person. By intentionally embracing dignity in our actions, words, and attitudes, we align ourselves with God's vision of love, respect, and compassion. This commitment empowers us to see others as God sees them, fostering deeper connections and creating environments where healing, understanding, and unity can flourish. In heeding this call, we not only

---

2. Hicks, *Leading with Dignity*, 214.

honor the dignity of others but also become vessels of Christ's love, bringing light and hope to the world around us.

Romans 12:3–18

For by the grace given me I say to every one of you: Do not think of yourself more highly than you ought, but rather think of yourself with sober judgment, in accordance with the faith God has distributed to each of you. For just as each of us has one body with many members, and these members do not all have the same function, so in Christ we, though many, form one body, and each member belongs to all the others. We have different gifts, according to the grace given to each of us. If your gift is prophesying, then prophesy in accordance with your faith; if it is serving, then serve; if it is teaching, then teach; if it is to encourage, then give encouragement; if it is giving, then give generously; if it is to lead, do it diligently; if it is to show mercy, do it cheerfully.

Love must be sincere. Hate what is evil; cling to what is good. Be devoted to one another in love. Honor one another above yourselves. Never be lacking in zeal, but keep your spiritual fervor, serving the Lord. Be joyful in hope, patient in affliction, faithful in prayer. Share with the Lord's people who are in need. Practice hospitality.

Bless those who persecute you; bless and do not curse. Rejoice with those who rejoice; mourn with those who mourn. Live in harmony with one another. Do not be proud, but be willing to associate with people of low position. Do not be conceited.

Do not repay anyone evil for evil. Be careful to do what is right in the eyes of everyone. If it is possible, as far as it depends on you, live at peace with everyone.

Following Dignity

The apostle Paul's missionary work was a pivotal force in spreading Christianity beyond its Jewish roots, reaching gentile communities across regions like Asia Minor, Greece, and Rome. His letter to the Romans invites us into short-term missions with the heart of dignity, offering a powerful and clear vision of how we should approach others—with humility, respect, and sincere love.

Paul's call to present ourselves as living sacrifices (see Romans 12:1) shows us that our role is not to come as outsiders who have all the answers but to listen, learn, and honor those we serve. Romans 12 highlights genuine love and selfless service as the way to honor others, reminding us that dignity must guide our efforts as we seek to share the love of Christ through our missionary service.

By living out the principles Paul teaches, we foster spaces for genuine, transformative relationships where every person's worth is honored and upheld. In short-term missions, we are called to serve with hearts that reflect Christ's love, approaching each encounter with humility and dignity.

How to Use This Book
A Flexible Guide for Team Leaders and Site Coordinators Serving in All Contexts

Welcome to your essential guide for leading short-term missions teams! Whether you're a site coordinator or a team leader, this book provides practical tools rooted in the key leadership principles of dignity, and can be applied in any missions environment. Whether you are serving locally or internationally, this guide will help you navigate each missions project with wisdom, compassion, and flexibility, ensuring alignment among everyone serving as they reflect the heart of Christ.

What's Inside

Key Definitions

Each chapter begins with essential terms defined. These definitions serve as a foundation for clear communication, ensuring everyone is on the same page as they navigate cultural nuances and logistical complexities. By establishing this mutual understanding up front, leaders can collaborate more effectively and approach their short-term missions projects with confidence and unity.

Guiding Principle

The seven guiding principles at the heart of this book are essential for both sending and hosting teams as they collaborate together in missions work. Each chapter will explore one of these seven principles in depth. Rooted in dignity and grounded in Christian values like humility, service, and respect, these principles empower leaders to foster meaningful relationships, honor one another's contributions, and create a shared experience that uplifts everyone involved.

Insider Perspective

We have gathered some stories and anecdotes from Nazarene missionaries serving in the field. They have generously shared their perspectives in order to help contextualize the seven principles and help teams understand that there is no such thing as a one-size-fits-all approach when it comes to short-term missions. Some of the names and locations attached to these stories have been changed or omitted to safeguard the ministries of those serving in sensitive contexts. Following each Insider Perspective anecdote is an opportunity to apply the ideas from the story to your own context through reflection questions and some discussion prompting.

Action Plan

Each chapter concludes with a set of reflective questions that have been thoughtfully designed to help you apply the chapter's guiding principle as you craft and tailor a missions plan to your specific context. These questions go beyond logistics, inviting you to reflect deeply on the unique cultural, relational, and spiritual dynamics of the community you serve. Sincere engagement with the prompts will encourage you to think about how your team's presence can build trust, foster mutual respect, and create opportunities for genuine collaboration.

For Site Coordinators

Use this guide as a tool to collaborate with the hosting team, fostering a missions plan that is culturally sensitive and responsive to the community's needs. Centering your approach on dignity will help you align your work with the values of respect, service, and mutual honor, ensuring that every action uplifts and affirms the worth of those alongside whom you serve.

For Team Leaders

This book will assist you in preparing your missions team, equipping them to serve with flexibility, understanding, and a heart for others, no matter the context. It also emphasizes the importance of caring for your team with dignity, ensuring they feel supported and valued as they in turn serve others with compassion and respect.

Built for Adaptability

Each mission trip presents unique challenges, and this book's strength lies in its adaptability. The definitions, principles, and guiding questions are designed to help you respond thoughtfully, ensuring that your leadership is effective and dignified in any situation. Whether you're serving in a rural area, an urban setting, in your home culture, or on the other side of the world, this book will equip you to lead with integrity and care.

The guiding principles in *Following Dignity* do more than provide structure—they align everyone with the common focus of serving with dignity. By using this book in your preparation and planning for each new missions project, you'll build stronger teams who are united in their approach to leadership and service.

We hope you will want to return to this book again and again as you adapt to each new missions context in order to ensure that your teams always serve with compassion, respect, and dignity.

The Journey

*And surely I am with you always,
to the very end of the age.*
—Matthew 28:20b

The Adventure Begins

The suitcases had an agenda all their own. The team leader stepped off the plane with team members in tow. Together they raced through security and met the site coordinator, who rushed them to the pier. They reached the dock in the nick of time. They boarded the ferry, relaxed into their seats, and breathed the tropical air as they cruised to their final destination. Their luggage, however, decided not to join them and would stubbornly hang out in customs for another week or so.

The team arrived emptyhanded. They had a project to do without the needed materials. They were missing clothing and other personal essentials. Everyone was pushed well beyond their comfort zone. The team leader and site coordinator looked at each other, unsure what to do next. After a few bumpy days of scrambling to make do, everyone came to realize the items in the suitcases weren't nearly as important as they originally thought. To everyone's surprise, they learned that what they carried in their hearts and minds was far more important.

"The experience of a lifetime" is how team members often describe their adventures in short-term missions. The pursuit of kingdom building with newly found Nazarene friends is incredible. Witnessing the marvelous ways that God works in other parts of the world is how this powerful and exciting ministry forever changes the perspectives and worldview of team members.

Team leaders have their hearts in the right place; they have learned what God is doing in short-term missions ministries, and they plan their trips with sincerity. They are excited about the adventure and eagerly share their enthusiasm. They understand that they will be joining a ministry already in place, and they are hopeful that they will bring some value to those they are serving. They anticipate and plan for God to transform the lives of his people during their time together. However, it doesn't take long for team leaders to learn that the complexities of doing short-term missions go far beyond logistics alone. Because of context, culture, and language barriers, challenges arise more often than not. Small encounters become more puzzling than expected. Cross-cultural relationships add a deeper layer of complexity, and the spiritual side of things isn't as glorious as everyone had hoped. Without a good site coordinator, people can be left wondering what just happened.

Through its long history, the Church of the Nazarene has put in place several excellent practices that serve short-term missions well. The fundamental role of the site coordinator is an exceptional one. This distinctive role serves as the bridge connecting two cultures. The site coordinator is the person who works with both the hosting team and the team leader. They don't live where the visiting team is from; they live among the people being served. They have relationships in place, and they know the culture and the context. They understand the strategies of the local church, the district, and the field. They guide the team leader as they come alongside the hosting team to minister together. The site coordinator helps the team enter as insiders more than outsiders.

If you have ever experienced another culture, you may have found yourself in interesting situations where you are unsure what to do next. The potential abounds for awkward moments in cross-cultural encounters! You may not know how to properly greet someone. Should you hug, kiss, bow, shake hands, or something else entirely? Hospitality in the form of food adds another layer of unpredictability, especially when you are offered food you don't recognize. Should you be the first to eat, or should you wait for the host? Should you finish the meal or leave a little on the plate? In some countries it's polite to burp after a meal; should you try that? Short-term missions team members are visiting for such a short period of time that they barely have time to notice when they make a cultural blunder. Unintentional blunders can be funny, but more often than not, they are embarrassing or insulting. Fortunately for everyone, team leaders can rely on the site coordinator to help educate the team on what's proper in the culture.

Teams always leave a lasting impression. Whether that impression is a good one is important. Teams take something home and leave something behind. It's not always the tangible gifts exchanged that people remember most. Rather, it's the interactions, the heartfelt connections, and the way people were made to feel that get remembered in the years to come. The things we carry in our hearts and minds are always what's most important.

This book will guide team leaders and site coordinators to work together as they embrace their short-term missions projects with the dignity needed for a truly effective ministry. The team leader will have tools to guide the team, and the site coordinator will learn how to prepare the hosting team to receive the missions team well. It matters not where the team comes from, where it goes, the type of project, or the people involved. Dignity is at the heart of all human interactions and has a profound role in all projects everywhere.

Dignity is the universal language of the heart. As humans, it's our first language. Long before we learn our mother tongue, the heart understands dignity. It's a language spoken through kindness, respect, and the way we treat others. As leaders, it's our responsibility to nurture that understanding, ensuring that dignity is at the core of every interaction. Whether we're leading a team or welcoming one, this shared language of dignity is what will make our work truly meaningful.

Dignity communicates far more than words ever can. A heart led by dignity speaks a universal language, connecting with others regardless of the words spoken. Sadly, the opposite is also true. Because dignity doesn't rely on words, hearts can be hurt without us ever realizing it. That's why it's so important to let dignity lead our ministries—it's a reliable, trustworthy guide. When we lead with it, we create safe spaces, build deeper connections, and ensure that everyone feels valued and respected.

Why This Book?

When we follow dignity, both the heart and mind find their place in step with Christ's leading. At times, the mind leads; at others, the heart takes the forefront. This perspective shapes how short-term missions projects unfold, recognizing that Jesus often speaks first to the heart, while the mind follows closely, bringing clarity and understanding. The seven guiding principles of this book reflect this rhythm, guiding those who serve with compassion and thoughtfulness. These principles honor dignity's role in creating space for Christ's Spirit to move, touching the hearts and minds of all who encounter the mission project.

Following Dignity takes us on a journey exploring the seven guiding principles that shape the philosophy of short-term missions in the Church of the Nazarene. Each guiding principle comes to life through insights and stories from those who have been there. There are questions and discussion points for each story that leaders can use to prepare teams for upcoming ministry. Peppered throughout are heartfelt quotes from Nazarene site coordinators—those who have served with hearts fully engaged in missions—offering nuggets of wisdom and insights they wished all hosting and mission teams understood before stepping onto a project. Each section guides site coordinators and team leaders through thought-provoking questions and will enable you to align expectations and develop healthy ministry strategies that will be effective in your particular context.

Coordinators and leaders working in a global context may find the definitions presented at the beginning of each chapter beneficial. Defining commonly used terms helps eliminate assumptions and offer clarity to conversations. Site coordinators and team leaders need a set of tools to bring out the best in short-term missions teams while avoiding common pitfalls that disrupt good intentions. *Following Dignity* provides a trove of tools to help get the job done.

Short-Term Missions and Our Nazarene Family

As Nazarenes, we are a Christian people, holy and missional. We think of ourselves as a great big family. We are a global family held together by our strong bond as believers in Christ. As we recognize our identity in Christ and see Christ in one another, we feel the dignity that comes from belonging. As brothers and sisters, we want to get to know each other, help and serve each other, and show our love for each other.

Our church has a long and beautiful history in short-term missions. In the early 1970s the movement began with Men in Missions. Teams went to churches in other countries to help build structures. Soon the name changed to Work & Witness and became our Nazarene family's way of serving shoulder to shoulder with different districts across borders and around the world.

Short-term missions in the Church of the Nazarene is in a good place. Teams come and go from more countries than ever before, serving in a wide variety of ways. Standing on the shoulders of Work & Witness and Men in Missions, today's teams do far more than build structures; they serve in the fields of education, emergency response, evangelism, medical, sports, technology, and much more. It's incredible to think about what God has done in the past fifty years, across which time the Church of the Nazarene has sent more than 10,000 teams serving in more than 130 countries.

Let's Get Started!

With its rich history and the incredible impact made globally, the short-term missions program in the Church of the Nazarene can offer incredible insights for all teams looking to serve God and God's world in this way. Our philosophy is founded on biblical ideas that hold up over time and across cultures. Whatever direction your ministry takes you, it's our prayer that it grows in dramatic ways that only God can accomplish. As you follow dignity and allow the seven principles be your guideposts for ministry, we hope Jesus leads you on a journey far beyond your wildest dreams.

Principle 1: Dignity

Be careful to do what is right in the eyes of everyone. If it is possible, as far as it depends on you, live at peace with everyone.
—Romans 12:17b–18

Key Definitions

✦ **Accountability**: Responsibility taken for actions and following through with commitments. Recognizing when it's necessary to apologize and committing to change hurtful behaviors.

✦ **Culture**: The observable social practices of a people group. These practices are often unspoken but are understood by everyone in the group. They are born out of an agreed-upon set of values. While these values may be less visible to the outsider, they are intuitive to the members of the group.

✦ **Dignity**: The innate worth of a person, place, or culture. It goes deeper than respect. It is the unearned yet priceless value that each person carries simply by being a child of God.

✦ **Fairness**: Treating people justly, with equality, according to practices and policies that are agreed on by those participating and those observing.

✦ **Global Church**: Today there are 30,000 Nazarene churches in more than 160 world areas. While the language, music, and cultural settings vary greatly, the Church of the Nazarene is connected as one body through the structure of what we call the global church. This beautiful structure allows all Nazarenes to serve God together as a family in one accord.

✦ **Global Missions**: The missions department in the Church of the Nazarene is led by the Global Missions director. The Global Missions office is located at the Church of the Nazarene's Global Ministry Center in Lenexa, Kansas, USA. They support the mission of the church by working with the regional and field leaders. They work to expand the church globally through Nazarene Ministries. An important role of Global Missions is to appoint and place missionaries in locations that are strategic to the global church.

✦ **Hosting Team**: The hosting team lives in the location where a short-term missions project will be taking place. The vision for the project originates *from* the hosting team, not from the missions team. The hosting team members are the rightful owners of the project. The hosts have been there long before the missions team arrives, and they will be responsible for the outcome and ongoing maintenance of the project after the team leaves. The voice of the hosting team carries the most weight; it should be trusted and heard above everyone else's.

✦ **Impact**: The lasting, transformative change that is present long after an event takes place.

✦ **Inclusion**: The practice of providing equal access and a sense of belonging for everyone—those participating in the project, their families, the supporting churches, and the community at large.

✦ **Missions Team**: A group of people, visiting from elsewhere, who contribute to an identified project initiated by the hosting team. Missions teams help by bringing resources. All team members should come with the posture of a learner.

✦ **Project**: A defined activity that will assist in accomplishing a goal set by the hosting team to develop and expand the ministry of the Church of the Nazarene.

✦ **Safety**: Put people at ease on two levels: (1) physically, so they feel free from the possibility of bodily harm, and (2) psychologically, so they feel free from concern about being shamed or humiliated, and feel free to speak up about their desires and needs.

✦ **Short-Term Missions**: The umbrella term for any team gathered from a local church or district going to minister alongside Christian brothers and sisters in another context for a short period of time. A short-term mission trip can last anywhere from a few days to a few weeks.

✦ **Site Coordinator**: The person who facilitates the project on the ground. The site coordinator is appointed by the district or field and is approved by the region. The role of site coordinator can be filled by any approved field ministry coordinator who receives a visiting team. The main objective of the site coordinator is to be the point person between the hosting team and their culture, and that of the missions team. The presence of the site coordinator is significant. The hosting team needs to be heard and appreciated by the missions team. The site coordinator plays a key role in assuring this will happen.

✦ **Structural Dignity**: The guidelines, policies, and regulations set in place to ensure that dignity is maintained for everyone who is impacted by the structure of the system.

✦ **Team Leader**: Works directly with both the site coordinator and the missions team. The team leader will gain understanding of the entire scope of the project through detailed communication with the site coordinator, and will guide the missions team as they work to complete the project.

✦ **Vulnerable**: People who can easily be physically or mentally hurt, influenced, or attacked. They are compromised already, and more harm can easily fall on them. They are dependent, exposed, and in need.

✦ **Work & Witness**: A construction ministry in the Church of the Nazarene. Teams from one church or district come alongside another church or district locally or globally to help their brothers and sisters in Christ build physical structures that will serve them in ministry.

Guiding Principle #1: Dignity

The missions team arrived at a small village in Central America, eager to serve. The sun was high, and the air buzzed with anticipation as they unloaded their supplies. They had come with good intentions, ready to build homes and share their faith. But something felt off.

The village leader, an older man named Mateo, greeted them at the edge of the community. His handshake was firm, but his eyes held a quiet hesitation. The team leader, busy directing everyone, offered a quick nod and moved on, not noticing the slight tightening of Mateo's jaw.

As the team set to work, they quickly realized that their carefully laid plans didn't quite fit. The materials they brought weren't what the locals were accustomed to using. The layout they proposed for the homes clashed with the community's needs. But instead of asking for guidance, the team pressed forward, assuming they knew best.

Mateo tried to voice his concerns, but his words, spoken in halting English, were brushed aside. "We've got it covered," one team member assured him with a polite but dismissive smile. The villagers, once curious and hopeful, began to retreat, watching from a distance. The gap between the team and the community widened with each passing hour.

That evening, as the team gathered for reflection, one of the younger volunteers, Sarah, couldn't shake the unease she felt. She wandered over to where Mateo sat under a tree, carving a piece of wood. Gathering her courage, she asked, "What do you think of the project so far?"

Mateo looked up, his eyes soft but tired. "You mean well," he said slowly. "But you did not ask what we need. You are building for us, not with us."

The weight of his words sank deep. Sarah realized that, in their excitement to serve, they had overlooked the most important thing: dignity. They hadn't listened. They hadn't respected the wisdom and experience of the people they had come to help.

If you've ever felt the sting of indignity, you know just how powerful dignity can be. Leading short-term missions with dignity is more than a strategy—it's the heart of meaningful ministry. Being treated with dignity makes us feel seen, valued, and understood. It fosters our sense of belonging and affirms our worth, both as individuals and as part of a community. Without dignity, relationships easily falter, and the mission becomes a checklist rather than a shared journey. But when dignity leads, relationships have the opportunity to flourish, and the work has the potential to become a sacred collaboration. Every project, every partnership, and every step should be guided by the gentle, steady hand of dignity.

In short-term missions, we're given the privilege of connecting with our Christian brothers and sisters across the world. Honoring each other's dignity with a listening ear and trusting heart has the potential to breathe life into our connections, making us feel like family. It's what can transform a simple gathering into a place where we feel truly at home—a space where love, respect, and belonging flourish.

Dignity is deeply personal—a gift from our heart that we offer one another through our actions and attitudes; it even shows up in the way we carry ourselves and the tone of our voices. Serving others in the name of Jesus calls for a tender awareness of how our presence is received. Short-term missions often pull us out of our comfort zones, placing us in spaces where vulnerability, cultural differences, and power imbalances can surface. These moments are fragile, but they also carry immense potential. When we choose to see through the eyes of our brothers and sisters, we open our hearts to deeper understanding. In our shared perspective, we find the truest ways to serve—with humility, compassion, and dignity.

Dignity is part of our community as well. As leaders, dignity asks us to take a step further, to look beyond our interpersonal relationships, to the body of believers and the community in which they live. In doing so, we see that the decisions, practices, and policies made by leaders can impact entire communities for years to come. Whether it's a water well added to a local church property, offering the dignity of clean drinking water for the neighborhood to enjoy; or another instance, where dignity has been overlooked—an abandoned, half-finished building sitting as a sad reminder that the annual floodwaters weren't considered. When dignity is remembered and acted upon, it's a blessing to the whole community, and when it's overlooked, we often find an uncomfortable tribute in its place. The dignity of the local people as well as the missions team needs to be a top priority. Wherever your ministry leads, it's crucial for team leaders and site coordinators to fully understand the role of dignity in short-term missions projects.

When dignity is at the forefront, what we give becomes a gift that keeps giving, shaping lives and communities long after the work is done. But when dignity is forgotten, what's left feels incomplete—an echo of missed opportunities left undone for both those who served and for the community they came to bless. As leaders, it's essential to prioritize the dignity of everyone participating in and affected by the project. Whether you're working close to home or crossing the globe, sending teams or receiving them, understanding the role of dignity in short-term missions projects is key to making a lasting, positive impact in the community and beyond.

Dignity Is for Everyone

It's not uncommon for people to confuse dignity with respect. They are similar but not the same. Knowing the difference is essential. Donna Hicks explains in *Leading with Dignity* that respect is earned by doing something. It gives value to another person because of an accomplishment, their status in the community, or even the families and nationalities they were born into. Respect is earned; it's based on circumstances and merit. Dignity is different; it recognizes the innate value that every person is born with. We are all created in the image and likeness of God, and that gives us dignity. Dignity isn't dependent on something needing to be done because the value is already there. Dignity recognizes the unearned value of simply being a person. It's the difference between the feeling one may have for someone who is outstanding in their field of expertise as opposed to the feeling we have when holding a newborn baby. The first is valued for what they do, the second for simply existing. Respect involves judgment where dignity offers understanding.[1]

Dignity is woven into the very heart of Jesus's ministry. Time and again, he stepped beyond the comfort of his circle to meet people exactly where they were—often on the edges of society. He reached out to those who were different, to the marginalized, the outcast, the ones his culture deemed unclean. Everywhere Jesus went, dignity followed. He chose the vulnerable, those in need of

---

1. Hicks, *Leading with Dignity*, 2.

Principle 1: Dignity

healing, the hungry, and children, who were especially close to his heart.

Perhaps one of the most powerful moments of Jesus restoring someone's dignity was when he rescued the woman accused of adultery. With a crowd of men ready to condemn her, we read in John 8 that Jesus stood between them and reminded her accusers that none of them were without sin. In that simple, profound act, he restored her humanity, showing us all that we are vulnerable yet deeply worthy. He meets us in the place of our shared brokenness. Jesus's ministry was a constant invitation to restore dignity where it had been stripped away. He showed us that dignity holds far more power than judgment or condemnation ever could.

Jesus often spent time with the very people society labeled as outsiders—eating, drinking, and sharing life with them. While others called them "gentiles" and "sinners," Jesus saw them differently. He called them "beloved." He showed us that his love is never something we have to earn. The simple, powerful truth of Jesus's boundless, unconditional love is at the core of what it means to restore dignity. We can know that another's dignity is being honored when that person feels safe, included, understood, and accepted. On the other hand, when people are treated unfairly, left out, or not given the benefit of doubt, these are signs that dignity has been violated or disregarded. When our dignity is disregarded, we may feel unseen, unvalued, or even dehumanized. It can leave us vulnerable, hurt, and disconnected—as though a vital part of our worth has been ignored or dismissed. This absence of respect often fosters feelings of shame, frustration, or a longing for justice and understanding.

Following the thread of dignity weaves warmth and beauty throughout experiences, and these experiences, along with the people involved, will be remembered with love. When dignity is disregarded, the experience changes, and people feel hurt, disappointed, or angry. That will be remembered too. Leaders following dignity bring safety to the hearts of diverse groups of people, allowing them to connect with one another in the shelter of love.

Vulnerability and Dignity

Having needs that we cannot fulfill on our own creates a deep sense of vulnerability. It's not just a feeling of exposure; it's the reality of being dependent on others, which can stir up a strong, uneasy awareness of just how fragile we are. This is something we all experience, no matter where we come from or what we've been through. Vulnerability touches every walk of life.

When a situation has us needing something we cannot provide for ourselves, we are left looking to others, hoping they will meet us with compassion. In those moments, we search their eyes, wondering, *Is this compassion or judgment? Will they offer dignity or withhold it?*

Being in a position of vulnerability can very well place dignity at risk. When needs become overwhelming, people may find themselves in the precarious position of trading their dignity just to have those needs met. In desperate moments, they may make painful sacrifices or compromises, only to lose a piece of their self-worth in the process.

When we walk alongside vulnerable people, it's not enough to simply recognize their needs. We must look deeper. We are called to see through their eyes, to understand their hearts, and to grasp how they perceive their own situation. This awareness reminds us that dignity is not something to be given or taken but something to be honored, protected, and restored when necessary. Without dignity, vulnerability can easily lead to victimhood and shame. Shame says, *This is my situation, and I'm not worthy.* Dignity says, *This is my situation, yet I am worthy.* When people are vulnerable and have unmet needs, dignity hangs in the balance.

Both the hosting and the missions team will have areas where they are especially vulnerable. Members of missions teams *arrive* vulnerable. Not understanding the language or the culture, being unsure of what to do, and existing in unfamiliar surroundings are conditions that make outsiders vulnerable. On the other hand, the hosting team may feel vulnerable because of the power and financial imbalances that teams bring. The missions team may bring gifts that cannot possibly be repaid. Additionally, hosting teams go above and beyond to serve hospitality, which makes them vulnera-

Principle 1: Dignity

ble because they have no way of knowing whether their guests will find it adequate.

Dignity offers a warm, healing covering for vulnerability; it brings trust, safety, and friendship to teams working together across cultures. When dignity is present in our shared moments of weakness, it reflects the very heart of Christ, reminding us that his love is made perfect in our unity and care for one another. When dignity gently covers our vulnerability, we find ourselves embraced by the very presence of Christ.

When vulnerabilities are met with dignity, there lies the power of short-term missions. When people say, "You have to go to know," this is what they are talking about. Meeting one another's needs in the precious space of vulnerability is where something beautiful takes root—a bond that transcends the surface. This is the place where true connection is born. In this sacred exchange, both teams and hosts become dependent on one another, offering and receiving in the shared dignity of the moment.

"Whether we are sending or receiving a team, one essential aspect to remember is that true dignity in missions is not found in what we give, but in how we honor, listen, and walk alongside those we serve. The greatest impact comes when we approach with humility, recognizing the strength and worth already present in every community."
—Shahade Twal, Missionary, Eurasia Region

Dignity creates the foundation for each person to step into their full potential, laying the groundwork for real, lasting transformation. When this kind of connection happens, it changes everyone involved. No one walks away the same. These moments of vulnerability, met with dignity, reshape hearts and forever transform lives.

The Gift of Dignity

Dignity is an inherent gift we carry and a treasure we extend to others. Like other spiritual virtues, the more freely we offer dignity, the more deeply it flourishes within us. Conversely, when we act without it—treating others with indignity—we diminish our own sense of it in the process. Yet the beauty of dignity lies in its resilience: it cannot be taken from us without our consent. No matter how others may try, dignity remains ours to hold, to share, and to nurture. The way we steward this gift shapes every aspect of how we live, lead, and connect.

Dignity has a quiet yet profound presence. We feel when it's there, and we also know when it's missing. The wrinkle of distaste we see in someone's face when we serve them our favorite meal. The drawing made by a child hanging prominently on the refrigerator as opposed to being set aside or thrown away. It's so quiet, yet it speaks volumes.

Dignity invites us into a posture of acceptance. It gives us the tender grace to receive a gift from someone of humble means, appreciating the deep sacrifice behind their generosity. It's allowing ourselves to accept the helping hand of a stranger when we're in need, recognizing the beauty of help given freely. It's finding the courage to accept when we're wrong, offering a heartfelt apology. Above all, dignity asks us to embrace what's before us with a spirit of grace, acceptance, and understanding, honoring both the giver and the gift.

Dignity also gently calls us to restraint. It's sitting beside someone who has much, and choosing to appreciate the generosity they've already shared—without asking for more. On the other hand, it's holding back from giving more than we're asked, even when it feels good to do so, understanding that true generosity sometimes asks that we be still. It's recognizing that listening and understanding are far more valuable than assuming we know what's best. Dignity encourages us to pause, honor the boundaries of others, and choose the greater good over our own immediate desires.

Principle 1: Dignity

Finding ourselves vulnerable in cross-cultural settings can be uncomfortable, bringing with it the real possibility of putting dignity put at risk. Team members with the ability to both extend and maintain their own dignity when finding themselves in uncomfortable situations bring esteem to everyone present. Feeling the prickle of a dignity violation always comes with a choice; we can either hold on to our dignity or let it slip away. Those who choose dignity hold it for themselves as they bring it to others.

Sometimes dignity requires that we speak up; other times it requires us to keep quiet. It requires both strength and gentleness of character. It affects us as we affect others. Dignity touches all aspects of short-term missions, from how we respond to uncertainty to how we post pictures on social media. Its presence matters in the way we treat team members as well as in our interactions with people in the communities we serve. Dignity is always a trustworthy guide.

> "Our mission is less about what we do and more about who we are, whether we cross the street or go around the world; it is always about God; it's his mission living in and through us."
> —Dr. David Wesley,
> Nazarene Theological Seminary

Structural Dignity

When we reflect on the incredible success of the Work & Witness ministry in the Church of the Nazarene, it's clear that the principle of dignity has been key. This amazing grassroots effort has endured over the years because its structure thoughtfully protects dignity at every step. A good structure strives to find balance between two important goals: safeguarding those who may be vulnerable while also honoring the worth and autonomy of everyone involved. It's this careful balance that has helped the ministry thrive and continue to bless so many.

It's important for leaders to remember that hosting teams are the true experts when it comes to their own communities. They know what's needed, can set the right goals, and should be the ones to lead their projects. The role of the missions team leader is to support and partner with them, not take charge. The structures in place are there to make sure the hosts are charged with leading so that the work is meaningful and benefits everyone in a lasting way.

The site coordinator plays a vital role, serving as the key point of connection between the hosting and missions teams. They help foster trust and ensure smooth collaboration by understanding the unique needs and vulnerabilities of both sides. As the bridge between the teams, a great site coordinator brings valuable insight, ensuring that every interaction is rooted in dignity. They skillfully balance the vision of the project while tailoring approaches to fit the local context, helping create a sustainable ministry that honors both the community and those serving.

For the structure to work best, it's ideal for the site coordinator to live among the people hosting the project. Being close to the project allows the site coordinator to maintain vital relationships and stay informed about local changes. They also need to have a good understanding of the cultural backgrounds of both the hosting and visiting teams, along with the practical skills needed to achieve the project's goals. When site coordinators live in proximity to the hosting team, they're in the best position to establish systems, policies, and practices that honor the local culture, address safety concerns, and ensure the project continues smoothly even after the visiting team has returned home.

Structures built on dignity have the ability to level the playing field. Teams can let go of any notions of superiority or inferiority that come from differing cultural backgrounds, financial abilities, education, or other influences that interfere with the relationship of brothers and sisters in Christ. With good structures in place, vulnerabilities can be addressed while honoring the dignity of everyone.

Good systems, policies, and structures aren't intended to be burdensome but are meant to clear pathways and remove barriers while safeguarding those impacted by the project. Structures that aim to balance the two noble objectives of protecting the vulnerable while preserving fairness are on the path of dignity. The purpose of all practices and policies should be to guard the dignity of all people.

The Generosity of a Widow
Mark 12:41–44

Jesus sat down opposite the place where the offerings were put and watched the crowd putting their money into the temple treasury. Many rich people threw in large amounts. But a poor widow came and put in two very small copper coins, worth only a few cents.

Calling his disciples to him, Jesus said, "Truly I tell you, this poor widow has put more into the treasury than all the others. They all gave out of their wealth; but she, out of her poverty, put in everything—all she had to live on."

The Dignity of Inclusion

In the Gospel of Mark, Jesus offers us a glimpse of dignity in the story of a widow with limited resources standing beside those of generous means. This temple scene is a vivid example of how the luxuries of wealth provide privileges that are denied to the impoverished. In this case, the luxury is the esteemed social standing one receives when giving large offerings in front of others. It doesn't matter the time or place; the uncomfortable reality is that poverty closes many doors that are open to those coming from more privileged circumstances. Participation in certain arenas is denied because the price is simply too high. Jesus always has a way of turning things around.

Did you notice that Jesus didn't stop the widow from participating in the offering? He didn't tell her keep her two mites because of her poverty. He didn't remind her that she was as poor as those who would receive the offering because offerings like this went to the poor and to the widows, and everyone could plainly see that she was both. He also didn't turn to the rich men and ask them to give her something out of their abundance. He didn't ask them for more than what they had just given. Instead, he stood back and watched the widow participate in the offering.

The woman was included. She was one of the givers. She was able to give her offering in dignity. Jesus then gave her something more, saying that what she gave was of more value than the others. He honored her because in the midst of poverty she had a generous heart. She gained social esteem because of her offering, and a door that had been previously closed to her was now open. Jesus takes notice of those who at first glance might seem to have little to offer. He includes them. He lifts them up. And he blesses them.

Another quality this story reveals about dignity is that Jesus didn't honor the poor by shaming the rich. The rich men in the story had just given a substantial offering. Jesus didn't coerce them into giving another offering to help the widow. He also didn't put it on them to find a solution to her problems. Nothing needed to be solved or fixed. In fact, Jesus pointed out that the heart of the widow was just about perfect. He wasn't concerned about money. He was concerned about dignity.

Seeing the many circumstances around us, we must be careful not to close doors or dismiss the offerings of those from humble means. Whether it is a person wanting to join a missions project or a church located in an impoverished area wanting to send a missions team of their own, inclusion is the message that Jesus gives. The structures we put in place need to be broad enough to include those who are often excluded by their circumstances. We need to look at the hearts and not the finances of the givers. Like the widow, the sacrificial offerings of the poor become the richest of treasures. Jesus says they are far more precious than all the others.

As leaders, we must always remember it's the Lord speaking to the hearts of his people as they give. All gifts given in ministry are offerings to the Lord. They are his. The conversation doesn't start with us because it's not ours to have. We can trust God to guide the hearts of the givers. We don't tell the poor not to give, and we don't tell the rich how much to give. Jesus stands back and watches the givers. He extends dignity to all, and we can do the same.

As we construct a ministry in short-term missions, we must look to see which doors in our ministry might be closed because of the structural, cultural, or financial restrictions in place. The widow's two mites were more than enough. She was able to participate. Leaders need to be mindful when creating policies to ensure that there is room for everyone.

Building Your Structure

Leaders have many different motivations and ways of getting things done. Some create policies and practices that are carefully thought out while others work it out as they go along. Either approach creates structure, habits are formed, and the way we do things becomes more or less permanent. Eventually, everyone knows what is expected. As new leaders come in, they often follow in the footsteps of those who have gone before. Whether the ministry has been around a while or is just getting started, leaders need to think through the practices and policies they are putting together and examine the structures already in place to ensure that dignity is considered from every angle.

Structures should have policies and practices that protect the dignity of vulnerable parties without creating obstacles that prohibit participation. Like the story of the widow's mite, where the small, seemingly insignificant offering was honored for its sacrifice, every person deserves to be included and valued. Carefully thinking through every step of a project—especially from the perspectives of those impacted by the decisions made—ensures that dignity and structure align. When we design systems that allow everyone to contribute in meaningful ways, we create an environment where dignity is upheld and all can participate with respect and honor. It's not about the size of the gift or contribution but about ensuring that each person's ability to participate is welcomed and celebrated.

Look closely at the areas where good structure is needed to protect the dignity of those impacted by the project. Issues around safety, fairness, accountability, and inclusion will need consideration. Good policies and structures don't just say, "Everyone is welcome to participate." They look further to see what might be hindering certain people from feeling included, and then they remove those obstacles. They don't *assume* that things are fair. They make plans to ensure that things are fair on all sides. They consider and plan for what's fair for all the members of both the missions team and the hosting team. Site coordinators can reflect on how churches on the district might perceive the ministry objectives when one church gets all the missions teams and others don't get any. They can come up with strategies for fairness and inclusion that will bring dignity to the entire district.

Impact and Dignity

All short-term missions projects make an impact. Everyone involved will remember what's been left behind. For good or for bad, people living in the community will feel the impact because the project that is left behind will carry with it the story of how it came to be. All those involved go home with memories that won't soon be forgotten. How the project is done matters. Like a boat crossing a lake, a wake is left behind. Dignity creates the space for an impact that can be beautifully remembered for years to come.

Insider Perspective[2]
Candies for Children: Haiti

I had just graduated from high school, and I traveled to Haiti for a week with a group of teens from my church. One afternoon, our group set out to Neply, a small village neighboring Leogane. The villages were separated by a rocky dirt road that characterized most of the roads in Haiti. We piled into the back of an old truck, and as we jostled past the palm-leaf-thatched houses, the Haitian children came out to wave at us. Some wore no shoes. Other wore no pants.

Someone ripped into a bag of candy, throwing it behind the truck, leaving a trail of junk food in our wake. As we crept along,

---

2. Excerpted from Mariette Williams, "Why I'll Never Go on a Mission Trip Again," *Medium*, July 16, 2019, https://zora.medium.com/why-ill-never-go-on-a-mission-trip-again-9bff6b6ea55a.

more children came out of their homes. We heard frantic howling as the kids fought over the small pieces of candy. I laughed, watching more kids scurry behind the truck, grabbing at the cheap candy. I dug my hand into the bag and threw some candy out like birdseed to hungry pigeons. They hungrily scraped at the dirt, reaching up at us to throw more.

Then we reached a curve in the road, and I saw a boy standing in front of his home, watching the truck come around the corner. When he saw the candy, his eyes lit up. He reached out to begin sprinting toward the truck, but just as he was going to take his first step, a hand came down on his shoulder. His father, I presume, held him back, fighting against his tiny jerks. The man turned to him and said something I couldn't hear or understand, his face a mixture of anger and disgust. In a few seconds, I had been taught a lesson about dignity.

That day, it was easy for us to think we were doing good. Had that father not reached out to stop his son, it would have been an otherwise unremarkable event. That father shamed me that afternoon, made me question my good deed. I sat on the edge of the truck, thinking about that look, bumping along until we reached our destination.

Insider Perspective
Candies for Children: The Philippines

We gathered in the lower level of the church in Manila, Philippines. The typhoon had hit our city, and it was the worst I had ever seen. Eighty percent of the people in our community had their homes damaged and flooded. Mud was everywhere, there was no power, the water supply was low, and the drinking water was being rationed.

It had been a couple of days since the terrible storm. People weren't standing around waiting for things to happen—they were cleaning up themselves. Everyone participated. The government wasn't coming to help, and there was no Red Cross. Manila is a beautiful city in southeast Asia that has endured a lot. If things were going to be cleaned up and managed, it was by the people themselves. And they did. Everyone was out in the streets cleaning things up and taking care of one another.

That's why we were at the church that day. We were missionaries, and we learned by example from the people who lived there. In the midst of tragedy, they were a shining example of God's love. Pastor Oni, the district superintendent, was at the church with us helping as we put together bags of supplies for families in the neighborhood—rice, canned fish, pasta, and other staples to help them get by for a few days.

Pastor Oni brought chocolates. He smiled as he laid them on the table and said, "The kids need chocolate! During hardship, we can't forget the kids!" He explained that he learned this from his dad. He shared that his dad always made sure to put chocolates in the bags so there was something for the children.

His dad had been a child in the Philippines during World War II. He experienced his village being invaded and destroyed by enemy soldiers. He never forgot that in the midst of the devastation, the U.S. helicopters flew overhead, dropping bags of food and supplies for the people on the ground. In the bags of food was always a chocolate treat for the children. It was important that the adults had a little gift they could give to the children.

His dad never forgot that, and now Pastor Oni always shows up with a little something extra that parents can give to their children—a little bit of love in the shape of a chocolate.

Questions to Consider
Candies for Children

1. When comparing these two stories, what stands out to you?

2. What is similar about these two stories?

3. What is different?

4. What impact does dignity make here?

5. What can we learn from these two stories?

6. What impact does dignity have in your ministry?

Discussion
Candies for Children

Both of the above stories include the distribution of candy to children. They are similar stories, but not the same. In the first story about the trip to Haiti, we feel the pain of the father. The writer of the story never got over that look of pain in the father's face. Dignity violations are long remembered by the ones who were hurt, but it's also important to remember that the ones who caused the hurt may have a hard time forgetting as well. It's hard to know exactly what the father in the story was thinking; the best we can do is imagine how we would feel in that situation: candy in the dirt, for our children, from strangers; something like a parade, but not really like a parade at all.

> "Love is a human language;
> you don't need to speak the same
> as the people to love them."
> —Robin Radi, Missionary, South America

The second story is about preparing gifts for families after a typhoon. It demonstrates dignity being passed down from one generation to the next and still making an impact. The presence of dignity can be felt in the way the chocolates were distributed after the typhoon. Everyone felt good about it, both givers and receivers. The gift was for the whole family. Parents—during a time of hardship, when they had very little to give to their children—received the precious gift of dignity because they had the ability to give their children a little something special.

In these two stories, the hero of the story shifts from self to other. Dignity is as subtle as it is powerful. Getting dignity right during a short-term missions trip will have a lasting effect. The impact that dignity has, for good or for bad, will be etched in the memories and hearts of all the people who participate in the project.

Dignity Action Plan

1. Purpose Rooted in Dignity
How does this mission project uphold the God-given dignity of every person involved—both those serving and those being served?

2. Partnership with Dignity
How are we empowering local leaders as equals, recognizing their expertise and respecting their leadership?

3. Sustainability for Dignity
How does this missions project empower the community to continue the work on their terms, with dignity as the foundation of sustainability?

4. Communication That Upholds Dignity
How are we ensuring that our communication—both verbal and nonverbal—reflects respect, understanding, and care for all involved?

5. Flexibility with Dignity
How willing are we to adapt our plans in a way that preserves and elevates the dignity of the individuals and the community?

6. Dignity in Rest and Renewal
How are we caring for the dignity of our team members and leaders by ensuring their spiritual, emotional, and physical well-being?

7. Reflection for Growth in Dignity
How will we evaluate this mission's impact to learn, grow, and better honor the dignity of others in future projects?

Principle 2: Hospitality

*Share with the Lord's people who are
in need. Practice hospitality.*
—Romans 12:13

Key Definitions

✦ **Biblical Hospitality**: To welcome, love, protect, and care for travelers or foreigners in need. Treating the stranger with brotherly love.

✦ **Cultural Hospitality**: Rules, roles, and expectations of hospitality are determined by culture. Hospitality is practiced worldwide, yet the expectations for guests and hosts varies greatly depending on culture.

✦ **Culture**: The observable social practices of a people group. These practices are often unspoken but are understood by everyone in the group. They are born out of an agreed-upon set of values. While these values may be less visible to the outsider, they are intuitive to the members of the group.

✦ **Guest**: The one who visits, the stranger, or the one who is away from home. They have been invited. Their role is to graciously accept everything that comes with the welcome. The visiting team sets aside their way of doing things in order to learn the intricacies of their role as guests in the culture.

✦ **Host**: Those who have permanent ownership of the project. They live there, they manage the project, and they will care for it after their guests leave. They anticipate and provide for the hospitality needs of their visitors in the spirit of brotherly love.

✦ **Service**: The action of helping or doing work for someone else's benefit.

Guiding Principle #2: Hospitality

Hospitality creates an environment where new connections blossom and lifelong relationships begin. It makes the missions team feel safe, welcomed, and cared for, giving them a true sense of belonging. At the same time, the hosting team gets the chance to express their gratitude in a tangible way as they care for their guests.

Each role in hospitality is important, and when everyone plays their part well, it brings dignity to the whole experience. The hosting team is responsible for making the missions team feel at home, while the missions team does their best to be gracious guests. Because culture plays an enormous role in how we offer and receive hospitality, the site coordinator is there to help both teams understand and respect each other's cultural norms.

Hospitality and dignity go hand in hand. When the missions team brings their time, friendship, and resources, they're offering a generous gift to the project. By allowing the hosting team to show hospitality, it strengthens their sense of connection to and investment in the work being done. For the visiting team, being open to receiving hospitality—while staying flexible and respectful of the hosting culture—creates a deeper, more meaningful experience for everyone involved.

Service and Biblical Hospitality

The word "hospitality" often brings to mind the glitz of the hospitality industry, with its bustling hotels and vibrant restaurants striving to deliver impeccable service. Other times we think of perfectly organized events or the ability to throw a great party, showcasing beautiful cakes and spectacularly arranged hors d'oeuvres. However, the true essence of hospitality stretches beyond professional service to a deeply rooted biblical principle. True hospitality invites us to see beyond the surface, recognizing and responding to the emotional and spiritual needs of others. This spirit of genuine care and recognition truly embodies the heart of hospitality.

Principle 2: Hospitality

Famous restaurateur and author Danny Meyer has a unique take on hospitality. He shares in his *New York Times* bestselling book, *Setting the Table*, that, while great service is important in restaurants, perfectly cooked meals and skilled waitstaff alone don't guarantee success. He learned that it's not just about excellent service—it's about hospitality. Meyer believes that true hospitality is the key ingredient that makes the difference, and without it, businesses don't thrive. While service is a vital part of hospitality, it doesn't give us the full picture. Service is just one piece of the hospitality puzzle.

Hospitality includes service, but service alone isn't hospitality. Hospitality involves the heart. It makes people feel welcome and at ease. It's about saying, "I see you, I see your needs, and I want you to feel safe and comfortable." When people experience hospitality, they *feel* it; they know they're truly welcome and that their presence is valued. Service without that spirit of hospitality says, "This is about me and what I'm doing for you." But the spirit of hospitality says, "I see you, you matter, and I want you to feel welcome." It's a small but significant difference.

The New Testament word for "hospitality" comes from the Greek word *philoxenos*, made up of *philo*, which means "brotherly love," and *xenos*, which means "stranger" or "foreigner." Biblical hospitality is about being generous to guests and showing love to strangers. Short-term missions projects thrive when the spirit of biblical hospitality is present.

Biblical hospitality invites us to look beyond a shared meal to see the whole person in front of us and accept them as they are. Think of the Good Samaritan, who helped a stranger in need. He didn't just offer food; he saw the injured man's many needs and, at his own expense, provided care. Hospitality can be present when someone simply offers the comfort of a listening ear, making room for understanding, even when they may not totally agree with what's being said. Biblical hospitality offers dignity, providing a sense of physical and emotional safety. Hospitality honors the presence of others, making space for them in whatever way they need. It's about offering dignity to those who are different from us, to strangers, and to those in need.

Acts 28:2

The islanders showed us unusual kindness. They built a fire and welcomed us all because it was raining and cold.

Understanding Cultural Differences in Biblical Hospitality

Biblical hospitality is rooted in the principles of welcoming the stranger, offering care, and creating a place where others feel valued and respected. It transcends cultural boundaries because, at its heart, it is about recognizing the inherent dignity of every person. In different cultures, hospitality may look different, but the heart remains the same—whether it's the offering of food, a place to rest, or simply the warmth of conversation.

We can be certain that the way hospitality is expressed varies greatly from culture to culture, and these differences can have a big impact on the success of a short-term missions project. While the core principles of hospitality are universal, how it plays out—whether it's spontaneous or carefully planned, where it happens, and the customs involved—depends on cultural norms. For example, in some cultures, guests are expected to arrive on time, and only those who have been invited are welcome. In other cultures, arriving on time might be viewed as arriving early, which can be construed as rude, and bringing along extra friends or family without getting prior permission is perfectly fine.

Every culture has its own set of etiquette rules that both hosts and guests are expected to follow. Social cues, food preferences, and knowing what's considered polite may require some learning for visiting teams. While some of this can be researched in books or online, the best guidance for short-term missions teams will come from the site coordinator and hosting teams, who can provide helpful tips on being a good guest and what to expect in different situations.

Regardless of the expression, biblical hospitality is about offering love and respect to those who enter our lives, extending grace even when it's not expected, and creating an atmosphere where people feel seen and cherished. Hospitality is a tradition that transcends culture and dates back to the earliest scriptural texts. It's woven into the fabric of God's kingdom, and we can trust that it remains as important today as ever.

Being a Good Guest

Those joining short-term missions projects are stepping into a unique opportunity to be a guest, whether the journey takes them somewhere that is close to home or to the far corners of the world. Even if missions team members don't consider themselves missionaries, the local community may very well view them in that light. The beauty of this experience lies in visiting teams embracing their role as guests—because the joy and relationships built along the way will always surpass momentary discomfort.

Being a guest often means letting go of some control. The guest doesn't decide how things are done or what meals are served. Letting go can feel uncomfortable for a variety of reasons. Many missions teams arrive with the mindset that they are there to serve, not to be served, and some worry about being a burden. However, it's important to remember that hospitality isn't just about service given and received—rather, it should be viewed as a gift of love.

If a team arrives focused solely on completing a service project, without being open to receiving hospitality, they could miss out on meaningful connections and unintentionally hurt the hearts of their hosts. True biblical hospitality goes beyond finances and physical tasks. Biblical hospitality is an offering of the heart—a gift of connection in the embrace of relationship. Overlooking this gift could compromise the dignity of both the hosts and the missions team. When a hosting team offers hospitality and the missions team receives it with gratitude and grace, it creates a beautiful balance where both groups feel safe to lean in and trust each other. This mutual exchange upholds the dignity of everyone involved.

Guiding team members to be flexible and follow the guidelines of their leaders is essential. Things may look and feel different from what they're used to, but it's important to remember that, even when the language is unfamiliar, kindness and respect are universally understood. Embracing these differences with dignity honors the effort and culture of the hosts, creating an atmosphere where trust and understanding can flourish. When missions teams learn to graciously accept hospitality in their host's "heart language," it brings a joy to both guests and hosts that is rooted in mutual respect and shared purpose and is remembered long after the project is completed.

> "Eat most of what is served to you. Being flexible about what you will eat is an important act of receiving hospitality. Allergies and longstanding food choices can be pre-communicated and respected. No sudden food refusals. Empathy and hospitality are needed at the table."
> —Brian Becker,
> Point Loma Nazarene University

Peter the Dinner Guest

Throughout the Old and New Testaments, the Bible is full of stories of hospitality. In John 13, we find the story of Jesus having dinner with his disciples. In the middle of dinner, Jesus got up and prepared to wash the feet of everyone present. Peter was there, and Jesus knew it was going to be new for him. Sure, Peter had probably had his feet washed before—but not by Jesus. So Jesus told him essentially, "You may not understand why this is important, but you need to do it anyway."

Yet Peter refused to let Jesus wash his feet. Trying to persuade him further, Jesus went on to say, "Unless I wash you, you have no part with me" (v. 8b).

This statement changed Peter's mind, and he said, "Then, Lord . . . not just my feet but my hands and my head as well!" (v. 9).

Jesus must have been laughing as he told Peter no, he wasn't going to wash his whole body.

Principle 2: Hospitality

Complex feelings around hospitality are not new. At dinner, Peter saw something he didn't fully understand. He thought he knew, but he didn't. He had his mind made up about what foot washing meant and was sure he didn't want any part of it. When Peter was finally convinced that it was the right thing to do, he didn't merely accept what was being offered, but he asked for more! Jesus gently told him no; just take what is being offered; that is more than enough.

This story beautifully captures what it means to be a guest in a cross-cultural setting. Visiting teams may be like Peter, where they have trouble understanding the significance of a hospitable act. Like Jesus, site coordinators and hosts may say something along the lines of, "You may not understand why—but you need to do it anyway." In these moments, dignity plays a vital role, inviting both humility and trust. Good guests honor the dignity of their hosts by finding the middle ground—they trust their leaders, do what is asked of them, and receive what is offered with gratitude, never demanding more. They don't need to take charge or be first; instead, they respect the rhythm and wisdom of the hosting team, fostering a spirit of mutual respect and shared purpose.

> "Serving through a team often requires less of a posture of action because it is more about cultivating a way of being Christlike as a guest in another community. This involves being a servant and receiving from others with love and grace."
> —Nell Becker Sweeden, CEO,
> Nazarene Compassionate Ministries, Inc.

Jesus made a powerful statement when he said to Peter, "Unless I wash you, you have no part with me." A generous act received graciously is the heart of hospitality. The spirit of hospitality enables connection. It brings hearts together. It's alive when the offerings of the hosting team are met with the kind acceptance of those serving on the missions team. Hospitality brings the transformative power of Christ to the center of short-term missions. It brings unity. It's the place where relationships are built and lives are transformed. When this happens, anything becomes possible!

In the Safety of Hospitality

An important element of hospitality is that it offers a sense of safety. Biblical hospitality means we protect our guests from harm. Creating a sense of security for the missions team is one of the hosting team's most important jobs. The hosting team is familiar with local risks and works hard to minimize them so that the missions team not only *feels* safe but also *is* safe. The hosts know the local culture, climate, and any political issues that could arise. They're prepared to handle emergencies and offer a sense of protection as part of their warm and welcoming hospitality.

Missions team members react to new environments in all kinds of ways. Some arrive filled with anxiety about germs, food safety, crime, or unpredictable traffic. Others arrive a bit too fearless. As a leader, you'll see people at both extremes and everywhere in between, and it's important to have a plan that makes everyone both safe and comfortable by building trust with the anxious while reining in the more adventurous spirits. Building trust is key to creating a safe environment. The team won't always understand the full scope of risks—whether it's pickpockets, political unrest, or environmental hazards like weather or wildlife. The anxious may fixate on the wrong dangers, while the fearless might overlook real threats. Your role is to prepare for actual risks and guide the team without scaring them. The team leader must encourage everyone to follow the advice of the site coordinator and hosting team, trusting that any precautions are in place for good reason.

The site coordinator and hosting team will work together to assess potential dangers and set up safety guidelines for everyone involved. It's important to remember that the hosting team also faces risks of their own, which may be different from the ones the missions team encounters. Guidelines should take both teams into account.

Principle 2: Hospitality

> "The impact of our work and the strength of our witness are rooted in genuine relationships. We should strive to approach every situation with dignity and not assume we know what's best. Instead, our focus should be on connecting with both the team and the local church."
>
> —Greg Taylor, Nazarene Missionary

Sometimes, team members bring valuables that require extra care, which can become a burden for the hosts. Whenever possible, it's best to leave expensive items—like personal computers, high-end phones, cameras, or jewelry—at home. Bringing these along can put everyone at risk. Each situation is different, so it's wise to plan ahead and pack only what's truly necessary, based on advice from the hosting team and site-coordinator.

Some, if not most, risks and guidelines will need to be communicated to the missions team to ensure everyone's safety. However, to avoid creating unnecessary stress, there may be certain precautions the hosts take behind the scenes that don't need to be shared with the team. It's often best for these details to be discussed with the team leader, leaving the team members to focus on their mission while trusting their hosts. The missions team might not always be aware of everything happening in the background, but they can rest assured that the hosting team is watching out for them, offering safety through the spirit of biblical hospitality.

> "Crisis must be managed with the help of the host. Sometimes what a missions team member feels is urgent might not be so urgent for the host culture. Learn to adapt even your expectations of what's considered urgent with the help of the host."
> —Tim Eby, Missionary, Africa

Insider Perspective
Security with Dignity

The team looked through the windows to see the joyful singing and waving from their new friends running alongside the van that was driving them to town. After a job well done and a completed project behind them, they were going home. The missions team was on their way to town for a final dinner before the flight back to their country. They had all of their belongings packed, and the van was nearly full. A few of the young men who had worked on the project with them ran ahead, stopped the van, and asked for a ride into town. The team gladly made room for them, and they quickly jumped in. It just so happened that the place the young men were wanting to go, the Bible Institute, was right next to where the team planned to have dinner.

Unbeknownst to the missions team, there had been an incident with the previous missions team. Someone had broken into their van and had taken all their belongings. When the hosting team learned that this next team was planning on sticking around town several hours before their flight, they quickly made a plan to come along and stay close in order to provide security. They did not *need* to go with the team; they chose to go in order to help with the unknown security needs of their guests.

Principle 2: Hospitality

Questions to Consider
Security with Dignity

1. Why did the men decide to spontaneously jump in the van?

2. Why didn't they tell their guests the reason?

3. What could have happened if the guests had said no?

4. What might team members need to keep in mind when their hosts suggest they do something that seems inconsequential?

5. How does security with dignity look in your context?

Discussion
Security with Dignity

In many cultures, hosts feel a deep sense of responsibility for the safety of their guests. If something bad were to happen to them, the hosts may feel ashamed because they believe they failed in their role of caring for their visitors. In this example, when the missions team allowed their hosts to ride with them into town, they gave the hosts the dignity of ensuring their guests got home safely. They were being very good hosts.

There could be several reasons why the local men didn't tell the team about the security risk. They may not have wanted to scare the team or burden them with unnecessary worry. It's also possible that the hosts were familiar with who might be responsible for the previous thefts and knew how to watch out for them. They may have also felt a sense of shame if locals were taking advantage of visitors, especially when those visitors were there to do good work.

Just as culture shapes hospitality, it also influences security norms. In some places, a security guard might be clearly identified with nametags and everyone knowing their role. In other places, security might be handled more discreetly through relationships and more subtle means. Either way, when hosts provide security, it's a gift. They are doing their best to make sure their guests feel safe and secure.

When team members show respect for the safety guidelines set by their leaders, they can be confident they'll stay safe. Stepping outside of those guidelines doesn't just put them at risk—it can also jeopardize the safety of the ministry and the hosting community. It's important to remember that not following safety measures isn't a sign of bravery or faith; it's a sign of disrespect to the hosts. Team members should trust that their hosts know how to care for them, and any safety guidelines they set are there for everyone's benefit.

Insider Perspective
Guests of Honor: Guatemala

Many months prior to departure, the team had been preparing for this trip. They worked together to gather the money they needed, and they spent many hours in prayer, focusing on what God wanted to teach them on their journey. They learned what to wear and chose to pack clothing that was respectful in the culture. They learned how to receive hospitality in the culture. Their plan was to be good guests while in the country.

The team heard stories about places where they might be expected to try new and exotic foods, such as grub worms, insects, or even guinea pig. They were prepared to eat with a smile whatever was put before them. They were especially happy (and some relieved) to learn that the typical Guatemalan diet consisted of homemade corn tortillas, rice, and black beans. They read about the open markets and were looking forward to trying plantains and the many tropical fruits available.

As the team stepped out of the airport, they were overwhelmed by the many sensations they experienced all at once. The aroma of ripe fruit mixed with the heaviness of the humidity was palpable. The area was crowded with people dressed in brightly colored clothes. Everyone stood so close that the team felt enclosed. Strangers tugged at their sleeves, asking for something in a language the team members didn't understand. Children pointed at them. Many people wanted to help with their luggage, trying to take it out of their hands and escort them to a taxi. Their new surroundings seemed to have an energy all its own. As they huddled together, clutching their bags and waiting to meet their hosts, they were filled with both excitement and nervousness.

When the site coordinator arrived, the team was relieved to see a familiar face, and they wasted no time boarding the old school bus. After the suitcases, supplies, and tools were loaded, they were on their way. It would be several hours before the team reached their final destination. The drive was as interesting as it was beautiful. Everyone was the kind of exhausted you have when you are too excited to sleep. The flow of traffic was different, the street signs were in Spanish, and the driver was fearless. It was exciting. Team members were eager to get to the project. This last part of the journey was the longest. It was getting late, and everyone was tired.

The team arrived at the church after dark and unloaded the bus right away. They were as hungry as they were tired. They were shown the rustic Sunday school rooms at the church where they would be sleeping. The mattresses were on the floor. With grateful hearts they organized their things while they were told to meet next in the church sanctuary, where they would be served their first meal.

The sanctuary walls were made of hollow block and still waiting to be painted. The windows had no glass but did have fresh curtains hanging in them. The team didn't know that someone had hung them special in preparation for the team's arrival. A single fluorescent bulb dangled from the ceiling. Several benches had been moved from their rows and now sat around a table with a green vinyl tablecloth on it. It was plain to see that the table was a simple one made of plywood.

On the table sat several pizzas from Pizza Hut. Pizza Hut? There was also warm Pepsi in bottles and no ice. There were plastic straws. This was totally unexpected. Where were the homemade tortillas? What about the tropical fruit? Wasn't this supposed to be an exotic cultural experience? Why pizza? They thought, *We could have this at home*. Tired and disappointed, the team members sat down.

There were several young people there they didn't recognize who must have been from the church. There was a prayer, prayed in Spanish. Then the team was invited to eat first. They remembered what they learned about being good guests. They didn't complain or grumble. They didn't take too much, and they tried to be grateful.

After they finished their meal, the pastor, who was their host, shared in Spanish while the site coordinator interpreted: "The youth group is so thankful for you coming to help our people, our families, and our community. They wanted to do something special for our first meal together. They learned that people from the U.S. love pizza. For many months they have been gathering cardboard from the neighborhood to sell. Although pizza is very expensive, they were able to pay for it with the money they earned. They wanted you, our honored guests, to have this very special meal."

As they heard this, team members looked around the room and saw their youthful hosts as if for the first time. As it dawned on the team members the sacrifice that these youth had made to serve in this way, the team knew they were loved and felt very welcomed. They went to be bed feeling sincerely grateful for the privilege of receiving their humble meal, presented as if they were royalty.

Questions to Consider
Guests of Honor

1. Did it make a difference that the pastor shared with the team about the sacrifice the youth had made for them?

2. How do you think the team would have felt if they weren't told?

3. What other sacrifices might the hosts be making that the team may be unaware of?

4. What might the impact of this first act of hospitality have on the team?

5. How can you prepare your team members in light of this story?

Discussion
Guests of Honor

Hospitality looks different when it's viewed from the heart. Guests become less concerned about what's being served and more interested in the people who are present. Those on this missions team had such a beautiful response. They were uncertain, but they politely accepted the pizza. Once they understood the hard work and generosity that had gone into the acquiring of the pizza meal for them, their courtesy turned into genuine gratitude because they saw that it was truly a gift from the heart. The spirit of connection was born, and it was felt by everyone.

Had the team not known about the youth raising money for the pizza, they may have been confused and assumed that not too much thought had gone into dinner. Had they not been prepared to receive hospitality well, they may have said no to the warm soda and cold pizza, and gone to bed instead. Not partaking in the meal would have been disrespectful, not just to the youth but also to the entire community who encouraged them as they gathered and sold the cardboard. They would have ended the evening in the spirit of hurt feelings and disappointment rather than the beautiful spirit of connection that was fostered instead.

It helped that the pastor shared with the missions team about the hard work and generosity of the youth group. Things might have been different if they hadn't known. Everyone participating on short-term missions teams can be sure that hosting teams have made significant sacrifices and preparations they will never be aware of. Things that seem small and ordinary to guests may come at a considerable cost to those who are hosting.

Hospitality is more than an act of service; it's a gift of the heart. It's not about what is being served but about the people serving it.

Understanding the roles of host and guest is an important key to short-term missions, but sometimes biblical hospitality calls us to look beyond cultural norms to see the bigger picture. The goal isn't to be rigid in our roles but to remain flexible. Flexibility helps create an atmosphere where Christ is present, people feel comfortable, and relationships can grow.

There will be times when both the missions team and the hosts come together in the kitchen, learning from each other and preparing meals together. Other times, the missions team might handle their own cooking, depending on the nature of the project. Sometimes the team invites the hosts in to teach them how to cook local dishes. Each culture expresses hospitality in its own way, and there are many ways to care for a team.

Biblical hospitality comes from the heart and is shaped by culture. What's most important is creating an environment where both the team and the hosts are cared for with a spirit of hospitality.

Insider Perspective
An Uncomfortable Lesson[1]

Several years ago, I learned an uncomfortable lesson about hospitality. I worked for a congregation-based shelter for families experiencing homelessness in St. Paul, Minnesota. Because the fifty-five beds that Ramsey County had in its shelter were always full, various local churches acted as overflow shelters, housing up to twenty people each night. Each month a different congregation hosted and staffed the shelter in their building. In the evening, families (mostly women and children) arrived via taxi. Volunteers from the congregation served food, helped kids with homework, or organized activities. The families slept on cots, usually in one large

---

1. Adapted from Kiely Todd Roska, "Dignity: An Uncomfortable Lesson in Hospitality," Benedictine Center of St. Paul's Monastery, n.d., https://www.benedictinecenter.org/dignity-and-hospitality/#:~:text=It%20is%20about%20honoring%20people's,receiving%20whatever%20gifts%20they%20bring.

room with little privacy. In the morning, everyone packed up their belongings and took taxis back downtown.

My role was to be there for a few hours each evening to welcome the overnight guests and get the volunteers settled into their responsibilities. I thought of my role as a ministry of hospitality. I tried to make the environment as comfortable as possible for people who had no other option than to sleep in a church basement. I made sure the sheets and blankets were clean, arranged the rooms, coordinated food prep, and prepared volunteers to welcome people effectively. Families often returned for several days in a row, but the volunteers were usually new each night. Because I was at the shelter almost every evening, I considered myself the host for both the volunteers and for the guests. I was the one who understood the routine and welcomed others into it.

Over time, I came to feel like I had learned some things about hospitality. For example, I learned that hospitality is not always comfortable. The guests often had strong body odor because they did not have regular access to showers. Adults and children alike were tired and hungry and carrying stress I could not even comprehend. This stress often surfaced as frustration with the rules, or as a child's need to move and be loud in cramped quarters. In my mind, good hospitality meant enduring strong smells without comment and navigating people's intense feelings. But these lessons were just the beginning; I had much more to learn.

One night, the guests were in the basement youth room of a large church with beautiful architecture. I arrived at the shelter after a full day of grant writing and staff meetings to find that the volunteers responsible for food and welcoming had not arrived. I opened the refrigerator to find only a quart of milk and a few cheese slices. I considered running to the grocery store, but then no one would be there to greet the families when they arrived. Irritated, I began welcoming people alone, trying to craft a backup plan to feed the hungry families.

Vikki walked in first. She was about forty and wore a large backpack while also carrying her toddler and several grocery bags. Her other five children followed her, each carrying their own backpacks and bags of belongings. Soon Vikki engaged the same routine she and her children shared every night. She walked over to the row of cots and asked each of her children to change into their pajamas and set out their outfits for the next day on the end of their cot. Then Vikki sat the children down at a table to begin their homework. I watched Vikki settle her family into a church basement with more skill and dignity than most parents with stable housing and far more financial resources can muster.

On this particular night, as her children solved math problems and read out loud to one another, Vikki set up a meal on an adjacent table. Vikki had spent most of the day at her sister's house with her younger children while her older children were at school. There she had baked lasagna and garlic bread and brownies and had prepared a salad—not only for her own family but enough to feed the other shelter guests, the volunteers, and me.

Jolted out of my embarrassing irritation about dinner preparations, I helped Vikki get plates and silverware for everyone. As we set the table, she turned to me and said, "Since we lost our place, I haven't been able to cook very much. I just wanted to cook today." I nodded as if I understood, but in that moment I realized how much I really did not understand. Suddenly, my long day and my frustrations about the absent volunteers and the missing food felt irrelevant and ridiculous. I was now living the parable of loaves and fishes. Vikki, like Jesus, had turned so little into a feast for everyone. She used her family's food stamps, intentionally and thoughtfully, to make a gift for people she did not know, many of whom likely had more resources than she did.

That night, Vikki taught me another uncomfortable lesson about hospitality. True welcome is not just about setting tables and arranging things for people to arrive. It is about honoring people's dignity so fully that you are willing to be changed by their presence. Vikki taught me that a person's beautiful presence can affect the way we see the world and our place in it. Real hospitality means receiving people as they are and receiving whatever gifts they bring. Sometimes hospitality means giving up your role as host and becoming a guest.

Principle 2: Hospitality

Questions to Consider
An Uncomfortable Lesson

1. What lesson was learned from this experience?

2. What made the situation challenging?

3. Do you prefer offering hospitality or receiving it? Why?

4. How might this story apply to short-term missions?

Discussion
An Uncomfortable Lesson

Hospitality asks us to truly see the people in front of us—not just in their roles but in the places they find themselves on their journey. Recognizing their need means that at times we will stand up and let them sit in the hosting chair or join us in the kitchen.

In this story, the author felt vulnerable when the volunteers hadn't arrived with the food. But the Lord provided an unexpected gift of lasagna to share with everyone. Vikki, in the midst of her own challenges, wanted to share her joy in being able to cook, a blessing she hadn't had in a while. Even in her hardship, she chose to give.

If the volunteers had arrived with food, Vikki's gesture would have been a nice addition, but it might not have been nearly as powerful. The author could have declined, saying, "We have a policy not to accept outside food." Can you imagine the hurt that would have caused Vikki? Thankfully, the author recognized the gift Vikki was offering and welcomed it with open arms. The result was a shared meal filled with dignity, love, and community.

Hospitality goes far beyond gracious manners at a dinner party. It's a posture of the heart that hosts and guests both embrace, and it's essential throughout the entire missions experience. Every aspect of the project will be shaped by the relationship of host and guest, and understanding this dynamic can make a world of difference.

As the missions team steps into their short-term project, they are always the invited guests. This posture of being a guest should be carried through every interaction, whether it's joining a local ministry, singing in the church choir, or visiting someone's home. But it's not just limited to the project itself—it extends to everyday moments like shopping, eating out, or taking a walk through the neighborhood. The team should always be mindful that they are guests in someone else's culture and community.

> **"The local church needs to fully understand that they are the hosts and are charged with leading the project."**
> —Elizel Soto, Missionary, Mesoamerica Region

Both teams have important roles to play. The hosting team works hard to meet the needs of the missions team, guiding and preparing them for each situation with care. On the other side, the missions team is called to graciously receive that guidance with open hearts. This exchange, rooted in hospitality, creates a beautiful partnership that strengthens both teams.

One of the joys of hospitality in short-term missions is the delightful uncertainty it brings. Cultural differences can create moments of ambiguity for both hosts and guests, but this is where flexibility and open communication come in. By embracing your role—whether as host or guest—with empathy and a willingness to adapt, you can create meaningful connections and truly enjoy the experience.

Flexibility allows everyone to savor their time together around the table of short-term missions, where relationships are built and hearts are opened.

Hospitality Action Plan

1. Creating a Culture of Welcome
How can we foster the spirit of hospitality for both the hosting and visiting teams, ensuring that everyone feels valued and cared for?

2. Preparing Thoughtfully
What needs to be prepared beforehand to create a smooth and welcoming experience, from logistics to emotional readiness?

3. Facilitating Spaces for Connection
What kind of spaces are needed for meals, devotions, debriefings, and other moments of connection that build community?

4. Going beyond Basic Needs
What additional accommodations, beyond basic necessities, can demonstrate a spirit of care and generosity to the missions team?

5. Demonstrating Cultural Sensitivity in Hosting
How is hospitality understood and expressed in the culture you are serving, and what are the expected roles of hosts and guests?

6. Avoiding Cultural Missteps
What actions or behaviors might be considered polite or rude in this culture, and how can we prepare teams to honor local customs?

7. Having a Mutual Understanding
What does the hosting team need to know about their guests' preferences, and what do the guests need to know about being gracious visitors?

8. Ensuring Safety with Hospitality
What basic safety measures (such as clean water, adequate restrooms, and secure lodging) must be in place to provide peace of mind for all participants?

9. Being Medically Prepared
What medical conditions or emergencies need to be planned for, including access to local healthcare resources?

10. Securing Valuables
How will passports, money, tools, and other valuable items be safely secured for both the missions and hosting teams?

11. Honoring Hosting Efforts
How can the site coordinator and missions team support the hosting team, ensuring their hospitality is sustainable and their dignity preserved?

12. Making Thoughtful Farewells
What kind of farewell or closing gesture would reflect genuine gratitude and mutual respect, leaving a lasting positive impression for both teams?

Principle 3: Culture

*So in Christ we, though many,
form one body, and each member
belongs to all the others.*
—Romans 12:5

Key Definitions

✦ **Cold-Climate Culture**: Cultures that view tasks as priority. Usually experienced in world areas where traditionally the climate has dictated getting things done in order to survive winter. Cold-climate cultures are conscientious of time and efficiency, direct in their communication, and prefer to be appreciated as independent individuals.

✦ **Cultural Competence**: Having knowledge of other cultures, including their holidays, histories, currencies, and politics. Cultural competence gives someone the ability to navigate another culture well and get things done.

✦ **Cultural Humility**: Cultural humility goes a step further than cultural competence. It takes the posture from "I know all about this culture" to a more dynamic stance of "I am willing to learn about the intricacies of subcultures, relationships, and the hearts of people."

✦ **Culture**: The observable social practices of a people group. These practices are often unspoken but are understood by everyone in the group. They are born out of an agreed-upon set of values. While these values may be less visible to the outsider, they are intuitive to the members of the group.

✦ **Dominant Culture**: The group that is most powerful in terms of wealth, prestige, status, and influence. They readily assume the role of leadership and often move forward without understanding the full impact they have on others.

✦ **Fear-Power Worldview**: The heartfelt needs of those living with this worldview strive to rid themselves of fear by gaining power over unseen spiritual forces. Fear-power cultures are often found in tribal settings.

✦ **Guilt-Innocence Worldview**: The heartfelt needs of the people with this worldview strive to remain innocent and free from guilt. Western cultures are often described as guilt-innocence cultures.

✦ **Honor-Shame Worldview**: Found in much of the world, especially including Asia and the Middle East, those who view the world through the honor and shame lens find value in honoring relationships, people, and societal status. They gain honor by being esteemed in the social community. They avoid shame, which comes when they do something that the social community disapproves of.

✦ **Interpreter**: A person who orally translates language through speech, such as a sermon given from a guest speaking another language during a church service.

✦ **Power Dynamics**: The balance of power between two or more people. There is a distinction between those with power and those without; those with power have an advantage.

✦ **Subculture**: A smaller group within a larger group having a distinct culture differing from the larger one. For example, a Christian population residing within the mainly Buddhist country of Myanmar would be considered a subculture of that larger community.

✦ **Translator**: A person who translates written material from one language to another.

✦ **Warm-Climate Culture**: In these cultures, relationships are highly valued. Usually experienced in climates where the temperatures are warm but this culture can be found in rural or tribal settings in cooler climates as well. Warm-climate cultures are event oriented, focused on relationships, indirect in their communication style, and value obligations to the collective group above personal wants and desires.

✦ **Worldview**: The lens through which a person views the world. The subjective perspective of an individual based on their own values creates the paradigm by which they make sense of the world.

Guiding Principle #3: Culture

Culture is woven into every part of our lives. It shapes how we see and understand the world, wrapping us in the traditions and values handed down from one generation to the next. Culture gives us a sense of belonging, guiding us in ways both big and small—like baking a birthday cake to celebrate a loved one or proudly wearing our favorite team's colors at a sporting event.

When something steps outside our familiar norms, it can feel peculiar. Imagine someone arriving to a casual gathering dressed in something completely unexpected—like a formal ball gown or a bathing suit. It would catch everyone off guard because it would feel out of place, uncomfortable, and sometimes just plain wrong.

Culture helps us know where we fit and who shares that space with us. When norms are broken, it can create distance, making someone seem disconnected from the group. It's a reminder of just how deeply culture ties us together and why understanding it is so important to how we relate to one another.

Countries and nations, churches and businesses, families and friend groups all have their own sets of values that are shared and agreed upon—things that are often unspoken and not always easy to articulate. Our actions, our jobs, our education, and the stories we tell all serve to express the shared values of our culture. Those who belong do things that express these values. Culture is the unspoken set of rules that a group of people live by. Following cultural norms provides status and esteem. Not following them has the potential to bring dishonor or shame.

What's considered socially appropriate in one situation may be perceived as inappropriate in another. Waving at someone with the palm of your hand up communicates something impolite in one culture while waving with your palm turned down means something entirely different in another. It can be as simple as knowing if fried chicken should be served for breakfast or dinner. Knowing the cultural distinctions of those we serve alongside has a tremendous impact on our ability to connect in a meaningful way. The clothing we wear, the food we eat, the things we say, the gestures we use, the gifts we give—all these communicate the values of our culture.

Understanding that people interpret our actions through their own cultural lenses highlights the need for thoughtful cultural guidance when we step into new environments. It's a journey that requires patience and a deep commitment to learning. This journey may not be quick, but it can be incredibly rewarding. Fortunately for missions teams, site coordinators and hosting teams usually enjoy sharing cultural norms with their visitors.

What Exactly Is Culture?

Culture can be defined as the observable social practices of a people group. These practices are often unspoken but are understood by everyone in the group. They are born out of an agreed-upon set of values. While these values may be less visible to outsiders, they are intuitive to the members of the group. The collective knowledge, beliefs, and customs of a culture are expressed in areas such as food, music, art, laws, festivals, and holidays. The visible parts of a culture are what people experience when visiting somewhere new.

Each culture has its own way of seeing the world, shaping unique ideas about what feels right and what feels wrong. In cross-cultural ministry, embracing and appreciating the diverse ways that values are expressed can be challenging, but it opens countless doors and touches hearts for those willing to take the time to learn. It can take an outsider many years to understand well the expressed values of a given culture. Under the surface is where the values that drive culture are found. Although values are expressed in subtle ways, they hold the key to successful ministry. Taking care to understand culture and respecting the values that drive it will open the many doors necessary to effective ministry.

Short-term missions teams come alongside to support the ministry of the site coordinator and their hosting team who have been living and working in the culture and among the people. Those who live there understand the culture and know what is needed to show love and respect. It may look different from what the people on the missions team are used to. Because culture is an expression of values, those serving on the missions team should be aware that not going along with culture isn't a matter of preference but one of dignity. Not participating in cultural norms can hurt the hearts of people and harm the ministry of the site coordinator and the hosting team. Entering another culture as a guest requires that we set aside our own cultural comforts and be willing to do things differently. Flexibility, adaptability, and a non-judgmental attitude are valuable for everyone who wishes to leave a positive impact.

Our Worldview

Culture is how we experience our world socially. Worldview is how we experience it personally. Our worldview is the lens we look through as we experience the world; the lens is fashioned from our own personal vantage point. Our worldview is socially constructed, shaped by our culture and our personal experiences. It tells us how we fit into the world. It's how we understand our personal stories and know what's important to us. Our culture, values, and beliefs shape the way we see the world; in turn, our worldview influences the values, beliefs, and culture we embrace.

Everyone sees the world through a unique lens that is shaped by a lifetime of experiences. This perspective gives meaning to the events and interactions around us. While culture plays a big role in shaping how we view the world, each of us carries a one-of-a-kind worldview—no two are exactly alike. It's easy to assume others see things the way we do, but stepping into someone else's shoes takes both imagination and empathy. When we take the time to understand our own worldview and genuinely appreciate the perspectives of others, it breathes life and vibrancy into the relationships we build—especially in the beautiful, diverse spaces that come with cross-cultural ministry.

Climate Cultures

Connecting with people from different cultures can be complicated, and learning as much as we can about the cultural dynamics at play will be incredibly helpful. Every culture has its subcultures and exceptions to rules. Generalizations can provide some insight, but truly understanding a culture takes time and experience. As outsiders, grasping the full depth of another culture may always feel a bit elusive, but each step toward understanding brings us closer to meaningful connections.

Sarah Lanier has a wide range of cross-cultural experience and has written an excellent book called *Foreign to Familiar* in which she dives into the similarities between cultures that are located in either hot or cold climates. Interestingly, she points out that the climate has an impact on cultural values. People living in warm climates have many things in common that are very different from those who live in cold climates. Knowing the values often expressed in these two different cultural styles is useful to navigate connection points.

As we think of culture, it's important to keep in mind that cultural practices and values are not something to judge as right or wrong; instead they should be viewed as a beautiful expression of the life that is shared in a particular community or people group. Approaching culture with curiosity is like discovering a new treasure; rather than judgment, we can bring a sense of ease while inviting understanding to take root.

Cold-Climate Cultures

In world areas where there is a cold climate, those cultures often focus on getting things done in order to endure a harsh winter. In order to survive, fields need to be plowed and planted, crops harvested, meat hunted and preserved, firewood gathered, coats mended, and warm blankets quilted before the short months of summer end and the arrival of another cold winter begins. If things aren't prepared, people and their loved ones may perish.

Cold-climate cultures traditionally value getting things done in a timely manner. The "work before play" attitude exhibited in many cold-climate cultures ensures survival. They may choose to see people as unique individuals and be comfortable letting them make their own decisions because who other than they know best how to take care of themselves? Often, there is an organized way to hospitality, things are planned, and guests follow the lead of the hosts as they care for them in a structured way. Worship may reflect cold-climate culture too. In cold-climate churches, Sunday school and other meetings tend to be organized, timely, and accomplished with purpose and intent.

Culture is like a window into the shared values of a group, and remembering this can make all the difference. In cold-climate cultures, warmth and love often shine through organization and timeliness. Starting and ending on time isn't just about the clock—it's a way of saying, "I value your time and the many important things you have to do." Honoring these values is a beautiful way to show dignity and respect, creating connection in a way that feels natural to them.

Cold-Climate Cultures Value Time and Tasks

Cold-climate cultures tend to hold tasks and time as high priorities. Respecting the task at hand shows that you care about the people involved. Structure, efficiency, and strategy often rule the day. People will likely have a plan for projects and schedule things to be finished in a timely, efficient manner. People in cold-climate cultures can be conscientious of time and productivity. If there is a faster way to get things done, it's usually appreciated.

Industrialization first took root in cold-climate cultures, revolutionizing the world with faster, more efficient production. Alongside this shift came a collective appreciation for punctuality, often summed up in the phrase "time is money." In these cultures, being on time is more than polite—it's expected. Tasks often begin promptly, even if everyone has not arrived, and finishing on time is seen as a sign of respect for everyone's schedule. Punctuality reflects a shared value of efficiency and care for the commitments of others.

In cold-climate cultures, direct communication is often appreciated. People tend to value getting to the point and sharing the facts of a situation, which helps build trust. While feelings are considered, they usually aren't the focus; facts and emotions are often seen as separate. In many cases, being straightforward and honest about the facts is valued more than the feelings that might follow. However, those who can communicate the truth with warmth and understanding tend to bring the best of both worlds. People with this skill are often well respected and rise to leadership roles. Clear communication about expectations is seen as both kind and thoughtful.

Cold-Climate Cultures Value the Individual

Cold-climate cultures often have a preference to recognize the individual. With a long history rooted in independence and self-reliance, personal responsibility is highly valued as a means of perseverance. The focus on individual achievement reflects a belief that each person's contributions are vital and that personal freedom and choice help drive innovation and progress.

In cold-climate cultures, people often prefer to be seen as independent, believing that each voice matters—their own as well as everyone else's. They tend to view themselves as distinct from the group, and they're usually not shy about having their preferences acknowledged. When it comes to ordering a meal at a restaurant, they might be comfortable choosing exactly what they want, they may expect their order to be served on time, and they may suggest it be prepared with a special request or two. It's about honoring each individual while recognizing the value of being part of the larger whole.

With individualism comes a deep sense of privacy. People from cold-climate cultures tend to treasure their personal space and expect that their belongings—whether in a hotel room, suitcase, or bag—will remain undisturbed unless they give permission. This sense of privacy extends to many areas of life, from medical history to whom they voted for, their finances, their body weight, and sometimes even emotional or spiritual matters. It's all about keeping things close to the heart and sharing only when they feel comfortable.

Relationships are treasured in cold-climate cultures, although they may unfold a little differently than in warmer places. Trust takes time to build, and deep friendships grow gradually. People love to share stories about their adventures and the best ways to get things done, often with a directness that can be refreshing. They're not often shy about offering their opinions, and they're usually more than happy to challenge new ideas, all in good fun and with a spirit of honest curiosity. In cold-climate cultures, open conversations pave the way for meaningful connections.

Cold-Climate Cultures and Hospitality

Hospitality in cold-climate cultures will vary of course, but there are some things that might be expected. When invited to someone's home, the meal will often be served at a set time, and guests should plan to be there on time or even a few minutes early.

Principle 3: Culture

The hosts may prefer to know exactly how many people are coming and will make arrangements for each person to feel comfortable. In all likelihood, they will have done a lot of work beforehand to prepare enough food for their guests and a may have arranged the seating as well. In many instances, bringing uninvited guests without permission, arriving late, and last-minute cancellations are considered impolite.

When eating in someone's home, it can be expected that everyone sits together, often around a dining table while enjoying a lively conversation. Other times, more causal circumstances bring people together; there may be takeout food from a restaurant while watching something on TV. It's common for guests to bring a hospitality gift, such as something to drink, flowers, or something sweet for dessert—usually something that can be shared or added to the meal and enjoyed with the company present.

When churches gather for a meal in many cold-climate cultures, potlucks tend to be the enjoyable norm. Everyone is invited to bring a dish or two to share, and people may sit wherever they like, using the time to chat and make new connections. There's often a preference for hot food, which is why meals may be served on time; even in a relaxed setting, the potluck has a certain rhythm. When the meal winds down, everyone may be invited to stay and join in the cleanup, whether it's washing dishes, folding up tables, or stacking chairs. It's all part of the joy of community with a scattering of shared responsibility to bring it all together.

In cold-climate cultures, hospitality in restaurants tends to have its own flavor. When invited out to eat, each person may expect to order what they like and pay for their own meal—sometimes hosts may offer to cover the tab for their guests but not always. Whether the meal is in someone's home, at a restaurant, or in another location, what really matters is the conversation. Good, engaging talk is always valued, and there's a gentle expectation to leave personal devices aside, making space for genuine connections around the table.

Cultures may vary in the ways they tip; in some places it's expected, and in others a service charge is added to the bill and additional tipping would be considered disrespectful. Following the cultural norms surrounding tipping is essential for team members.

They need to know whom should be tipped, when, how the tip should be given, and precisely how much is expected. Team members want to be good guests, and proper tipping will help them leave a positive impression on those who serve them.

Cold-Climate Cultures and Worship

Worship may look orderly and subdued comparatively, but it doesn't mean a culture lacks spiritual depth. People may be more contemplative; there is a quiet reverence without too much outward expression. Often there is a practical, organized, and timely way of getting things done. Church services start on time and end on time. The order of the service is planned and followed. Guests may be acknowledged and welcomed during the service, but they wouldn't be asked to address the congregation unless they were invited and it was planned ahead of time.

If there are several services, or it's recorded for online use, each part of the service may be limited to a specific timeframe. When speaking or sharing in services, it's good to keep things orderly and within the timeframe suggested in order to show respect to everyone.

Warm-Climate Cultures

Warm-climate cultures tend to be found in places where there isn't a prolonged winter season. In warm climates, we often find that people place their focus on relationships. People and relationships tend to be valued far above tasks and time. These warm, relational, event-focused cultures are usually experienced in climates where the temperatures are warm, but they can also be found in rural or tribal settings in cooler climates. This cultural type can be present when there isn't a desperate need to survive the winter; rather, survival depends on high-quality relationships. Getting along with people becomes a highly valued trait. In warm-climate cultures, we often recognize that respecting relationships and putting others at ease is the greater priority.

Warm-Climate Cultures Value Events

You may find that warm-climate cultures are event cultures as opposed to time cultures. Events held in warm-climate cultures tend to place the people attending those events above time and tasks. There may be a gentle nod toward time, but it does not usually rule events. You may find that things start when everyone arrives and end when everyone leaves. The value is placed on people and why they are together, rather than on a timing orientation brought by the clock.

In a warm-climate culture, it might be said that "good hospitality assures good events." Event invitations may not be limited to just those explicitly invited; there may be an assumption that invitations extend to families and friends as well. Inclusion tends to be assumed, and guests who arrive without a proper invitation would most likely be warmly welcomed. Hosts often prepare an abundance of food so that everyone has enough.

In warm-climate cultures, we tend to find that honoring special guests is a key part of hospitality. It's often expected that everyone will wait for the special guests to arrive before beginning ceremonies or events. Guests are typically invited to eat first, and if they're especially important, they may receive even more care, with a separate table set just for them and special food prepared in their honor. It's a beautiful tradition that shows deep respect and appreciation for those who are valued.

During events in warm-climate cultures, presentation tends to matter a great deal. Tasks are set aside, conversations may be more indirect, and conflict is usually avoided at all costs. Being too direct in conversation or making someone feel shame can be seen as rude. Honor shown to a person's position in the family, their title, or their role in society is often readily accepted. Hospitality toward visitors is the norm and is usually extended with great care and expertise. When arriving at an event, it's polite to greet and introduce everyone, and when leaving, it's customary to say goodbye to each person, along with a special thank you to the hosts. It's all about creating a warm, respectful atmosphere that everyone can enjoy.

Warm-Climate Cultures Are Group Cultures

In warm-climate cultures, we often find a sense of belonging and community that are deeply woven into the everyday life of the people living in these cultures. The needs and well-being of the collective group are often prioritized over individual rights, and one's actions are seen as a reflection of the group they belong to. Whether it's family, friends, or a community like a church or school, the bonds formed within these groups provide a strong sense of safety and dignity.

Obligations to the collective group tend to be valued much more than a person's individual rights. It's often well understood that a person's actions reflect on their group. Having one's identity tied to a collective group provides a sense of belonging and safety, which are both fundamental elements of dignity. What's best for the whole group is more important than what one individual might want. Important decisions such as marriage, schooling, and jobs might be left to the elders and those with the highest status in someone's valued group.

Often, people speak on behalf of their group rather than offering their own personal opinions. Privacy and independence are less desirable, while belonging and inclusion are highly valued. A person might think, *I belong, therefore I am*. Outsiders expecting someone from a collective culture to a make significant decision as an individual, separate from their group, can harm the dignity of not only that one person but also the entire collective group they belong to.

We can expect that people living in warm-climate cultures will tend to value how they present themselves in public. They want to represent their collective group well and show respect to others by dressing appropriately for any occasion. It would be unlikely to see those visiting banks or businesses wearing casual clothes that are stained, torn, or dirty. People dress properly for the occasion and will be respectful in the way they present themselves. It's not about them; it's about showing value to the other person.

People in warm-climate collective cultures will readily share their resources within their group. Tools, housing, and even clothing may very likely be available for everyone's use. Extended family members might live together, and those working abroad may send a portion of their income home to be shared. There may be a tendency not to feel the individual ownership of their possessions like someone from a cold-climate culture might, where permission to use items must be sought. The collective concept is "we" rather than "I," and the "what's mine is yours and what's yours is mine" mindset has the ability to ensure that everyone in the collective group has what they need.

Warm-Climate Cultures and Hospitality

Warm-climate cultures tend to be less planned, and hospitality may be more spontaneous. Preparations for a meal may not start until guests arrive, and they may all work together to prepare the meal. Everything is shared, and everyone is welcome.

When there are special guests, the host often takes great pride in caring for these guests; they tend to be generous in their provisions and offer up their very best. If the occasion calls for taking guests out for a meal, they choose the best restaurant and may order for everyone and then pay for the dinner as well.

In restaurants, the bill may not arrive until it's asked for. Servers may have the outlook that the dinner is an event and guests should be allowed stay as long as they want. Bringing the bill would communicate that they are rushing their guests, asking them to hurry or leave. Even when the restaurant is very busy, guests should be comfortable and feel welcome to stay as long as they like. When the emphasis slants toward relationships, having a meal together often becomes an event and shouldn't be rushed.

Receiving hospitality in a warm culture often means letting the host take care of you. It's not uncommon for hosts to assume responsibility for expenses and to welcome guests for as long as they wish to stay. Hospitality in these cultures is deeply tied to dignity—seeing the person, recognizing their needs, and ensuring they feel valued.

In many warm-climate cultures, hospitality is a cornerstone of social interaction, extended even to strangers. For example, while riding a city bus, someone opening a snack might offer it to the person sitting next to them, even if they've never met. Good manners dictate that the offer be made, and an equally polite response will follow. The first response is typically, "No thank you; I've already eaten." If the friendly bus passenger truly wants you to try the snack, they may insist, which should be politely declined. By the third offer, it becomes impolite to continue refusing. It's a genuine invitation, and accepting it honors their generosity.

Warm-culture hospitality is about seeing beyond the circumstances to honor the individual, making them feel valued, welcomed, and that they belong. It's a profound expression of care and respect.

Warm-Climate Cultures and Worship

Worshiping in a warm-climate culture can be a vibrant and lively experience. The service may begin when everyone arrives and may go on for much longer than expected. Joyous dancing, clapping, and singing can break out during the service. Visitors are often honored and, in some places, may be spontaneously given opportunities to share, sing, or pray. If the church has been planted by missionaries from a cold-climate culture, there might be a mixture of warm- and cold-climate cultures layered into the experience.

> "One of the most valuable tools we can bring with us on a short-term mission trip is the ability to look at each situation through the eyes of the other culture. We can respond with dignity from our hearts and not with a gut reaction from our own cultural perspective."
> —David Cooper, Nazarene Missionary

Your Cultural Bridge

Culture is fluid and is impacted by many things—current events, social media, the younger generation, and political situations, to name a few. Rural settings tend to be more steeped in culture than larger cities. Subcultures abound! Every church has its own specific culture, and they are often ministering to people in another subset of culture. Generalities are helpful for those entering a new culture, but cultural competence comes from living among the people.

Teams are sure to find cultural generalizations interesting and helpful, but the best knowledge will always come from those serving and living in the culture. For missions teams on a short-term trip, this person should be the site coordinator. They understand the lives of the people they minster alongside, they know the history of the area, and they are working to impact the culture for Christ. They have been serving in the culture and know the ins and outs of accomplishing their task in a meaningful way. The site coordinator can be depended on as the cultural bridge.

> "It's very important that both the visiting and hosting teams trust their site coordinator."
> —Robin Radi, Missionary, South America

Challenges of Connecting through Culture

Navigating different cultures can be a nuanced and complex experience that often raises pertinent questions. When cultural norms clash, whose practices should be prioritized: those of the guests or the hosts? Typically, teams visiting new cultures are guests, and an essential part of being a gracious guest is to honor the customs and expectations of the hosting culture. This requires guests to sometimes set aside their familiar ways in favor of adaptability and openness to new experiences. Although stepping into the role of a guest may make some team members feel awkward or find some experiences challenging, the hosting team and site coordinator are there to provide guidance and support. Those choosing to embrace the journey with flexibility can transform these encounters into truly enriching and exciting adventures.

The way dignity is observed in culture is not universal. It can be challenging when there is a dignity conflict. For instance, the warm culture of Malawi cares about hospitality in the way many warm cultures do. They must show that they care for their visitors; in many instances, an international guest would likely be considered very special. When meeting new people, a sign of respect is to invite the visitor into their home for a meal. A special guest would require them to offer their finest, the best food should be served, and it should be served with just the right cutlery and care. Often, they do not have the resources to host the visitor, but they need to be polite, and to be polite is to be hospitable.

When visiting Malawi, guests need to know that the expected answer is "no thank you." They must decline the offer and give an excuse as to why they can't come. Like many warm-climate cultures, they will ask a second time, insisting that you are invited. Again, the guest must decline. If they ask a third time the guest is truly invited and very much expected to come. At this time the guest must accept the invitation. In cold-climate cultures, it's proper to accept the first offer because it most likely won't be offered a second time. Dignity is universal, but the way it's communicated differs dramatically between cultures.

When two cultures come together, the financial side of hospitality can feel like a dance with unfamiliar steps. In cold-climate cultures, the unspoken rule is often that everyone pays their own way, while in warm-climate cultures, it's more common to expect the host to cover all the costs. This cultural choreography can lead to a few missteps when it comes to dining out, sharing resources, or even covering daily expenses of the missions teams, like transportation.

The key to harmony lies in planning ahead and having open, friendly conversations about expectations. A little bit of clarity can turn an encounter with the potential for confusion into a seamless act of understanding, ensuring that everyone feels comfortable and cared for. After all, good hospitality is all about creating a space where everyone feels valued—which includes navigating the tricky terrain of who picks up the check!

When cultures come together, there's always the potential for imbalances in wealth, status, and influence—especially when one culture holds more power than the other. This dynamic can become even trickier when a dominant, assertive culture visits a

Principle 3: Culture

place where a quieter, more indirect approach is the norm. Without care, guests might unknowingly take the lead, overshadowing their gracious hosts. It's important to tread lightly, ensuring that the hosting culture doesn't feel silenced or sidelined. Guests can practice thoughtful humility, leaving space for the hosts to shine, while hosts should feel empowered to speak up and share their perspectives. With a little extra care, these cross-cultural exchanges can become a beautiful dance of mutual respect and understanding, where both sides feel heard and valued.

> "True connection in service is built on humility, understanding, and mutual respect."
> —Marty Hoskins, Director of Missions Personnel and Partnerships

Insider Perspective[1]
When Elephants Dance: Mali, West Africa

"Would you like to know what it is like to do mission with North Americans? Let me tell you a story," said David Coulibaly, a ministry leader in Mali, West Africa.

"Elephant and Mouse were best friends. One day Elephant said, 'Mouse, let's have a party!' Animals gathered from far and near. They ate and drank and sang and danced. And nobody celebrated more exuberantly than Elephant.

---

1. Excerpted and adapted from Dr. Kenneth Acha, "When the Elephant Dances, the Mouse May Die," Servants University, n.d., https://www.servantsuniversity.com/when-the-elephant-dances-the-mouse-may-die/. Dr. Acha is quoting a story from Dr. Miriam Adeney, "an anthropologist, missiologist, author, and associate professor of World Christian Studies at Seattle Pacific University," who was recounting a story an African Christian told her.

"After it was over, Elephant exclaimed, 'Mouse, did you ever go to a better party? What a blast!' But Mouse didn't answer. 'Where are you?' Elephant called. Then he shrank back in horror. There at his feet lay Mouse, his body ground into the dirt—smashed by the exuberance of his friend Elephant.

"Sometimes that is what it is like to do mission with you North Americans," the African storyteller concluded. "It is like dancing with an elephant."

Questions to Consider When Elephants Dance

1. What happened here?

2. What did the elephant do wrong?

3. Is your home culture more like the mouse or the elephant in this story?

4. What can we learn from this story?

Discussion When Elephants Dance

Although it's usually not their intention, people coming from a task-oriented, resource-secure, dominant culture can easily take charge without understanding the subtle intricacies of cross-cultural leadership. It takes wisdom and discernment gathered from leaders on the field to create connections with dignity during a short-term mission trip. By letting the host do the hosting, and following their lead, the team will be in a much better position to not step on too many toes.

Communication Strategies

Communication breakdowns have the potential to lead to a lot of stress during mission trips. Even when the language is the same, the culture can be different, and assumptions can easily lead to misunderstandings. Clear communication should start from the early planning stages and continue through the duration of the trip. Culture has a tremendous impact on communication styles and practices. Leaders will need to be mindful as they develop strategies to bridge the conversation gap.

It's important to think through the impact the communication style of the culture has when sharing information. In many parts of the world, the preferred style is indirect, where people consider it impolite to say uncomfortable things. In many warm-culture climates, you may find yourself facing instances where people share what they think you want to hear rather than giving bad or uncomfortable news. This shouldn't be viewed as people trying to be misleading but that they are trying to be respectful. Some cultures frown on the word "no" and would never speak it out loud, so they may agree to things that might not actually be possible. An important role of the site coordinator is to work through the cultural communication styles of both teams and act as the bridge bringing them together.

Most leaders find that having clearly defined roles, timelines, and expectations is essential to a good experience. Financial costs should be outlined and communicated well before the team arrives. Unexpected changes do happen from time to time but should be the exception, not the rule. Good planning with excellent communication can prevent most mishaps most of the time. Not communicating extra expenses and not having things prepared should be avoided if at all possible.

Missiologist Matt Price reminds us that when communicating cross culturally, it's helpful to keep in mind that the burden of clear communication falls on the one sending the message, not the one receiving it. Believing that others intuitively understand what you mean can be a costly mistake. The message should be clear, and assumptions should be kept to a minimum. The one receiving the communication should ask clarifying questions when necessary to make sure they understand what is expected.[2] As plans are being made, the hosting team and the visiting team should share any necessary input to ensure that dignity is protected for everyone affected by the decisions and strategies being suggested.

> "It is vital for the host and sending cultures to have a steady flow of communication in the weeks leading up to the trip. These conversations do provide much needed information for planning the details of the experience. The less obvious benefit is getting to know the people you are about to serve with. Connections are made and friendships begin as we learn about their families, their churches, their lifestyles, and how they worship God. We can look for ways to learn from each other as we learn about each other."
> —David Cooper, Nazarene Missionary

Whether communication takes place through video calls, phone calls, texting, or email, documenting the conversations and writing down the plans and expectations is a simple but powerful practice. Summarizing decisions in an email or attachment and sharing with everyone involved helps clarify expectations and provides a handy reference point for the future. This small step adds

---

2. Matt Price, professor at Mount Vernon Nazarene University. These thoughts were shared at a cultural orientation event in 2017.

a layer of accountability, reduces misunderstandings, and ensures everyone is on the same page. It's a thoughtful way to bring order to the swirl of ideas and keep the path forward clear for all. Good communication is challenging enough within a single culture and language—add the dynamics of different cultures and second languages, and the need for clarity and grace grows exponentially. Navigating these waters requires leaders to cultivate thoughtful practices and commit to thorough follow-through.

With intentional effort, leaders can help ease the stress of miscommunications and misunderstandings, creating a bridge where words carry meaning and hearts feel understood. A little patience, a lot of grace, and a commitment to clear communication can transform potential confusion into a shared journey of connection and trust.

The Power of Nonverbal Communication

It's not unusual for missions teams to help with projects in places where they don't speak the language. Some team members may learn some words in the local dialect, but for the most part, they depend on interpreters to help them with communication. Relying on interpreters and translators is helpful, but it's important to remember that they assist with only a fraction of what's being communicated. The majority of communication happens outside the spoken language. Words account for only a small percentage of what is being said. We communicate most effectively by the things we do rather than what we say.

Albert Mehrabian, a professor at the University of California in the 1970s, was the first to suggest that we overwhelmingly gather our feelings, attitudes, and beliefs about what someone says not by the actual words spoken but by the speaker's body language and tone. He asserts that only 7 percent of what people hear is actually from our words; 38 percent is our vocal tone; the majority, 55 percent, is through body language.[3] This has a lot of implications for those serving cross culturally. It's not what we say; it's what we do. Even when the language isn't understood, we can be sure that

---

3. Albert Mehrabian, *Silent Messages* (Belmont, CA: Wadsworth Publishing, 1971).

communication is happening. The gestures we use, our expressions, tone of voice, tears, and laughter all communicate something.

Our behavior speaks volumes. For instance, knowing how to properly greet someone according to their cultural norms communicates respect. Whether it's kissing on the cheek, bowing to each other, or shaking hands, there is protocol to be followed. In some countries, shaking hands is the norm. Not shaking the hand of someone reaching out to you is very insulting and shows everyone who witnesses it that you are not friends.

Getting the greeting right is just the beginning. There are many other nonverbal communications to think about. We show our wealth with the name-brand handbags we carry, the cell phones we use, or the expensive watches we like to wear. We declare our religion with our clothing (consider the clerical collar, hijab, yarmulke, etc.). The head coverings we wear—whether turban, wedding veil, tiara, cowboy hat, or baseball cap—all have something to say. A woman's makeup and jewelry are busy making their own statements too. A ring may communicate marriage in some places; in other places, a man sporting a beard symbolizes his marital commitment.

Tattoos, piercings, exotic hair color, and fashion styles make statements all their own. In some places these things might be perceived as artistic, a form of self-expression, or belonging with a particular community. In other places they may signal affiliation with something sinister. In our own culture, we might know what we are expressing through the attire we choose, but when we minister cross culturally, we should question what it communicates in other contexts. We must be willing to ask if the clothing and accessories we wear are saying what we intend. We need to know how things translate in other cultures.

More than our greetings and the clothing we choose to wear, our actions often communicate the loudest. We are communicating with our gestures, our laughter, our whispers, and our tone of voice everywhere we go. We are communicating something when we take pictures of our new friends, their surroundings, and their homes. Are we choosing to take pictures of impoverished areas, strange-looking food, people in humble circumstances, or the even the local toilets that are different from our own, instead of preserv-

Principle 3: Culture

ing the dignity of our new friends? Teams communicate dignity, or the lack thereof, in the pictures they take and share. Teams stand out, and people are watching. They interpret our actions through the eyes of their own culture and their own worldview. People may not understand the language fully, but they are paying attention, and all people understand dignity.

"Be wise in what you wear, what you say, and how you react to things that are not in your culture. Giving up your rights for this time of service will allow you to experience the world from a different perspective."
—Tim Eby, Missionary, Africa

Missions teams need to be prepared. A good cultural orientation is needed before or as soon as they arrive. Going over details of the project is expected, but the more important aspect is learning about the culture and how dignity is communicated within it. Just as team members need to be willing to eat different foods, receive hospitality according to the new culture, and do things differently than they may be used to, they also need to be willing to pay attention to what they are communicating with their expressions, gestures, clothing, and behaviors. Good cultural orientation will help the team show dignity, which will in turn grant them a sense of dignity of their own.

Communicating Cross Culturally

For many missionaries, learning the language is more than a tool for ministry—it's a gateway to understanding the culture itself. Each language carries unique vocabulary, reflecting what matters most to its people. By learning the language, missionaries gain insight into the values and priorities of the community they are serving. But the deeper impact lies in the posture of the missionary as a guest and a learner. Embracing this role opens the door to understanding the heart of the people in their own words, uncovering what is most important to them and why. With every new word and phrase, they aren't just learning a language; they're building bridges to connection, trust, and belonging.

Learning the language offers missionaries more than just words. It's a bridge into the soul of the culture, a bonding experience that forges heartfelt and often lifelong connections. Hosts take on the role of language teachers, much like parents with a young child. The missionary becomes dependent on the hosts, belonging to them in a deeply relational way. In this dynamic, the hosts teach, correct, and encourage, just as they would with children. Along the way, they become like family. Trust grows as the missionary finds their place not just in the language but also in the heart of their new culture, creating a shared journey of understanding and connection.

Much cross-cultural work takes place among people who speak second or even third languages, adding a layer of cultural awareness that visitors must consider. The ability to speak a shared language doesn't guarantee an understanding of the culture behind it. A common language is a bridge, but it doesn't mean the two sides of the bridge are the same. Learning the language without cultural immersion can build competence but often misses the deeper layers of meaning and tradition. Words are only part of the conversation. True understanding comes from engaging with people's hearts, hearing their stories, and discovering the subtle nuances that shape their lives. This depth transforms simple communication into meaningful connection.

Missions teams may bring translators or interpreters along, which can be invaluable. However, it's essential to remember that speaking the language doesn't always mean fully understanding the culture. Cultural knowledge takes time and is learned by living among the people. Hosting teams and site coordinators are vital because their established relationships and cultural insights can ensure that projects will be guided effectively.

When a team includes someone who has previously lived in the country, they can be a tremendous asset, especially if they humbly follow the leadership of the team leader and hosting team. Above all, hosts should remain at the helm of the project. Site coordinators rely on their wisdom to guide the team leader and members, ensuring that the work honors the culture and community it serves.

Communication goes far deeper than words alone. Working in cross-cultural ministries is a work in relationships. Language offers us words. Context brings meaning to words, which speaks to the heart of our relationships. Realizing that each project is unique, teams can trust that the leaders on the ground understand the context of the project, the nature of the people, and their relationships within the community. Teams respecting the relationships that the hosting team and site coordinator have worked hard to foster will humbly be mindful of their words.

Insider Perspective
A T-shirt Says It All

Short-term missions teams can usually be spotted a mile away, at least across an airport. You can often recognize them by their matching t-shirts, which are usually brightly colored and often have customized religious imagery or sayings on them. These people are almost always friendly, and many who travel frequently may have seen them a time or two. When they get to the place they are going, they usually have a few extra t-shirts to share with the locals. It's fun to be part of something like that.

A pastor from South Africa shared about a missions team flying to Africa on the same flight as him. He knew they were a team because of their matching t-shirts, which said, "Save Africa."

He had questions about that statement. Did Africa *need* saving—the whole continent? Didn't they know that God is alive and well in Africa and that there are many Christians there? Wasn't the team going to work with Christians on the ground? Why would they wear shirts like that?

The message implied that all of Africa needed saving, and by golly, this missions team was the one to do it!

Discussion
A T-shirt Says It All

Customized team t-shirts can be great, but paying attention to what the message implies is essential. Consider the images and the wording. Even the color may make a statement you haven't thought about. Leaders should strive to show dignity in these choices.

It's not just shirts; teams have been seen wearing matching hats that were highly unusual as well. Bright flags of their home country prominently displayed on their heads. Statement hats worn and passed out to their new friends. Anything political is best left at home. Short-term mission trips aren't the time to talk politics, flaunt flags, or bring other trendy agendas from the home culture.

When teams give some of their matching t-shirts or hats to people who help with the project, think through the implications of those who get them versus those who don't.

Many teams have worked together with the hosting team beforehand to create shirts together. Every context is different, and having a willingness to do something different can be an excellent opportunity for connection. If you have questions, thoughts, and ideas, the site coordinator will be able to help you navigate what's appropriate and what isn't.

Culture, Communication, and Gift Giving

When we fully understand that the actions of a culture are represented by the collective values underneath the surface, we can see why giving gifts is an act of communication with potential cultural connotations attached. Giving a gift always communicates something.

Teams arrive with generous hearts. By the nature of things, teams come alongside an ongoing ministry to help. Often, they look around, see a lot of perceived needs, and come up with unsolicited solutions based on their limited understanding. Hearts are open, and team members want to give things to their new friends. Their hearts are in the right place, and their intentions are good, but it's important they consider a few things first.

Principle 3: Culture

Nobel Prize winner Milton Friedman is known for the famous quote, "There's nothing that does so much harm as a good intention." Thankfully, God understands our hearts, but actions driven by good intentions alone really can be burdensome to others. Not understanding the nature of what is being communicated when a gift is given (or received) can be disruptive. Many site coordinators have had messes to clean up because of gifts left at the end of a trip. Things like accidental marriage proposals, people leaving churches, or shame brought to whole villages have occurred because of a naively given gift loaded with cultural connotations. Not understanding what a gift communicates culturally can cause immense problems in ministry.

In some countries, a diamond ring means a marriage proposal; in another country it's a string of beads; in yet another, it's a whale tooth. Sending flowers on a birthday can bring joy to some, but to others it communicates that you wish them dead. In some places, if you purchase someone's basic needs, like soap and shampoo, you are committing to be their parent and have signed up to pay for all their future needs. In yet another culture, giving cash to a woman, even if she's already married, means you want to take her on as your wife. Gifts are tricky. Even when they are culturally appropriate, gifts given to some and not others have left behind more than a few hurt feelings.

It's not only the gifted item that communicates; how it's given communicates something as well. Thinking that giving a gift in front of others will create jealousy (which it very well might), some team members choose to give privately. However, in many cultures, gifts given in private communicate, "This is a secret." Others see a person with something left from the missions team and may make the assumption that it was stolen or taken without permission, leaving a stain on the character of the one receiving the gift.

Other issues arise when a gift is given directly to a person rather than to the ministry being served. Imagine a missions team giving a computer to the finance person working in the church office. It's wonderful—they will be able to do things simpler, faster, and better than before. However, if that person changes positions, moves, or leaves the church, they may take the computer with them rather than leaving it for the ministry to use. The ministry then finds itself stepping back in time as they again keep record books without the help of a computer. Personnel changes should be expected; if the gift had been given to the church, things would have continued to progress even when a new person joined the team.

We are not implying that gifts should never be given. A generous heart is a beautiful thing. What's needed is for gifts to be given with great care. Leaders need to communicate clear parameters for gift giving with arriving teams, ensuring that team members work with the team leader and the site coordinator before giving any gifts. Ministry leaders, pastors, and district leaders should approve and have full knowledge of any gifts given to those in their ministries. Mixed messages have the potential to rob people of their dignity. It can simply be avoided when teams trust the guidance of knowledgeable and understanding leaders serving in the context.

Wise leaders think through all aspects of gift giving and create a process as to how contributions should be given. A good policy in short-term missions is to instruct team members and hosts not to give gifts directly unless it has otherwise been approved by leaders. It's also advised that everyone know not to ask for gifts, money, or other items directly from team members or hosts. When there is a need, the policy should indicate how to properly request resources through proper channels, such as through the site coordinator and/or team leader.

Sharing Light with a Cultural Perspective

A beautiful time during short-term missions is when teams get to share the good news of the gospel. Team members may even be asked to preach from the pulpit. Sharing our Christian message in cross-cultural settings is an awesome experience and a great way for teams to learn from and grow with each other. Although it does bring with it more than a few cultural hurdles to navigate, it can be one of the greatest joys of cross-cultural ministry. On one hand, we need to know if the stories we tell make sense and are understood in light of the other's cultural views. On the other hand, we need to know if we are reaching people at the heart level, connecting and letting Christ speak into their deepest concerns. This is a balance that can be achieved with some forethought in both areas.

Principle 3: Culture

Speaking about specific cultural norms allows those inside the culture to understand but often leaves others confused and feeling left out. The speaker may believe that everyone knows that avocados are a poor person's food and should therefore never be served to guests; however, in some places, avocados are expensive and would be considered a delightful cuisine to share with guests. If the focus of the message is how to biblically honor our guests and the speaker hinges that idea to the assumption that avocados are somehow inferior, they may confuse those listening. Linking sermons and messages to specific cultural norms can make sense within a person's own culture but leave outsiders wondering what it means.

The idioms we offer as we explain things can be confusing for outsiders as well. For example, in some English-speaking cultures, to have a "green thumb" means you can grow plants well. Outsiders may be unfamiliar with this phrasing and be left wondering what in the world a green thumb has to do with anything. In China, you might hear the phrase "to inflate a cow," which is to exaggerate or brag. In Thailand, when someone is putting in a lot of effort for very little gain, they might say, "Got to ride an elephant to catch a grasshopper." Group knowledge and idioms share ideas that define who is part of the group and who is not. Knowing lets you in while not knowing leaves you out. Dignity obliges that we be inclusive in our language in order to bring others along. We can do this by leaving our assumptions and in-group thinking behind and tailoring our message so it's easily understood in the new culture.

As team members are asked to speak in front of congregations and ministries, they may need to use an interpreter. It's helpful to meet together beforehand to go over the message to be certain it can be easily understood in the context. The speaker should have it written out and, when possible and if needed, provide a printed copy for the interpreter to review. As clarifications and adjustments are made, the interpreter may want a fresh copy for reference during the service. When there are specific Bible references, the interpreter should know ahead of time so they can present them according to the text in the translation of those listening. When speaking cross culturally, team members should remember that jokes can be confusing, and sarcasm is almost always offensive. Going over all the talking points with the interpreter beforehand can help the guest speaker share the message in a way that will be received well by the congregation.

As in all areas of ministry, sharing the gospel message or preaching from the pulpit requires that we enter as good guests. We are taking part in hospitality, and it should be viewed as an honor and a privilege to be invited to share. As outsiders, moral declarations that are based on our home culture, rather than what's biblical, can hurt and close the hearts of those listening. Ideas such as, "It's wrong to be late," or, "You must pray out loud in one voice together in order to be heard by God," or, "Cleanliness is next to godliness" are more cultural than biblical. Before speaking or sharing in the name of Jesus, everything must thoroughly be sifted through the light of our home culture, the hosting culture, and, above all else, Scripture.

Our cultural upbringings, along with the subcultures of our particular church bodies, help us establish our own cultural norms. When serving in other cultural settings, we sometimes find ourselves surprised by our very own Nazarene brothers and sisters. We see them doing things that conflict with our worldview and what our own culture considers acceptable Christian behavior. Things such as ear piercings, losing one's temper, dancing in church, playing cards, having tattoos, and what clothes are appropriate can make some people feel uncomfortable and bring about judgmental thoughts. Judgmental thoughts often lead to statements that are better left unsaid. Missionaries and local pastors understand the culture and are far more equipped to speak into areas of cultural difference. Sharing the good news abroad means we must allow room for differences in the body of Christ. Letting things be different offers dignity to areas we cannot fully understand as outsiders.

The Altar of the Unknown God

In the New Testament, we can see how Peter and Paul approached sharing the good news. Both were charged with spreading the gospel but went about it differently. They each tailored their message according to those they were speaking to. Peter knew how to speak to his own people. He understood the hearts, beliefs, and background of the Jewish people. He knew they were expecting a messiah and spoke to them through a thought pattern they understood. Although Paul was also Jewish, he was preaching in a culture that wasn't his own, so he did things differently.

In Acts 17:16–34, we find the story of Paul visiting Athens. At that time, Greece had a very different culture than that of the Jewish people. They didn't believe in one God but several gods. They weren't expecting a messiah, and they constructed idols to worship. Their worldview, beliefs, and backgrounds were quite different from the Jewish people. Verses 22 and 23 tell us that Paul stood up on Mars Hill and said, "People of Athens! I see that in every way you are very religious. For as I walked around and looked carefully at your objects of worship, I even found an altar with this inscription: TO AN UNKNOWN GOD. So you are ignorant of the very thing you worship—and this is what I am going to proclaim to you." He went on to share with them that God is near and they are forgiven; he also praised them because they were already worshiping God! He expressed gladness that their poets wrote that we are all children of God, and he confirmed that this was indeed true (see v. 28). He then told them about the resurrection and called them to repentance, and people were saved.

Paul, as a Jewish man, shared the gospel in the cross-cultural context of Greece. We can see that dignity was present throughout. Before he was asked to speak on Mars Hill, he was out and about, building relationships and learning about the people. He learned about their beliefs, worldview, and culture. As he visited the city and saw the idols, he took the time to learn about their gods and discovered something interesting—an altar for what they called the unknown god. He got to know their customs and became familiar with local poetry. As he talked with local people about their idols, he learned that the people of Athens loved to talk about the latest new ideas. Some of what he learned troubled him, but he was also able to learn something about the hearts of the people.

Because Paul spent time building relationships, he was invited to teach at a meeting of the governing council. It's important to note that he was invited by the local people; he didn't speak to the council on his own initiative (see vv. 19–21). After the invitation, he needed to craft a message. It might have been easy for him to share all the things that troubled him. They were worshiping idols in the town square, a grave sin indeed. He could have heaped shame on them, but he didn't. Instead, he complimented them for being religious. Amazing. He then used one of their own altars as way to teach them who the one true God is. Absolutely brilliant. As he quoted the local poet, highlighting what was true, not only did he show respect to the culture, but he also used insider language that connected to the hearts of the people. Classy.

Peter's message to the Jewish people was well received because he understood his home culture and could easily tell them that Jesus is the Messiah they have been waiting for. However, in Greece, his message most likely would not have been understood because the worldviews and culture were different. Paul took the time to build relationships and learn about the culture from the people, so he was able connect to their heartfelt needs. He tailored his message in a way they could truly understand. And he did it with dignity.

The Shared Cultural Response to Guilt, Shame, or Fear

Jayson Georges, author of *The 3D Gospel*, shares his unique way of detecting the heartfelt needs of a culture. In the book, Georges states that "a person's cultural orientation shapes their notion of salvation even more than their individual personality does."[4] Our shared culture dictates to us what our biggest areas of concern are. He goes on to explain that people hear the good news of the gospel in light of their cultural view of sin. Knowing a culture's biggest concern helps us uncover their worldview and heartfelt desires. Like Paul discovering the engraving on the altar, Georges shows us a similar pathway to open doors cross culturally, allowing Christ to enter in.

Missional anthropologists have come to understand that the cultural lens a group may have often sprang out of coping with their community's focus on one of three painful emotions: guilt, shame, or fear. All of us, no matter the culture, struggle to one degree or another with each of these three emotional responses to sin. This

---

4. Jayson Georges, *The 3D Gospel: Ministry in Guilt, Shame, and Fear Cultures* (Tim Press, 2014), 11.

outside voice has a huge impact on how we hear the gospel and why it makes sense it in our lives. People groups develop a shared set of solutions that become cultural norms that address this underlying painful emotion.

World cultures have been shown to fall into one of the three main types according to which one of these three human emotions they place their emphasis. In the West, there is a great desire to avoid guilt while striving to maintain innocence. They seek justice and need forgiveness to maintain relationships. In Asia and the Middle East, the emotion to be avoided is shame, to which honor becomes the solution. Shame and honor are social constructs. Good relationships and esteem come from good social standing. Animism is experienced in tribal settings where fear is the most worrisome emotion. Gaining power becomes the remedy, and seeking power from spiritual rituals is common in these cultures. The problem you feel determines the solution you seek. Jayson Georges explains that these three moral emotions have become the foundation for three types of our world's cultures: guilt/innocence, honor/shame, and fear/power. Taking a broad look into these three cultural types and their common responses to sin can help guide us as we share the gospel more effectively across cultures.

Guilt-innocence cultural worldviews are individualistic societies most often found in the West. People are most concerned about what's right and what's wrong so they can behave properly and remain innocent. Their biggest concern is guilt, and they strive for innocence. They think wrongs should be accounted for, and they rectify wrongs by seeking justice or obtaining forgiveness. They are concerned with who is to blame and want to avoid blame themselves. The United States is known for being the most litigious country in the world with the highest number of prison inmates. The message of the cross offers a message of hope, recognizing that everyone is guilty and deserves to be punished but that Jesus offers forgiveness for our sins; we are washed clean again and made perfect, we are no longer slaves to sin, and the heavy burden of our wrongdoing has been lifted. Jesus offers us glorious freedom.

The honor-shame cultural worldview's principal concern is shame, which they seek to remedy by meeting it with honor. Honor-shame cultures are collective cultures, most common in Asian and Middle Eastern parts of the world where people feel social pressure to fulfil group expectations. They feel shame when they fall short of meeting these expectations and seek to restore their honor in order to save face in front of others. Social status and esteem are highly desired while shame and exclusion are to be avoided at all costs. In honor-shame cultures, showing honor to others is expected, and you bring shame to yourself and your loved ones when you overlook an opportunity to show someone else honor. Withholding honor and causing shame is culturally equivalent to sinning. Scholars suggest that much of the Bible takes place in honor-shame cultures and that as much as 80 percent of today's world's cultures would be described as honor-shame cultures. Mark's Gospel tells us that at the cross Jesus bore our shame for us. He took our shame and exchanged it for his honor. He who knew no shame became shame for us. Imagine sitting before the crucified Jesus, recognizing that he became what many fear the most—nakedness, exposure, vulnerability, and failure. He became sin in order to free us from sin. In him we are invited to participate in what he is doing. We belong to him. He restores our relationships with himself and our community. In Jesus, we have the highest honor of being called children of the living God.

Fear-power cultural worldviews are often found in tribal settings where people live in fear of unseen forces, such as dark magic, curses, witches, and ancestors. They seek to appease or exert power over those forces through hexes, spells, and other ritualist practices. In animistic or folk religions there is an awareness of voodoo, witch doctors, or shaman. People sometimes wear embalms or place them on their children to ward off evil spirits. When people fall ill, they may feel it comes from dark sources rather than a medical condition. Understanding this worldview of fear allows us to find the path where Christ enters. Colossians 1:13 tells us, "For he has rescued us from the dominion of darkness and brought us into the kingdom of the Son he loves." We serve the one true and living God who created this world and sent his Son to rescue us. He cast out demons, performed miracles, healed people, and overcame death on a cross. He has authority over the devil, sin, and death. He is alive and sitting at the right hand of God, and we can call on his help anytime we need it. Trusting in Jesus gives us authority over sin and death. The Holy Spirit is with us, he comforts us, and he is our rock, our refuge, our shield, and our strength.

Georges has shed light onto these three distinct worldviews. These insights are exceptionally helpful for those who wish to share the gospel cross culturally and even more so to those who hear it! Much of Protestant theology comes from the West and focuses on guilt/innocence. Those who are able set aside their own worldview in order to respond to the heartfelt concerns of others will find they have an easier time connecting hearts to Christ. This means that the usual way of sharing the message may have to change in order to address the deeper needs of the heart. We can be assured that altering our message to meet the needs of the heart doesn't change the scriptural message in any way. Whether it be fear, guilt, or shame, we can be certain that these very human emotions, and our cultural responses to them, are all covered by the blood of Christ. The salvation story is big enough to reach the deepest concerns of everyone who hears it.

Cultural Competence versus Cultural Humility

Cultural competence is having the ability to understand, navigate, and work with people from other cultural backgrounds. People with cultural competence know the history and holidays and possibly even the language of a culture. They are good at identifying others, generalizing them, and putting them into categories. People are identified by their differences. Those who have cultural competence have knowledge about a culture and have arrived at knowing who others are based on their cultural background. They have an air of confidence and expertise. Many people make the mistake of believing they are culturally proficient because they have learned a few generalizations.

Cultural humility is different because it leaves room for dignity. People with cultural humility may learn some generalizations but understand that it takes a lifetime to truly learn a culture. They have a teachable spirit and are comfortable being curious rather than an expert. They see subcultures and power dynamics and know that culture is fluid and always changing. They get to know individuals in light of their culture, which brings a feeling of belonging. The hierarchy is gone, and they feel more like equals.

The difference between these two postures is that cultural competence gives the feeling, "I already know who you are" rather than, "I am curious about who you are." Nobody likes to be put in a box. Feeling included rather than excluded is the gift that cultural humility offers, and with that comes dignity.

Cultural competence is important. Generalizations help us navigate a new culture. When looking at generalities, it's important to keep in mind that there are always exceptions to every rule and that subcultures abound. Generalities give us insights that can be helpful as we enter another culture. They offer us a hand to hold as we wade into deep water, giving us the ability to swim sooner rather than later. Using these tools as a gentle guide rather than a harsh ruler is helpful as we get to know the heart of a culture. When hearts move from a posture of competence to humility, there is a shift in the ability to minister cross culturally.

Insider Perspective
Mudslide on the Mountain

Tropical storms aren't anything unusual for this mountain community. They have evacuation plans in place. When a particularly large typhoon is in the forecast, the Nazarene church opens its doors to let community members gather in the basement for safety. This time, a Category 4 storm was approaching, bringing with it more rain than the area could handle. Mass flooding and landslides were underway. People were scared and knew they could count on staying safe at the church.

The basement was full of families taking refuge. During the night, as they tried to sleep, the rains continued to drench the hills around the church. To everyone's horror, terror came crashing upon them. The hillside behind the church collapsed, pouring its unwelcome presence into the building and onto the families seeking refuge. They were buried under a mountain of mud. Many were able to make it out but not everyone. Several in the church building

Principle 3: Culture

died that day. It was a terrible storm and a tragedy for the whole community.

After the funerals, the people cleaned and repaired the church building. These were sad days. Soon a Work & Witness team came to help shore up the mountain so this would never happen again. They came alongside a group of local men who were experts at building rock walls, and together they worked to put up a wall. They built gabion baskets and placed them against the mountain. Building gabion baskets isn't easy work. They are made from strong fencing wire formed into baskets, and filled with boulders and rock. It took everyone working together to get them built and to set in place. The team leader was hard at work making sure everyone had a job to do, and progress was being made.

Just after the first few baskets were in place, a member from the church who could speak English approached the team leader on behalf of the national men working on the project. He shared with the leader, "The men are saying that the wall should be moved back a few feet."

The team leader, not wanting to lose momentum, said, "No. it's fine. Let's just keep going."

Everyone smiled and, out of respect to their honored guest, said, "Okay," and together they all went back to work.

And they worked hard. In just seven days, they got that wall up! The team felt victorious for the great work they did. They had great pictures of working together with the locals. It was a sweet success after such a terrible tragedy. They celebrated with the church family and went back home.

After the team left, the men from the community looked up at that rock wall, knowing it needed to be moved several feet back. In the days after the team left, the men took down the wall, moved all the baskets back a few feet, and rebuilt the wall themselves so they and their community would be safe.

Following Dignity

Questions to Consider
Mudslide on the Mountain

1. What stands out to you about this story?

2. How do you think the missons team would feel if they knew the rock wall was torn down, moved, and rebuilt after they left?

3. Why didn't the local expert insist on placing the wall where it should go?

4. How did warm-climate culture and cold-climate culture affect the outcome of the mission project?

5. What could have helped?

6. How could things have turned out differently if the leaders from either culture had brought the site coordinator into the conversation?

7. How can you safeguard ongoing communication during your project?

Principle 3: Culture

Discussion
Mudslide on the Mountain

From one perspective it's hard to imagine what the team would have thought if they knew the rock wall was moved shortly after they left. They may have questioned why the local men didn't insist on it being moved earlier. They seem to have expected the men building the wall to see things from their perspective. The outsiders were also determined to get the wall finished before they left.

From the perspective of the local men, the expert wall builders had a worldview from a warm-climate culture, which dictated that they give honor to their guests. They very politely asked them to move the wall, and their guests said no. They wouldn't allow the shame of conflict to stain relations between themselves and their generous guests. Time wasn't of the essence; relationships were.

Culture has a powerful influence on a person. People do what seems right to them, even when it may not seem to make much sense to someone on the outside. They make decisions based on their own culture and worldview. Even when you can stretch your mind and see that their view does make sense, it still may seem unimportant to you. People from warm climates prioritize people and relationships so much that they would rather rebuild a rock wall than cause their guests embarrassment or shame them with conflict. People from cold-climate cultures are different. They can be very focused on getting things done and seem to have little concern when someone doesn't hold their ground.

In this situation, everyone felt they were doing the right thing. There was no malice, hearts were in the right place, and everyone's intentions were good. Had either side brought the conversation to the site coordinator, things may have turned out differently.

Culture and the Lens We Look Through

The culture a person lives in and the worldview they hold shapes their perspective on just about everything. Their worldview gives them the lens through which they see the world. Culture dictates how they behave in their world. People don't see the world as it is; people see the world as they are. One person sees one thing, and someone from another culture sees something entirely different. Neither one fully comprehends what the other is experiencing. It's difficult and doesn't always make sense.

Culture takes time to understand, and there is a lot to learn. Some of it is taught; most of it is caught. Those who can lay down their lens of certainty and exchange it with that of curiosity will be the ones to see the world in a whole new way. The longer someone lives cross culturally, the better their ability becomes to see clearly through both lenses.

One of the reasons the Church of the Nazarene has had such tremendous success in short-term missions is that we leverage the important role of the site coordinator. The site coordinator can see clearly in both cultures. They act as the cultural liaison between the missions team and the hosting team. The site coordinator's role of seeing that the project is done, while bridging dignity between the cultures of everyone involved, is short-term missions at its finest.

> "Our ability to observe actions and reactions becomes very important. We should be willing to ask questions and allow ourselves to learn through observation and humility. Our goal should always be to bring honor and respect to our new brothers and sisters in Christ."
> —David Cooper, Nazarene Missionary

Culture Action Plan

1. Understanding Cultural Dynamics
What are the key characteristics of the host culture, and how do they differ from the missions team's culture? How can both teams navigate these differences with respect and humility?

2. Bridging Worldviews
How do worldviews (e.g., guilt, shame, or fear) impact the project's goals, relationships, and communication? How can teams approach these differences with cultural sensitivity?

3. Adapting to Warm-Climate or Cold-Climate Culture
Is the project set in a warm- or cold-climate culture? How can the team prepare to adapt to different views of time, communication, and relationship building?

4. Anticipating Cultural Conflicts
What cultural norms (e.g., gender roles, leadership styles, or generational respect) need to be clarified beforehand to prevent misunderstandings and conflicts?

5. Engaging Cultural Experiences
What meaningful cultural experiences can the missions team respectfully engage to foster trust, mutual learning, and deeper relationships?

6. Facilitating Clear Communication
What will be the most effective communication method between the site coordinator, the hosting team, and the visiting missions team to ensure clarity and collaboration?

7. Maximizing Interpreters and Translators
How will translators or interpreters be prepared to bridge language and cultural barriers effectively? When and where will their presence be most crucial?

8. Showing Respect through Presentation
What guidelines do the teams need regarding appropriate clothing, gestures, behavior, and photography to show respect for the host culture?

9. Identifying Cultural Liaisons
Who will serve as a cultural bridge between the two teams to provide insight, address challenges, and foster mutual understanding throughout the project?

Principle 4: Learning Posture

*Do not conform to the pattern of this world,
but be transformed by the renewing
of your mind.*
—Romans 12:2

Key Definitions

✦ **Briefings**: Preparing others by giving them needed instructions for a plan or event.

✦ **Context**: The interrelated conditions around words and actions that bring meaning to the circumstances at hand. What happens prior to, after, the time, place, and setting in which circumstances occur is considered context, all having the ability to create or change meaning of what's being said or done.

✦ **Culture**: The observable social practices of a people group. These practices are often unspoken but are understood by everyone in the group. They are born out of an agreed-upon set of values. While these values may be less visible to the outsider, they are intuitive to the members of the group.

✦ **Debriefing**: The process of talking through events after a task is complete. The task can be a mission, a project, or simply the activities of the day. Information is shared in order to unpack, learn, and process what happened. It places events in context and brings the broader scope of the overall mission into perspective.

✦ **Discipleship**: A journey that Christians make with other people as they go from no faith, to new faith, to mature faith, walking alongside others with evangelistic intent until they repent and believe. The journey continues until they are fully devoted, sanctified disciple makers.

✦ **General Superintendent:** The Church of the Nazarene has six elected elders who constitute the Board of General Superintendents. This is the highest office in the denomination and is charged with the responsibility of administering the global work of the Church of the Nazarene.

✦ **Incarnation:** God became flesh and lived among us. God became human in the form of Jesus Christ, the Son of God, and second Person of the Trinity.

✦ **Nazarene Discipleship International:** A global ministry of the Church of the Nazarene whose mission is to carry out the Great Commission to children, youth, and adults in preparation for a lifelong journey of being and making Christlike disciples in the nations.

✦ **Prevenient Grace:** The divine influence that precedes and enables human response, offering grace that draws us deeper into our relationship with God. It is grace that goes before us, preparing both missionaries and those they serve by fostering openness, understanding, and readiness for transformation.

✦ **Project:** A defined activity that will assist in accomplishing a goal set by the hosts to develop and expand the of the Church of the Nazarene.

✦ **Regional Director:** Each of the six global regions identified in the Church of the Nazarene is led by a regional director (RD) who is appointed by the global church. On each region there is a regional office with missionaries and staff to assist with strategy, missionary placement, and the ministries of the fields in that particular world region.

✦ **Resources:** The people, expertise, labor, funds, equipment, and materials that contribute to the completion of a project.

✦ **Role Model:** A person whose behavior, example, or success is or can be emulated by others.

✦ **Work & Witness:** A construction ministry in the Church of the Nazarene. Teams from one church or district come alongside another church or district locally or globally to help their brothers and sisters in Christ build physical structures that will serve them in ministry.

✦ **Worldview:** The lens through which a person views the world. The subjective perspective of an individual based on their own values creates the paradigm by which they make sense of the world.

Guiding Principle #4: Learning Posture

People come together to participate in short-term missions projects with hearts full of good intentions. They have something to share, they want to help, and they want to give back to the Lord. Often, those who are blessed with special skills, talents, and resources want to share the blessing. They are prepared to offer the best of their abilities, and they are excited to share with those on the mission field and others in need. Most of the time, people serve with sincere hearts full of love.

Going as a learner can be complicated because we bring our expertise, offerings, and gifts that lift us to a position of authority because we think we fully understand the nature of what we are giving and doing. People are confident in their abilities and become comfortable taking the lead. They may think, *We know how this project should work, we are here for a short period of time, and we are ready to get things done.* But moving forward too quickly without fully knowing the underlying context can lead to avoidable complications.

When serving, it's good to realize that cross-cultural ministry can sometimes be like fitting a square peg into a round hole. In our home cultures all the pegs are square, and they fit perfectly into the square holes around us. When we arrive in a new context with our square pegs, we soon find that they don't fit quite right because the holes are round, oval, or an entirely different shape altogether. It's not that the gifts aren't needed; they just need to be reshaped a little.

Taking the time to learn what shapes are needed will help missions teams reshape their square pegs into something that can really help the people they are serving. To have a learning posture is to know that some adjustments will need to be made to what we are bringing and how it's presented. It's not up to outsiders to create square holes; rather, we need to reshape what we are bringing and offer it in a way that is truly useful. The site coordinator and the hosting team will be familiar with the landscape and will be able to guide teams as they bring ministry gifts and tools. They will help team members shave off the square edges and fit them in according to the culture and the needs of the people. Teams not taking the time to learn or having the willingness to adjust can make things much more complicated than necessary.

Those who host teams must adopt a learning posture as well. Not only is it essential to learn the needs of the guests in order to be helpful hosts, but learning the nature of the gifts brought to the project will also impact everything. Sacrificial resources brought by missions teams aren't given out of abundance; rather, they are treasured gifts of the heart, a love offering to the Lord, and should be treated with dignity. The hosting team needs a full understanding of the nature of the resources in order to guide the giving and receiving process so it fits properly into the culture and adds true benefit to the project. If tools are brought, people may need to learn how to use and care for them. When tools are too cumbersome for the project, the missions team needs to be aware of this too. Only by learning from each other is it possible for the project be a success.

Insider Perspective
A Simple Solution to a Simple Problem

A group of administrators joined a short-term missions team to help the staff at a Bible school run things more smoothly. The school's employees included a team of maintenance men who weren't highly educated but knew how to work hard. They kept the buildings in good repair, and the grounds were always beautiful. They made very little in the way of wages, just a few dollars a day. They reported to the office at the end of each workday to collect their payment, which was given to them in the local currency.

The visiting team assessed the situation and determined that paying employees daily was a time-consuming and tedious chore. To save time for the office staff and the employees, they implemented a plan for all employees to be paid weekly with a paycheck that could be deposited into their own bank accounts.

This change meant that the maintenance men needed to open bank accounts, which they had never done before. In order to get a bank account, they would need to get their national identity card. Many of them didn't have one because the cost was prohibitive.

Principle 4: Learning Posture

Another roadblock was that most of them couldn't read sufficiently to fill out the paperwork required for a bank account. Several of the men quit their jobs because of the indignity that their international guests were requiring of them.

Questions to Consider
A Simple Solution to a Simple Problem

1. What assumptions were made by team?

2. Did they truly understand the problem?

3. Was it actually a problem? Why?

4. Whose dignity was harmed in their solution?

5. How could they have acted less like foreigners and more like guests?

6. What strategies can you put in place to help teams reshape square pegs?

Discussion
A Simple Solution to a Simple Problem

The international guests, with all of their expertise, could easily identify problems with the payroll system. They quickly put in place a simple solution to streamline the process that would have worked perfectly in their own context at home. However, their lack of understanding of their project's context caused great indignities to those who being served by the system that was already in place. They were fitting a square peg into a round hole. Assumptions were made, and people were hurt in the process. Most of us have had an experience with the absurdity of someone offering solutions to problems they didn't fully understand.

We can all relate to the maintenance men in this story. However, the people working in the office had their dignity stepped on as well. They fully understood the existing situation, but their opinions were never sought. When a hosting culture desires to be respectful and deferential toward visitors, experts, and international guests, unknowing team members can easily misinterpret this behavior and assume leadership without realizing there are many things yet to be understood.

Many around the world who have worked with international guests in ministry projects have been asked, "What is the one thing you wish international helpers understood?"

No matter who is asked or where in the world they live, the answer is always the same: "I wish they trusted us. If they trusted us, they would ask us and learn from us. We are their brothers and sisters in Christ, and we know our own people." They go on to explain, "Our international guests aren't the ones bringing God here; he is already here, guiding the people who are doing his work."

Those who are going to serve should always keep in mind that that those who already live there understand their culture and are the experts in their own context. Those with whom we serve can offer us a great deal of wisdom if we are willing to sit humbly as their guests and learn from them.

A wonderful book called *Color*, coauthored by African Regional Director Dr. Daniel A. K. L. Gomis and General Superintendent Carla D. Sunberg, speaks to this point well. They share an African proverb that paints us an image: *The guest does not untie the goat.* They write:

> We enjoy inviting friends over for dinner and preparing special meals. Sometimes we work for hours to prepare for a special occasion. Can you imagine that the moment arrives when you invite your guests to the table, only to have them run back out to the car to get something. Before sitting down to eat, they

produce their own cutlery and dishes, rearranging everything that has already been set. In that moment, we feel dejected, as if we have done a poor job of hosting.

Sadly, this is how we have often entered new cultures. We come with many things because we believe that what we have brought with us is something that *they* should have. We don't arrive empty-handed as a guest so our hosts can take care of us, but instead, we feel the need to show people something we think is better. There is vulnerability in being the guest, for you are now dependent upon the host.[1]

> "Be a learner as you visit the new culture. Learn from your hosts what God is already doing in their community, and always remember how important it is to learn people's names."
> —Janet Wilkins, Asia-Pacific Region

The Incarnational Jesus

Entering a new culture requires a level of humility that is most beautifully shown to us by Jesus. Our Savior came to us as a baby. He lived incarnationally, didn't bring anything with him, and had humble beginnings. He arrived in a stable, alongside the animals living there. They shared with him their feeding trough, a manger, that he could use for his bed. Research tells us that, by the time the Magi appeared bringing gifts, he was close to two years old. Jesus was the Savior of the world when they arrived, yet he was still just a toddler. Was he potty trained? Maybe. Still nursing? Possibly.

Of this we can be certain: Jesus arrived into this world dependent on his mother and family to meet his needs. He was God,

---

1. Daniel A. K. L. Gomis and Carla D. Sunberg, *Color: God's Intention for Diversity* (Kansas City, MO: The Foundry Publishing, 2021), 55.

yet just like us, he learned how to live in this world from those who raised him. They loved him and taught him everything he needed to know to get along in this world.

His posture as a learner was ever present. In Luke 2:46–52, we find young Jesus lost in conversation with leaders and teachers of the temple. Jesus was found asking them questions and listening to them. The leaders at the time were impressed with his deep insight, but what some of us today might find even more astonishing is that Jesus Christ, the Son of the living God, arrived with a heart to learn from his creation. Jesus—the Savior of the world—valued the perspectives, understandings, and knowledge of the people he came to serve. He entered with the humble heart and posture of a learner.

To enter another culture in the way of Jesus, we must become dependent on those who are already there to teach us and take care of us. Our Nazarene family is there to welcome, host, and guide the missions team. They will teach the team everything they need to know with the compassion of a loving family. This requires that, like Jesus, missions teams enter with humility and the heart of a learner. They may bring answers and solutions that will surely transform lives, but without posture of learning, those offerings are given in a way that falls outside the example Jesus gave us.

After Jesus grew in the culture and learned from his family, the Gospel of John tells us in chapter 2 how Jesus's ministry first started. His approach is a perfect example for those serving in missions. The first thing Jesus did after gathering his disciples was go to a wedding with his mom. Weddings are always steeped in tradition and are cultural events at their finest. There is protocol to be followed, valued guests, delicious food, and fine wine. In Cana at the time, there should have been plenty of wine for the guests, but the host ran out—something that should never have happened at a wedding. The father of the bride would be shamed in front of his friends, his family, and his new in-laws. It would be an embarrassment that wouldn't soon be forgotten. Jesus's mother understood the situation and asked Jesus to help.

Jesus told her he wasn't quite ready to do it; he wasn't sure it was his time. But Mary knew Jesus, and she understood the needs of the hosts. The host was vulnerable to shame, and it was time for Jesus to act. Jesus, our Savior, humbly trusted his mother's leadership. It was his first act of ministry and his first miracle. It was dignity covering vulnerability. It wasn't Jesus's idea. He was invited by his mother to do it. He listened to her, followed her instructions, and served those in need.

The posture of a new missionary entering another culture should be like that of a young child. Like Jesus depended on his mother, missionaries are dependent on the local people to help them navigate life in the new culture. Locals have an understanding and a way of doing things that is in every sense foreign to the new missionary. The missionary has much to learn, and it often takes many years for them to understand a culture in depth. They practice cultural humility by depending on local people to guide, help, and teach them. After they grow in understanding, they are then able to make a positive impact in the culture. It took Jesus many years to do that, and we can be certain it will take the missionary some time to learn as well.

A learning posture is welcomed in all areas of ministry, both locally and abroad. Knowing that it takes time to understand and to learn the values expressed through culture requires us to be dependent on locals to guide the way. Learning and being curious without judgment offers dignity. Arriving with the willingness to do the unexpected is necessary. Bringing two cultures together for a short time to accomplish something is an extraordinary experience for everyone.

The Mindset of a Learner

The burden that comes from having to know everything is heavy. The gift of being a learner allows us to set that burden down for a while. Choosing to hold the mindset of a learner not only lightens our load, but it's also the best strategy for getting along in a new environment. Being a learner sets everyone on the right foot as the project gets off the ground. Interactions with people who seek understanding rather than making assumptions are wholeheartedly welcome by all. Trusting that the hosting team fully understands their own context and have seen the Lord's work all along gives the missions team an opportunity to learn things they may have never dreamed of.

> "When entering a new culture, it is essential to approach it with open hands, learning from the people and their ways rather than imposing our own."
> —Marty Hoskins, Director of Missions Personnel and Partnerships

---

Curiosity without judgment is always encouraged when encountering things being done in surprising ways we aren't accustomed to. Letting go of words such as "wrong" or "weird" and embracing phrases like, "That's different, but it's okay" not only imparts dignity to those doing things differently, but it also expands the worldview of those witnessing a new way of getting things done. It's not necessary for missions team members to teach everyone about the way things are done back home. Joining a short-term missions project can be a great time for participants to fully leave home and embrace the place and people with whom they are serving. Learning local customs, trying new foods, and participating with an open mind will go a long way toward connecting and building relationships.

Prevenient Grace: Meeting God Where He's Already Working

Speaking at a short-term missions conference in 2021, General Superintendent Dr. David Graves offered these comforting words, "God is the Lord of the harvest. God is the one inviting his people to join in. When we go, he is already there, he is at work, and he is inviting his people to come along and join him. He is in charge, and he has a plan. Going as a learner, learning what he is doing—what he has been doing all along—is where our hearts should be. There's

Principle 4: Learning Posture

no need to take God there because he's already there—waiting for his friends to come and see what he is up to."

As Nazarenes, we believe in prevenient grace—the holy idea that the Spirit goes before us to draw us closer into our relationship with God. We don't take God—we are moved by the Holy Spirit, who leads us to him. We follow. Even when we enter unknown territories where the work of the church is just beginning, the Holy Spirit prompts us to go and meet God, who has gone before us. When God is leading, we can trust that he is already there.

> "The most important aspect of serving cross culturally is cultivating the ability to listen and learn from the hosting communities. We must listen first, and not lose sight of the fact that it takes time, sometimes a lifetime, to build relationships of trust and mutual respect."
> —Nell Becker Sweeden, CEO,
> Nazarene Compassionate Ministries, Inc

Most of our short-term missions work will be joining our Nazarene brothers and sisters around the world. We can rest assured that God is alive and well in their churches and communities, and he is inviting us to come along. It's a family connection, his children coming together. Short-term missions teams follow the omnipresent spirit of God, experiencing the Father wooing his children and calling them into his presence.

Imagine for a moment that your church has a team coming from another Nazarene church for a short-term missions project. Everyone is excited to meet their Christian brothers and sisters and share what God is doing in their part of the world. Deciding to get to know the other team better, you tune in to their online worship service. Then you hear the pastor announce that they are doing a mission project with you and that they have been charged with taking Jesus to you—implying to everyone listening that they are the possessors of God, they have him and you do not, until they bring him to you. They failed to recognize that God is already with you, who are fellow Christians. Ouch!

Understanding prevenient grace brings dignity to those we serve alongside. God is already there, inviting his children to participate in what he is doing. We are all his children. Even when the work leads us outside the doors of the church, we can trust that God is there working and inviting us into his holy adventure.

What Is God Up To?

Missions teams are truly blessed when they get a glimpse of what God is doing in new places. Often, teams arrive and start sharing their own stories and teachings, which is great. But it's equally important for them to listen to and learn from those they are serving. Hearing from local pastors and ministry leaders can be deeply encouraging and strengthen everyone's faith.

Encourage local leaders—whether they're experienced missionaries or those just starting out—to share their stories with the missions team. These testimonies can be inspiring and provide valuable insight into the local context. Recognizing and honoring their work can be uplifting for everyone involved.

Missions team members should also be ready to share their own stories of what God is doing in their lives and communities. Focus on the positive and powerful ways God is moving, rather than comparing cultures or discussing personal opinions about their home culture. Sharing uplifting stories about how God is at work can create a mutual exchange of encouragement and inspiration.

As team members learn new skills, explore a different culture, and grow spiritually, they will also gain insight into themselves. Setting aside time for personal reflection helps them integrate these experiences into their ongoing journey with God. This self-reflection can reveal new things about themselves and their role in God's plan.

Be imaginative in creating opportunities for learning and connection. Plan intentional group activities, meals, and local ministry visits. Allow time for both group sharing and personal reflection.

Principle 4: Learning Posture

This way, team members can fully appreciate the lessons and experiences of their mission trip. God has something to teach everyone involved. By listening, sharing, and reflecting, both the missions and hosting teams can grow together in faith and understanding.

> "Plan for team members to interact and hear from a wide variety of leaders on the field."
> —Greg Taylor, Nazarene Missionary

The Journey of Discipleship

"To make Christlike disciples in the nations" is the mission statement of the Church of the Nazarene. Dr. Scott Rainey, who has served as a pastor, missionary, and global leader of Nazarene Discipleship International (NDI), describes discipleship first and foremost as a journey of grace. He explains discipleship this way: "We understand disciple making as a journey that Christians make with other people as they go from no faith, to new faith, to mature faith. Imagine everyone in the church mobilized to come alongside people who don't know Jesus, walking with them with evangelistic intention until they repent and believe, and we continue to walk with them until they are fully devoted, sanctified disciple makers."[2]

Discipleship is a journey that Christians travel together. We are called to be both disciples and disciple makers. In discipleship, we continue to grow more and more into the image and likeness of Christ as we bring others along with us. At times, we are the ones being discipled; at other times we are disciple makers. Short-term missions projects bring people together in all walks of the discipleship journey. Everyone is in their own place along the way, whether they have yet to meet Christ, they are young in the faith, or they are saints

---

2. These comments were made to the authors in 2024. The same ideas can also be found on *Holiness Today*'s YouTube channel, "NDI Core Principles," located at: https://www.youtube.com/watch?v=UWLV9U_Qcy0.

who have been walking with God for many, many years. We can be sure we will encounter God at work in the lives of everyone we meet.

With intentionality, we have a real opportunity for discipleship. God has been part of the story since long before the team arrived, and he will continue to be there long after the team leaves. We are given a short window of time together during the missions project. We can make good use of this time by planning with intentionality. God has been preparing the hearts of his people for this sacred encounter. Doors will be opened. Growing, learning, and teaching will surely take place. Opportunities for disciple making will arise, and everyone should be prepared for divine encounters. Participating in a missions project guarantees that hearts will be changed. Everyone will move a little further forward in their journey to becoming more like Christ.

Cross-Cultural Discipleship and Role Models

Cross-cultural settings offer a beautiful and complex space for growth. People going to new settings arrive with their senses on overdrive. The sights are different, the sounds are unique, the smells, temperatures, and foods are all exotic and new. Everything is stimulating and catches their attention. Team members are trying to process things with an acute sense of awareness. Simultaneously, they are encountering the challenges that cultural and language barriers bring. This brings everyone's actions, behaviors, and attitudes to the forefront. In an environment such as this, discipleship becomes more about being caught than taught. Everyone is a learner, and everyone becomes a role model. Those doing cross-cultural ministry should be reminded of the words from St. Francis of Assisi: "Preach the gospel at all times. When necessary, use words."

Short-term missions offer an excellent opportunity for discipleship and leadership development. This unique setting connects people to opportunities and leadership styles they may have never experienced before. Intentionally bridging people can raise up new leaders through the simple act of role modeling. Role models lead by example. Others watch, learn, then imitate. It's caught as much as it's taught. The hosting team has much to teach the missions team as they model their ministry roles in the new context. The missions team brings unique gifts and talents to share. Everyone has something to offer, and everyone has something to learn.

Role modeling is simple yet powerful. The global success of the Work & Witness ministry is a great example. Short-term missions in the Church of the Nazarene originated with teams from the United States going to help in other countries. As these teams have traveled the world, the ministry was modeled. Seeds were planted, and now those seeds have taken root and sprouted to life, growing into strong ministries of their own. Work & Witness has truly gone global. There are more short-term missions teams sent from more countries than ever before. People learn by example. Role modeling has been and will continue to be an instrument that has the power to change the world.

Discovering the Hidden Gems of Culture

To learn a new language is to learn a new culture. You learn what's important because they have words for the things that matter most, and it might be things you have never thought about before. Of course, missions teams won't have time to learn a new language while they are there, but with guidance from those who understand the language and culture, God can help people to see his world in a whole new way.

For example, Lera Boroditsky, an assistant professor of psychology, neuroscience, and symbolic systems at Stanford University, shares some interesting insights about an Aboriginal tribe in northern Australia. What she shares about the people who live in Pormpuraaw can teach us something about our own worldview. This tribe doesn't have words for "left," "right," "forward," or "back." Instead, they use cardinal directions. They might say something to the effect of, "You have an insect on your southeast leg." But, if you were facing another direction, a bug in the same location might be said to be on your west leg. To greet someone, they will say, "Where are you going?" Your answer might be something like,

"Northwest, the middle distance." If you don't have a sense of direction, Boroditsky says, "You can't even get past 'Hello.'"[3]

The implication of this usage of language is that this tribe will always know their orientation in the world. Anywhere in the world, they will be able to know the cardinal directions and never be lost. They can even be in a room without windows, playing games with friends, and still know which direction is north. Boroditsky describes a test where they were given several cards depicting the same person at different ages. They were asked to lay the cards out on a table in order, from the youngest age to the oldest. English speakers doing this exercise tend to lay out the cards from left to right because that is how we think of linear time. Speakers of languages that read right to left, on the other hand, tend to lay out the cards in this exercise from right to left. This Aboriginal tribe, however, laid the cards out according to the cardinal directions—east to west. They were tested facing multiple directions, and no matter which direction they were facing, the card showing the youngest age was always placed the farthest to the east, and the card showing the oldest age was always placed the farthest to the west.

This tiny difference in language has an incredible impact on culture and worldview. The Aboriginal tribe in Pormpuraaw do not see themselves as the center of the world; rather, they know their place in the world. In languages where we are oriented by our left, our right, what's in front of us, and what's behind us, we become the center of the world. That's quite a difference. The everyday language of this people reminds them that they aren't the center of the world. Instead, they are *part* of the world, part of something much bigger than themselves. Christians can learn something from that orientation.

Culture reveals concepts that we may have never thought about before. What's valued in a culture is given words and is shared through a common language. To learn language is to learn culture. To learn culture is to discover the hearts of people. Understanding

---

3. Lera Boroditsky, "How Does Our Language Shape the Way We Think?" *Edge*, June 11, 2009, https://www.edge.org/conversation/how-does-our-language-shape-the-way-we-think.

Principle 4: Learning Posture

hearts is our starting place. We are all God's children, and we have so much to learn from one another. Imagine all the languages, with all that they express—all the ideas, all the thoughts, and all the values they communicate. It's amazing to think of the privilege we have as believers to travel to faraway places to be with our extended Christian family and to be given this incredible opportunity to learn from one another.

The Power of Briefings and Debriefings

Briefings and debriefings are like the faithful companions of your ministry team. They warmly guide everyone into service and help everyone thoughtfully process events afterward. Consider them your indispensable tools for preparing your team and fostering a reflective space to consider their experiences together.

Briefings are about getting everyone set up for success. Before the project starts, and even each new day or when a new event comes up, hold a briefing to make sure everyone knows what to expect. It's like giving your team a game plan. You'll cover things like what supplies they'll need, what to wear, cultural tips, and what kind of hospitality to expect—anything they need to know for success. Briefings can help everyone feel ready and at ease. Plus, they are a great chance to clarify any questions or concerns before things get started.

Debriefings happen after the event or at the end of each day. This is where the power of learning happens. Debriefings help everyone process their experiences and understand what went well and what could be improved. They're also a time to reflect on what the team learned and how they felt about the day. It's like putting the pieces of the puzzle together. Good debriefings can help clear up any misunderstandings and give everyone a better understanding while honoring the dignity of the culture and experiences they encountered.

Having someone with experience in both cultures lead the debriefings brings a sense of dignity to the process. Usually the site coordinator is ideal for this role. Thoughtful questions encourage team members to reflect on what they've learned and how they've felt, helping everyone understand the bigger picture. In a safe and respectful space, participants are free to share their thoughts, ask questions, and process their experiences without fear of judgment. This kind of environment fosters dignity for each person involved, allowing them to feel heard and valued as they make sense of their journey together.

> "By incorporating reflective moments and learning opportunities, team members can fully grasp the depth of their experiences."
> —Elizel Soto, Missionary, Mesoamerica Region

The way you handle briefings and debriefings might vary depending on the culture and the project. It's important for everyone to be prepared for what's coming and to have a chance to reflect on what's been experienced. It's a good idea to keep these sessions private and respectful, allowing team members to ask questions without feeling awkward. Having someone who understands the cultural nuances can make a big difference in how these sessions are received. Ultimately, both briefings and debriefings are about growth. They help your team see the beauty in the culture they're working in and understand the impact of their work. When done well, they help everyone see how God is at work in their lives and in the community they're serving.

After the mission wraps up, debriefings are also a great time to evaluate how everything went and to assess what can be improved for the future. Regular debriefings help leaders learn and grow, making the missions experience better for everyone involved.

Insider Perspective
An Uncomfortable Exchange

It was near the holidays, and the missions team came to work on a project in the city. The church where they were working plant-

Principle 4: Learning Posture

ed a little church in a small village just outside the city. It was a great little church. The pastor was a young lady in her teens. There were a few older people who lived in the impoverished area and helped with the church plant. It's always exciting when a missions team has the opportunity to go to an outreach area to do ministry.

The pastor arranged for the team to deliver bags of food to needy families in the church. The bags contained more than enough for a traditional Christmas dinner. The team would break into smaller groups and were assigned a leader from the church to be their guide. Their guide would take them to the preselected homes to deliver the bags. When they arrived at each home, team members were asked to pray for the family living there and give them the bag. The village was small, the houses were simple, and the people were friendly. It was good to watch the team interact with the community.

At one particular house, a woman opened the door. Her frail-looking husband was lying on a cot in the small room. The leader from the church shared that he had a terminal illness and wasn't able to work or even get out of bed. This woman very much needed the groceries that were inside the bag the visitors held.

The church member stepped back to allow the team member to pray and present her with the groceries. The team member did more than pray with this woman. She asked the woman if she would like to invite Jesus into her heart. The woman looked at the much-needed groceries, then at the team member, and said yes. Right there on the stoop of her house the woman confessed she was a sinner and asked Jesus into her heart. The team member rejoiced and gave her the bag of food. She couldn't wait to share the good news with the rest of the team.

As the team walked back to the church, the guide confided in one of the other team members that the woman receiving the groceries was a founding member of the church and had been a Christian for many years.

Questions to Consider
An Uncomfortable Exchange

1. What happened?

2. Why do you think the woman agreed to accept the Lord when she was already a Christian?

3. What do you think the team member was thinking?

4. How was dignity lost?

5. What can we learn?

6. How can you encourage visiting team members to follow the guidelines set by their hosts?

Discussion
An Uncomfortable Exchange

The woman in this story was extremely vulnerable. Her spouse was ill, and she had many needs. In that moment, what she needed most was food for her family. She had strangers standing in front of her with that very thing. The plan from the church was to bring dignity to her door with a blessing and Christmas dinner. Instead, it cost her something. She quietly gave up her dignity in exchange for some desperately needed food.

When missions teams step into a ministry, they do so as guests, not leaders. Embracing the role of a humble guest means recognizing that they are not in charge. When guests fail to adopt a learning posture and assume they know best, they can disrupt the ministry and wound the hearts of the local community. It's a privilege for missions teams to be part of local efforts. As guests, they must honor this opportunity with respect and gratitude. Listening to and trusting local leaders is not just important—it's essential.

> "Short-term missions is not about fixing problems but about joining in the ongoing work of God's kingdom with a heart to serve and be transformed."
> —Marty Hoskins, Director of Missions Personnel and Partnerships

A missions team with the heart of dignity listens and adjusts. They trust their leaders. They hear and do what is asked. They know they are not in charge, and they understand that they don't always know what's best. What a gift they bring when they arrive as learners. Being a good guest with the heart of a learner allows dignity to always be present.

A Learner's Mindset: Cultivating Trust, Dignity, and Global Insight

Maintaining the posture of a learner brings adaptability as teams learn new skills and collaborate. It brings dignity to the culture while building trust in relationships and in the community at large. With the mindset of a learner, we gain new insights about others' lives as well as our own. Learning the nuances of the project and the resources brought by both teams communicates that we care about each other, we see hearts, and we understand intentions. Those arriving to the project without the heart of a learner compromise dignity and unintentionally cause harm, whether they are the part of the sending team or the receiving team.

Remember that the Lord is there, that he has gone before us, and that he is waiting for his people to arrive to see what he is already up to. God calls exactly the right people together for an extraordinary moment designed to bring glory to his name. Those who recognize that everyone has something to teach and everyone has something to learn will see God through new eyes, learning what he is doing and gathering extraordinary new insights that bring us closer to him as we grow closer to each other.

> "Site coordinators and team leaders should be willing to coach their team members. When the host trusts leaders enough to tell them that the team is making errors or is unhelpful to their long-term work, be kind but strong in making an intervention to coach toward correction."
> —Brian Becker, Point Loma Nazarene University

Engaging in the project as a learner means looking at short-term missions through a global lens. It's knowing that God is at work all over the world. He is ageless, timeless, and has been loving his people well all along. He has been there long before the team arrives and will be there long after they are gone. All cultures have unique beauty and treasures given to them by the Lord. Arriving as a learner prepares us to receive fresh insight into the goodness of God.

Learning Posture Action Plan

1. Aligning Hopes and Goals
What are the hopes and goals the hosting team has for the project, and how can the missions team come alongside to support them effectively?

2. Preparing Resources That Fit
What adjustments need to be made to the resources offered by the missions team so they are truly helpful and relevant to the hosting team's needs?

3. Navigating Cultural Understanding
What areas will be hardest for the missions team to comprehend, and what tools or insights might make it easier for them to adapt?

4. Fostering Safe Communication
How will you cultivate an environment where the hosting team feels comfortable sharing concerns or suggesting alternative approaches with the missions team?

5. Developing Leaders Through Role Modeling
What opportunities exist for discipleship, leadership development, and role modeling during the project, and how will leaders set an example worth imitating?

6. Recognizing God's Work
How will you share what God has been doing in the local ministry and community to inspire and encourage the missions team?

7. Celebrating Cultural Beauty
What are the best aspects of the host culture, and what lessons, experiences, or values do you hope the missions team will take home with them?

8. Structuring Briefings and Debriefings
Where and when will briefings and debriefings take place, and what questions will help the team process, reflect, and learn from their experiences?

9. Identifying Cultural Liaisons
Who will act as the cultural liaison, helping both teams navigate cultural insights, address challenges, and foster clear understanding if the site coordinator is unavailable?

Principle 5: Relationship

Be devoted to one another in love. Honor one another above yourself. Never be lacking in zeal, but keep your spiritual fervor, serving the Lord. Be joyful in hope, patient in affliction, faithful in prayer. Share with the Lord's people who are in need. Practice hospitality.
—Romans 12:10–13

Key Definitions

✦ **Briefings**: Preparing others by giving them needed instructions for a plan or event.

✦ **Context**: The interrelated conditions around words and actions that bring meaning to the circumstances at hand. What happens prior to, after, the time, place, and setting in which circumstances occur is considered context, all having the ability to create or change meaning of what's being said or done.

✦ **Culture**: The observable social practices of a people group. These practices are often unspoken but are understood by everyone in the group. They are born out of an agreed-upon set of values. While these values may be less visible to the outsider, they are intuitive to the members of the group.

✦ **Debriefing**: The process of talking through events after a task is complete. The task can be a mission, a project, or simply the activities of the day. Information is shared in order to unpack, learn, and process what happened. It places events in context and brings the broader scope of the overall mission into perspective.

✦ **Dependency Syndrome**: Individuals or communities relying on assistance and depending on others for donations and outside help rather than creatively seeking sustainable solutions to reach their goals in their own context.

✦ **Discipleship**: A journey that Christians make with other people as they go from no faith, to new faith, to mature faith, walking alongside others with evangelistic intent until they repent and believe. The journey continues until they are fully devoted, sanctified disciple makers.

✦ **Global Missions**: The missions department in the Church of the Nazarene is led by the Global Missions director. The Global Missions office is located at the Church of the Nazarene's Global Ministry Center in Lenexa, Kansas, USA. They support the mission of the church by working with the regional and field leaders. They work to expand the church globally through Nazarene Ministries. An important role of Global Missions is to appoint and place missionaries in locations that are strategic to the global church.

✦ **Honor-Shame Worldview**: Found in much of the world, especially including Asia and the Middle East, those who view the world through the honor and shame lens find value in honoring relationships, people, and societal status. They gain honor by being esteemed in the social community. They avoid shame, which comes when they do something that the social community disapproves of.

✦ **Incarnation**: God became flesh and lived among us. God became human in the form of Jesus Christ, the Son of God, and second Person of the Trinity.

✦ *Koinonia*: A Greek word used frequently in the New Testament to describe the bond and heartfelt joy that are created through deep fellowship within the body of Christ. *Koinonia* is experienced when hospitality and the prayerful hearts of a body of believers come together in unity, creating something together that has eternal value for the kingdom of God.

✦ **Nazarene Compassionate Ministries (NCM)**: A global ministry of the Church of the Nazarene. NCM partners with local Nazarene congregations around the world to clothe, shelter, feed, heal, educate, and live in solidarity with those who suffer under oppression, injustice, violence, poverty, hunger, and disease. NCM exists in and through the Church of the Nazarene to proclaim the gospel to all people in word and deed.

✦ **NCM's Child Sponsorship Program:** Based on a holistic child development model that seeks to simultaneously address key aspects of a child's life—spiritual, physical, intellectual, emotional, and relational—through learning opportunities and developmental interventions. Through this model, children are encouraged to grow into the people God created them to be.

✦ **Nazarene Discipleship International (NDI):** A global ministry of the Church of the Nazarene whose mission is to carry out the Great Commission to children, youth, and adults in preparation for a lifelong journey of being and making Christlike disciples in the nations.

✦ **Nazarene Missions International (NMI):** The organization for mobilizing the local church in missions in the Church of the Nazarene. NMI is also the denomination's representative for missions on the district and in the local church.

✦ **Partnership:** Two or more people, or groups of people, coming together to accomplish a goal. Together they bring the necessary and often different resources and skills to complete a project. Healthy partnerships always view each other as having equal value. All parties have something to give, and all have something to receive.

✦ **Power Dynamics:** The balance of power between two or more people. There is a distinction between those with power and those without; those with power have an advantage.

✦ **Project:** A defined activity that will assist in accomplishing a goal set by the hosts to develop and expand the Church of the Nazarene.

✦ **Regional Director:** Each of the six global regions identified in the Church of the Nazarene is led by a regional director (RD) who is appointed by the global church. On each region there is a regional office with missionaries and staff to assist with strategy, missionary placement, and the ministries of the fields in that particular world region.

✦ **Resources:** The people, expertise, labor, funds, equipment, and materials that contribute to the completion of a project.

✦ **Role Model:** A person whose behavior, example, or success is or can be emulated by others.

✦ **Saving Face**: Refers to the act of preserving one's reputation, dignity, or honor in social interactions, particularly in situations that could potentially cause embarrassment, shame, or loss of respect. Saving face involves maintaining a positive self-image and avoiding situations or actions that may diminish one's standing in the eyes of others.

✦ **Social Capital**: Credit earned through resources and/or social influences. The social capital brought by short-term missions teams can be leveraged through local networks, bringing the ability to increase public esteem in leaders at the forefront of local ministries.

✦ **Transactional Relationship**: A relationship where both (or all) parties are interested in what they have to gain. Partners do things for each other with the expectation of reciprocation. Transactional relationships serve a clear purpose, and when that purpose has been fulfilled, the relationship ends.

✦ **Work & Witness**: A construction ministry in the Church of the Nazarene. Teams from one church or district come alongside another church or district locally or globally to help their brothers and sisters in Christ build physical structures that will serve them in ministry.

✦ **Worldview**: The lens through which a person views the world. The subjective perspective of an individual based on their own values creates the paradigm by which they make sense of the world.

Guiding Principle #5: Relationship

Relationships formed during short-term missions projects provide an opportunity to connect with diverse combinations of people on a personal level. We learn about different cultures and perspectives as we work together toward a common goal. In this way, relationships serve as the bridge between different cultures and communities and offer us a better understanding of what God is doing in the world. As the project is underway, ongoing relationships are strengthened and new ones are formed. The transformative power of the Holy Spirit is passed from one person to another in the holy relationship of *koinonia*.

The heartfelt connections created by doing something together for the kingdom brings a spirit of *koinonia*. Knowing the spirit of *koinonia* is understanding an essential element of short-term missions. The Greek word *koinonia* is used in the New Testament and translates as "deep fellowship." This kind of fellowship is best described as the bond and sincere joy that come from the unity experienced in the body of Christ. It's experienced when hospitality and the prayerful hearts of a body of believers come together with the unified intention to create something that has eternal value for the kingdom of God. When team members return home after the project, *koinonia* is the joy they try to put into words when talking about the transformational experiences they had.

Developing relationships that cultivate *koinonia* between hosting and missions teams takes some forethought. In order to avoid uncomfortable situations, we must consider the nature of transactional relationships and the implications they carry on the project. The project is best served when everyone recognizes that all participants have something of value to contribute. Leaders need to identify the power dynamics involved and have practices in place to balance them. Good leaders realize it's a blessing to give, but generosity outside the bounds of relationship can be disruptive. Site coordinators can be depended on to fully grasp the importance of relationship between the two teams and can be relied on to serve as the buffer and go-between for both teams. Western and Eastern cultures view relationships differently, and special care needs to be shared with teams in order to avoid hazards that can easily get in the way of heartfelt connections. Site coordinators are positioned to be experienced in both cultures and are able to set proper guidelines in each group so that *koinonia* is fostered and felt by everyone.

Short-term missions have us looking beyond the tasks of the project in order to see the hearts of the people we are serving with. There is a project, and with that comes work that needs to be done, but the higher calling, the heart of the matter, is always the people we are serving alongside. *Koinonia* is found in relationships. The project is the excuse; relationships are the reason we participate.

Vacations, Transactions, and Family

Going on vacation is usually a fun adventure, but experiencing a short-term missions trip can be life changing. The difference is that vacation is a transactional experience, whereas short-term missions rests on the relationships of our extended Christian family.

Vacations involve paying entry fees to get into touristy places, hiring guides, eating in restaurants and staying in hotels. These are a series of transactions—money given in exchange for services received. Transactional relationships serve a purpose. They occur when both parties are interested in what they have to gain. Partners in a transactional relationship do things for each other with the expectation of reciprocation. When the purpose of a transactional relationship has been fulfilled, the relationship ends.

Short-term missions projects are different. People serve with the heart of Jesus, working together in a united and holy calling. This is a place where people expect to find and build authentic relationships with their Nazarene brothers and sisters. The gift of the project is more than a transaction. It represents our love for one another, a gift between family members, embraced in the warm arms of a kindred relationship.

Using a transactional approach in ministry is uncomfortable because it changes things. Relationships become about what we can get rather than getting to know each other. Everyone arrives to the project expecting to meet their Nazarene brothers and sisters. They anticipate a relationship of kinship. If either team finds that the other party is just in it for the transaction, they are left in an uncomfortable position. Learning that someone isn't interested in you but only in what you have to offer changes the nature of the relationship. Overlooking dignity in this way leaves people feeling foolish. The focus of the relationship becomes more about what people are getting for themselves rather than the shared dignity that a healthy relationship brings.

When the focus shifts to *What's in it for me?* it's easy to lose sight of integrity. For hosting teams, this might look like exaggerating needs in order to tug at the heartstrings of their guests. For missions teams, it could mean prioritizing the project over the people they came to serve. In both cases, relationships risk becoming transactional rather than transformative. When self-interest takes center stage, trust and genuine friendship are compromised. True partnership calls us to honor one another above ourselves, fostering relationships that are rooted in mutual respect and dignity.

Principle 5: Relationship

People come to projects with diverse backgrounds and worldviews, yet we all love and worship God together as brothers and sisters in Christ. This unity reflects the global church at its best. As we get to know one another, sharing our strengths and vulnerabilities, we experience true *koinonia*—a deep, intimate fellowship that transcends mere transactions. This is the heart of missions: a bond that money cannot buy, a connection that transforms us into family.

> To understand koinonia is to understand Work & Witness.
> —Carlos Radi, South America

Insider Perspective
Transactional Impact: Mabuhay!

Growing up in the Philippines as the daughter of Work & Witness coordinators, Jordan has had many visitors in her home from all over the world. It wouldn't be uncommon for her parents to host several hundred people in their home throughout the year, including volunteers living with them, special guests from remote villages, meals with missions teams, and parties and potlucks for all occasions. The home she grew up in was full of people living in the spirit of hospitality—both given and received.

The Philippines is known to be one of the world's most hospitable countries. *"Mabuhay"* is a beautiful word said to visitors that can be translated as "live long." This word is at the heart of how to best welcome strangers. Filipinos always show that people come first. The task comes second. You offer guests the very best of what you have and of who you are. Your intention is to make others feel welcome, appreciated, and comfortable.

God works mysteriously in this space, and Jordan understands the sacredness of what it means to be hospitable. After growing up in Manila, she moved to the southern part of the United States to attend college—a part of the country known for its culture of "southern hospitality." Jordan fit right in. She met and married her husband, and together they love people through hospitality. They have a large, diverse group of friends. They love good music and good food. Their home is open, and everyone is always welcome. Always.

Deciding on further education, Jordan and her husband moved from the south to the northeastern part of the United States, where they easily made many friends due to their willingness to continually invite people into their home or out to a restaurant. After coming to several gatherings at their house, one of their guests hosted a luncheon of her own and invited Jordan. Jordan was excited and felt like a new friendship might be blossoming. It was a lovely experience with delicious food. However, the hospitality quickly lost all its warmth when the host coolly asked the guests to for pay for their meals before leaving. Since Jordan had never been expected to pay for food that someone prepared in their own home, she felt surprised. She reluctantly paid the requested amount and was sad to realize this might not be a friendship after all. The nature of the relationship changed. It seemed to have moved from a place of friendship to a place of transaction.

Jordan and her husband have found, after living in the northeast for a few years now, that this type of hospitality is not unheard of. Although it is not the norm, it does happen from time to time, even in cases when they have contributed food items to the meal. They always smile and pay, and they try not to let the discomfort they feel affect the new relationship, but it has been difficult for Jordan to get used to this version of hospitality.

Insider Perspective
Transactional Impact: Work & Witness Bus

Renting buses for Work & Witness teams was expensive. Not only that, but the buses were unreliable. The safety of their guests was too important to risk any longer, so donations were gathered and saved to purchase of a bus that could carry the teams. It took several years to raise enough funds to purchase a bus that would be suitable for the teams. There were costs to operate it. A driver was needed, gas, ongoing maintenance, and it seemed to go through a lot of tires. Wear and tear on the bus was par for the course. Air conditioning was a must in the tropics. The seats were made for East Asians and couldn't always tolerate the size and weight of the visiting Westerners; therefore, the seats needed to be replaced from time to time.

Generous donations had made it possible to purchase the bus, but it needed additional funds to keep it going. The Work & Witness coordinator figured out a fair price that would cover the costs for the trip—the actual expenses along with a small amount to go into the bus maintenance fund. The teams from the U.S. were happy to pay the necessary fee as part of their overall transportation costs.

Then a team from Korea planned to come. They were invited by a Korean missionary, and they were very special guests who wanted to do a vision trip to see the work of the missionary. The Korean missionary would host them, and they expected to use the bus, which was available, so there were no problems. Except, there *was* a problem—the fee. The Korean missionary explained that he couldn't ask his VIP guests for money to rent the bus. The U.S. missionary said, "But there are costs to renting the bus. It isn't sustainable to let everyone use it for free. Plus, it isn't fair to everyone else who has to pay the fee. Feelings will be hurt."

The two missionaries understood each other, and they also understood the two different cultures. The Korean missionary said, "It's hospitality. I cannot charge them for hospitality." Then he said, "I promise you, when they leave, they will take an offering to cover the costs of their trip, and it will more than cover the rental of the bus."

And it happened as he said it would.

Following Dignity

Questions to Consider
Transactional Impact

1. What stands out to you in the *mabuhay* story?

2. How do you think Jordan felt when she was invited to the luncheon?

3. How did she feel when she was charged afterward?

4. Have you ever felt this way?

5. Do you think the charges were justified?

6. How is the bus story similar to the *mabuhay* story?

7. Why couldn't the Korean missionary charge for the bus?

8. What can we learn from both of these stories?

9. How do these stories relate to your context?

Principle 5: Relationship

Discussion
Transactional Impact

Each of these stories revolves around the question of how to culturally handle transactions in the midst of the hospitality relationship—when it should happen, how it should happen, and what exactly it should cover. There are expenses around hospitality and the many needs of the missions team. Because transactions communicate the nature of the relationship, how it's handled answers the question, *Is this business or friendship?* It's important to consider what cultural parameters are involved and then cover the costs appropriately.

These stories focus on asking for money to cover the cost of hospitality, but a misplaced transaction can show up in many areas. For instance, if you give a friend a birthday gift, you want to let them know that you value them and care about them. You are communicating friendship. If they ask, as you hand them the gift, "How much do I owe you for this?" it's uncomfortable because it communicates something other than friendship. Offering to pay for something can communicate business in a similar way that charging for services does—it's offering a transaction in place of friendship. In some instances it might be appropriate; in others, not at all.

> "The local community won't remember the amazing building you built or the beautiful wall you painted. They will remember the way you made them feel and the relationships you formed."
> —Hope Owens, Former Missionary, Philippines and Africa

In many cultures, placing the transaction in front of the relationship communicates a business relationship rather than a personal one. The message a misplaced transaction sends is uncomfortable and confusing in relationships. In the first story, it's as simple as a friendship you were hoping for that didn't turn out; in the second, it was seen as shameful and disrespectful to important guests. In many instances, charging for hospitality implies that the guests are burdensome and their presence isn't truly wanted. Other times, it's seen as the hosts taking advantage of their guests. Any way you look at it, placing the transaction in the right place is necessary for everyone's sense of dignity.

Everyone expects that hospitality has expenses involved. Culture sets the parameters for how these expenses are to be covered. In the first story, the cultural differences took place within the same country, just a few states away. We can expect that in most cultures, transactions in friendships are managed one way and in business settings another. The site coordinator works with the missions team to make sure they have the funds necessary to cover all the costs of their hospitality needs. They also work with the hosting team to provide and care for them within the missions team's budgeted amount. The site coordinator and the team leader work together as they cover costs in a way that communicates friendship with dignity rather than a transactional business arrangement that might be felt as dishonorable in the culture.

Partnerships, Dependency, and Dignity

A transactional approach to ministry isn't the only difficulty that should be paid attention to. Another common mistake is thinking that the relationship is one way, one-sided, or top-down. One side does all the giving while the other side does all the receiving. When the partnership is unbalanced, dignity is sure to be compromised, and dependency is likely to follow.

Teams may feel they are doing well by doing all the giving. They might feel like the superheroes saving the day, but in reality, one-sided giving communicates that the other side isn't worthy, that they have nothing of value to offer, and that they have to wait for others to come along and save them. This might require that they hold the posture of a beggar with an outstretched, empty hand. It's uncomfortable, it's not an equal partnership, it's messy, and dignity is compromised on all sides.

Principle 5: Relationship

All four Gospels share an account of Jesus feeding the multitude. Each story is a little different, but they all show people with needs, compassion being felt, and not enough resources to go around. Jesus felt compassion for the people who had been with him for several days. He knew they were hungry, and he wanted them to have something to eat before they went on their way, but there wasn't enough money to purchase food for a crowd of that size. Scripture tells us that Jesus is God and had been doing miracles all day, so it seems that he could have easily provided something out of nothing. He could have snapped his fingers and made appear a gourmet meal with nice dinnerware and white linens—but he didn't do that. He chose another way.

He asked his disciples what they had. The Gospel of John tells us that a boy came forward and offered what he held in his hands, which was a basket containing two fish and five loaves of bread. "Jesus then took the loaves, gave thanks, and distributed them to those who were seated as much as they wanted. He did the same with the fish" (John 6:11). They all had enough to eat, and there were baskets of leftovers.

Jesus still did a miracle, but he did it *through* his people rather than *for* them. His way allowed them to participate by offering what they had. Their hands weren't empty. Jesus gave thanks and blessed their offering. With dignity he took their food—the meal they were familiar with—and blessed it. He didn't bring outside food, and he didn't imply that their food wasn't good enough by giving them something better. He could have offered heavenly food, something wonderful they had never had before, something from the outside that they couldn't get on their own. But he didn't. The generous offering from the hands of a young boy was perfectly acceptable. His participation was needed, and the whole crowd was fed in abundance. Honor, dignity, and participation.

One-sided giving isn't sustainable in the long run. Equal participation brings everyone together with a sense of belonging. Participation and belonging bring feelings of esteem and ownership of the project. Sustainability is reached when ownership of the project is embraced by the hosting community. The Church of the Nazarene works diligently toward sustainability in all missions and ministry projects taking dependency off of outsiders and placing it at the feet of Jesus, where it belongs. Young ministries may need outside help at times, but the goal of reaching sustainability is something we should always aim to achieve together. Short-term missions are at their best when partnerships and relationships maintain balance and everyone feels ownership of their part in the project.

Dependency on outside resources creates an unnecessary stumbling block to resilience and sustainability. Too much help can easily perpetuate a continuous cycle of dependence, which can evolve into dependency syndrome, where the ministry becomes reliant on outside assistance and will fall apart once the resources are no longer available. Sustainability depends on local leaders seeking sustainable solutions that work best in their context. Dependency syndrome leads to unintended consequences by fostering a culture of entitlement and the potential to create power imbalances within the culture. At its worst, it can distort local economies and harm relationships within the church body. Leadership and teams need to work together to discourage dependency as they encourage independence and ownership of ministry projects leading to prolonged sustainability.

> "True partnership is built on reciprocity. We can create spaces where every voice—regardless of financial means—is heard and valued and where each person is given the opportunity both to teach and to learn."
> —Dr. David Wesley,
> Nazarene Theological Seminary

Choosing a ministry project or partnership is building a relationship. It's similar to a friendship, or even a dating relationship. When looking for a partner, we look at the strengths each has to offer. We don't look at all of their problems, we don't point out their

Principle 5: Relationship

flaws, and we don't share with them all the ways we plan to improve them. Instead, we see their beauty and the good things they offer to us and to our relationship. In this way, we give dignity to each other. Often, opposites attract. The strengths that one has will fill a need of the other.

A good partnership in short-term missions isn't based on pity or lack of resources but on the mutual benefit of giving and receiving. When there is strong ongoing ministry taking place in both the hosting and the missions team, with mutual opportunities to learn from each other, the partnerships will be strong. It takes time to build strong relationships. Uncovering each other's strengths is just as important to the relationship as seeing the vulnerabilities. When we lean into the strengths of the other, we are better suited to build our dreams together for the mutual benefit of each other.

Insider Perspective
A Partnership in the Making

The families living in the shanties on the mountainside watched curiously as outsiders delivered gifts to the people in their neighborhood. These people were doing a lot of giving; in fact, all they seemed to be doing was giving. They brought items from afar and handed out their gifts with delight. Everyone seemed to love it. Every time one of the visitors perceived a need, they gave something to help. As the hosting community got comfortable with the extravagant generosity of the visiting outsiders, things got a little messy.

The missions team didn't discriminate in their giving; it was often to families from the church but not always. They gave shoes to people on the street and toys to children playing nearby. They didn't really know or understand the people they were giving to; they were moved by the poverty they encountered and found that they could put a smile on a child's face by giving them a Barbie or a Hot Wheels car, and this made them feel better. The missions team's response to the uncomfortable circumstances they found themselves in was to give generously. They handed out money,

Bibles, clothing, and baby blankets. They gave crisis care kits and offered to sponsor children.

The community came to realize that that these visitors from the missions teams loved giving to their children. They also noticed that they seemed to give more when they encountered poverty, so they came up with a plan. The next time the missions team arrived, they would put their children on display and parade them in front of team members, hoping they would select them for sponsorship. Tthey would make sure to hide their valuables in order to appear more needy than they actually were. They also dressed their children poorly when the teams were around, had them play outside barefoot, and even went to the extent of putting dirt on their faces to make themselves look more impoverished.

Leaders were soon confronted with this challenging situation; dignity was lost on all sides, and they had to intervene.

Questions to Consider
A Partnership in the Making

1. What was the heart of the missions team?

2. What did the missions team's response to the poverty communicate to the people?

3. What went wrong?

4. How could the team have preserved dignity better?

5. How could the community have maintained their dignity?

6. What could have been done differently?

7. What can we learn from this story?

8. How do aspects of this story apply to your context?

Discussion
A Partnership in the Making

The missions teams arrived with hearts full of compassion. They saw that things were very different from their home environment, and they became uncomfortable. They were pained by what they perceived as poverty and wanted to alleviate their own heartache by giving gifts. They thought that's what the people needed, and they felt good because they were helping.

What they didn't understand was that one-sided giving, outside the boundaries of healthy relationship, can cause a shadow to form over dignity. It communicates that only one side of the relationship brings the value; they are the superheroes who swoop in to meet perceived needs while the other side is left to bring only this perceived deficiency. It's a common tale. A superhero can only be a hero if there is someone to save. When the superhero arrives, the other must bring their poverty, their deficiencies, their problems, or their neediness in exchange for the goods, services, or solutions offered by the hero. It becomes a transaction of sorts, an off-balance relationship, a partnership depending on an empty hand from one side in exchange for resources from outsiders who don't really understand their true needs.

When one side of the relationship gets their value from giving, in order for the partnership to survive, the other side must respond with the unwholesome posture of a beggar. And that's what this community on the mountainside did. They recognized that their worth in the partnership came from their lack, and they did their best to accommodate the givers by exaggerating their neediness. The commodity that the hosting community was asked to bring to the relationship was their poverty. Their God-given value, talents, competencies, and sense of worth were overlooked by the initial and possibly false perceptions of poverty by the outside missions team.

The mistakes made by the missions team set the groundwork for the situation, but the response of the hosting team was also regrettable. They could have done things differently. Instead they set aside their dignity in exchange for resources. They disregarded the dignity of their children just as quickly as they cheated it from their generous guests. Because they didn't have a real relationship with the missions team, they felt their value wasn't seen as important, and it became easy to take advantage of the situation. Dignity was theirs to offer and theirs to suppress—sadly, they chose the latter.

The site coordinator and the hosting leaders had some work to do. They brought the whole community together in an effort to remind them of their dignity. They learned from each other and built much-needed relationships. Leaders discovered the hopes and dreams of the town and learned about their concerns as well, one of which was that they didn't have a secure bridge going from the street to their homes on the mountainside. During rainy season, floodwaters would rise and they couldn't pass through. The leaders uncovered many talents of the townspeople. One was that the children loved to sing, and a young lady in the church put together a children's choir. They also taught their people how to be better hosts to their guests in the future. As they built relationships, they found people who could provide security for teams, others who enjoyed preparing food, and young people who learned the ins and outs of being good tour guides. They learned how to do it all with dignity.

When the next missions team arrived, they did things differently. The team followed the guidelines from the leadership on the field and restrained themselves from passing out gifts to everyone they saw. Together the hosting team and missions team built a footbridge from the street to the homes in the community on the mountainside. The bridge was constructed inside the boundaries of relationship and would be a treasure to the community in the years to come. It was better than the gifts of dolls and toys because the children could walk safely to school during torrential rains. It was truly a bridge to the hearts of the people. The team members were guided to channel their giving through the local church as well. The church had created procedures to distribute the resources given, and they would help the neediest in their community. They taught teams how to properly sponsor children through the Nazarene Compassionate Ministries (NCM) child sponsorship program and provided information to the locals so they could apply for sponsorship of their children through the global church.

The team and the church built trusted relationships in the community. Trust became the norm as teams were well taken care of by their hosts, and the spirit of *koinonia* sprang to life. The community was impacted by the church, and many came to know Christ. With pride, families brought their children to the missions teams, and together they watched the children sing in the choir. The children also taught the team members songs, which they loved. And, of course, the children in the choir were always presented well, clean and dressed in their finest clothes.

> "The core of missions teams is not only about bringing solutions but about building relationships. True dignity is upheld when we empower, respect, and learn from those we serve, recognizing that God is already at work in every community."
> —Shahade Twal, Missionary, Eurasia Region

Relationships: When West Meets East

Jayson Georges, a storyteller and missionary in the Middle East, reveals an intriguing truth: as much as 80% of the world's cultures view relationships through the lens of honor and shame.[1] With

---

1. Jayson Georges, "About HonorShame.com," *Honor Shame: Resources for Global Ministry*, https://honorshame.com/about/.

so many short-term missions teams coming from the West, where relationships often follow a different rhythm, there's a wonderful opportunity to learn how these two unique cultural styles can partner together.

Serving more than a dozen years as missionaries in the Asia-Pacific region, Greg and Terri Taylor have gathered some valuable insights from their time bridging the cultural gap between Western missions teams and their hosts in the Philippines—a culture steeped in the rich traditions of honor and shame. The Taylors discovered that navigating these contrasting dynamics required intention, creativity, and a good dose of curiosity as teams partnered with hosts in ministry across the region. It's a journey of blending perspectives, fostering understanding, and finding common ground in shared purpose.

In warm-climate and collectivist cultures, relationships tend to be treasured above all else. These cultures often use honor and shame as gentle guides to nurture and navigate connections. In honor-shame cultures, doing right is less about following rules and more about fostering a sense of belonging, offering esteem, and preserving relationships. Time, efficiency, and schedules may take a backseat to the more meaningful priority of ensuring that no one feels shame or embarrassment. By showing respect, one honors not only others but also oneself—a beautiful reflection of their commitment to relational harmony.

Bringing honor to relationships is always a worthy pursuit, but in honor-shame cultures, it's absolutely essential, and something outside teams must consider. In these cultures, humility isn't just valued; it's a way of life. Boldly pointing out flaws or positioning oneself as the hero may seem productive to some, but in honor-shame cultures it can unintentionally wound hearts. While some problems might get solved and egos boosted, the cost is too steep when it leaves others feeling diminished and burdened with shame. True respect lies in lifting others up, not overshadowing them.

Neither perspective is inherently right or wrong, but blending these two cultural approaches can require delicate and careful thought. Cold-climate Westerners often operate through the cultural lens of guilt and innocence, tackling problems by thoroughly

Principle 5: Relationship

analyzing the situation, having candid conversations, and striving for the best solution. To them, openly addressing issues and assigning blame feels logical—after all, how else can future missteps be avoided? But in honor-shame cultures, this approach can land differently. What Westerners see as constructive, others may experience as deeply offensive and wounding. The challenge lies in navigating these differences with sensitivity and understanding.

An underlying difference between these two cultural perspectives lies in how they view and address vulnerability. Western cultures often see guilt as something to confront and resolve—a temporary issue that, once remedied, can be removed entirely. In contrast, honor-shame cultures regard shame as a fundamental part of the human condition, something to protect and cover, much like our physical nakedness. Shame represents our deepest vulnerability. Though guilt and shame share similarities, they're not entirely the same. Guilt is seen as fleeting while shame is enduring. This distinction leads to vastly different responses: in the Western mindset, resolving guilt restores peace; in the Eastern mindset, peace comes through covering shame with honor, preserving dignity in the process.

Bringing these two different cultural paradigms together can create discord in relationships. One seeks to cover, and the other seeks to expose. Again, it's essential to remember that neither perspective is wrong and both hold deep cultural value. However, misunderstandings can arise unless each one is willing to recognize and appreciate the unique strengths of the other. Seeing the world through another's lens fosters connection and mutual respect, bridging gaps that might otherwise divide. Westerners often feel at ease tackling problems head-on, bringing them into the open to find solutions. Efficiency tends to take the lead, sometimes at the expense of considering others' feelings along the way. In contrast, honor-shame cultures often view problem solving through the lens of relationships and social standing. Their focus on preserving dignity and harmony might mean a slower or less direct process, but it ensures that the journey respects everyone involved. Both approaches reflect deeply held values, and there's beauty in finding the balance between them.

Following Dignity

Honor-shame cultures have a remarkable gift for creating emotional safety. They deeply understand the universal emotion of shame and instinctively cover it with honor—not only for themselves but for others as well. These cultures excel at making people feel comfortable, valuing harmony and dignity in every interaction. Saving face, a cornerstone of the social fabric, is about preserving one's reputation and honor, especially in moments that might bring embarrassment or loss of respect. By prioritizing a positive self-image and protecting the dignity of others, they foster an environment where everyone can feel valued and respected.

When teams arrive and shine a light on a person's or a community's vulnerabilities, they may unintentionally send the harmful message that the people they're serving aren't capable of caring for themselves or their loved ones, which can lead to a sense of shame, eroding self-worth. Exposing vulnerabilities for outsiders to solve has the potential to do more harm than good unless it's approached with great care and a commitment to preserving dignity. As we serve, it's essential to ensure that our actions uplift rather than diminish, honoring the people we seek to help by partnering with them in a way that respects their worth.

In honor-shame cultures, it's not just pointing out others' weaknesses that's frowned upon; the act of elevating ourselves above others that can be the most shaming of all. Sadly, on short-term mission trips, this harmful combination happens more often than we realize. When outsiders arrive and flaunt their good deeds—snapping photos of themselves in action and solving problems that the "less fortunate" can't address on their own—it sends a message that can diminish dignity. Sharing those images on social media or other public platforms can make it worse, leaving local people to endure public shame as the price of receiving help. It's embarrassing, disheartening, and often not worth the trouble. True service requires humility and respect, not a spotlight on ourselves.

We all have areas where we could use a little help. Some needs we might be comfortable sharing, others not so much. For some, it might be something as simple as pulling out the refrigerator to clean behind it. To give you an idea, let's pretend you aren't strong enough to do it yourself and need to get some help. You are

Principle 5: Relationship

fine with not being strong enough. The problem is that, once it's pulled out, you don't know what you will find back there; it could be an embarrassing mess. There might be insects or mice behind the refrigerator, and whoever helps you pull it out will see the mess. It's uncomfortable.

After considerable thought, you've decided to ask a group of young people from church to come over one evening to help with the refrigerator. They come, and you're thankful. They are quite friendly and eager to offer their services. They pull out the refrigerator for you, and you see the dust, the dried food, cobwebs, insects, and even the dreaded mouse droppings you suspected. You knew it would be bad. In your hurry to clean up this embarrassing mess, you notice someone take a picture of you as you're squatted down wiping the floor. Then you hear the snap of yet another picture and see that this one is focused on the mess. And that makes you cringe.

Later that night, you see these pictures posted on social media. The helpers look great and strong as they move your refrigerator, but the other pictures make you feel uncomfortable. They show you crouched down in your work clothes, and what's worse, everyone can clearly see your terrible mess behind the refrigerator. The feeling lurking in the pit of your stomach is shame. The reason some honor-shame cultures don't allow nonprofit missionary organizations into their countries might not be because they don't like God but because missionaries have not helped them save face.

Some may not care as much about the dirt behind the refrigerator, and of course many people don't even own refrigerators, but everyone understands and experiences shame to one degree or another. We care how we are perceived by our friends, families, and communities. In honor-shame cultures, this concern is forefront. Shame comes from the feeling of being exposed. Something we would rather not have revealed about ourselves or our situation is shown to the world with little or no regard.

Many of the standards and ideals we strive to meet are set by the culture in which we live. Each culture's ideals are different. For some, not having wealth or education causes shame, and having money and education brings honor. For others, it's health, weight, or skin color: being too big or too small, too light or too dark can feel shaming. Culture defines which of these is right and wrong. Sun exposure tans our skin, and the response is cultural. Some think it's a shame to be too dark because it means you work out in the sun all day—poor person's work. To others, it's an honor to be tanned by the sun because it means you are able to vacation while others are working, so you must be wealthy. Another important area that is on display surrounds the behavior of children. A lot of conversations about our kids stem from feelings of shame and honor, no matter the culture. Calling attention to a person's successes in these areas set by culture brings honor while highlighting the failures in the same areas is hurtful. Personal attributes that are in conflict with standards set by culture are carefully guarded to protect social standing.

Western cultures often emphasize individuality, while Eastern cultures frequently value a collective approach. These perspectives shape how each culture responds to the experience of shame. In Western contexts, people may view shame as a personal burden to resolve, focusing on the individual's responsibility to process their feelings. In contrast, many Eastern cultures see shame as something the group navigates together. The individual strives to avoid bringing shame to others, while the community shares a responsibility to safeguard one another from it. Both approaches reflect the unique ways that different cultures care for and support their members.

In honor-shame cultures, people tend to view the well-being of their collective group as closely tied to how they are perceived in the community. Together, they often prioritize maintaining dignity and respect for their group. In these contexts, "having no shame" typically refers to behavior that is considered socially unacceptable, which may bring dishonor not only to the individual but also to their group and community. When this occurs, the group may take responsibility to address the behavior, sometimes using corrective shaming as a way to guide the individual back toward actions that reflect honor. Occasionally, public shaming may be used to separate the individual's actions from the group, enabling the community to preserve its shared sense of honor. This approach reflects the deep sense of interconnectedness and shared accountability that are valued in these cultures. As a person's behavior is corrected in honor-shame cultures, they tend to be welcomed back into the group. The individual's sense of shame for their mistakes is acknowledged, and together the community seeks to restore honor. It's less about enforcing consequences and more about fostering restoration and celebrating the honor of belonging. Both the individual's honor and that of the group are lifted up and celebrated.

For further understanding, we can look to the New Testament. In Luke 15, Jesus explained to the Pharisees and teachers of the law why he spent time with tax collectors and sinners. After sharing the parables of the lost sheep and the lost coin, he told the story of the prodigal son, illustrating restoration and the joy of being reunited with the community. The prodigal son deeply hurt his father and brought shame to his family by demanding his inheritance and leaving to pursue a reckless, self-centered life. In doing so, he not only squandered his wealth but also tarnished his family's honor and compromised his father's standing in the community.

Yet, when the son returned, broken and humbled, the father didn't focus on punishment or shame. Instead, he sought to restore him to his rightful place in the family with open arms and a full heart: "But the father said to his servants, 'Quick! Bring the best robe and put it on him. Put a ring on his finger and sandals on his feet. Bring the fattened calf and kill it. Let's have a feast and celebrate. For this son of mine was dead and is alive again; he was lost and is found.' So they began to celebrate" (Luke 15:22–24). The father's response was a celebration of life, love, and belonging. They celebrated his return! Honor is the covering. If the father had punished his son, he would have added more shame to an already shameful situation. Scripture shows us how giving honor covers shame.

Different cultures often respond to relational conflict in distinct ways. In honor-shame cultures, the potential for shame to harm relationships means that conflict is handled with great care. To protect the honor of both parties, conversations about conflict tend to be indirect. If indirect communication proves ineffective, a go-between or third party may be called upon to mediate. This person's role is to listen to both sides, then approach the other party privately to share the concerns, ensuring that the issue is never discussed openly between the two in conflict. This approach helps preserve honor, resolve the problem, and maintain the relationship. In short-term missions projects, the site coordinator is often the best person to navigate these sensitive situations, ensuring both teams are treated with respect and the relationship remains intact. In some cold-climate Western cultures, the idea of using a go-between might be frowned upon as going against the cultural value of being direct. Honor-shame cultures seek to preserve honor by doing the opposite. Both approaches are scriptural.

In honor-shame cultures, there is often a clear hierarchy, and understanding who holds the most honor requires some cultural learning, especially for guests. In some cultures, the eldest person may be the most honored, while in others, someone from a respected family or holding a high-status job might carry that distinction. Recognizing who holds honor and for what reasons may not always be immediately apparent to outsiders, so it's important for guests to learn whom they should honor and how to do so appropriately.

Honor is often expressed through various social interactions, such as greetings and farewells, seating arrangements at events, and the order in which people are served in stores, restaurants, and at meals in people's homes. These subtle practices reflect deep respect for social roles and relationships.

Scripture reminds us to honor others above ourselves (see Philippians 2:3–4), a principle that is valuable across all cultures. In honor-shame cultures, team members from the West have a unique opportunity to embrace and practice the Christian value of honor in meaningful and tangible ways. By understanding and respecting local customs, guests can build deeper connections and contribute to the well-being of the community.

The impact of shame on relationships is significant, and it's important for teams to recognize the many ways it can manifest in a project. Sometimes it's as simple as forgetting to express heartfelt gratitude to a host who has welcomed them into their home. Other times it can be more subtle, such as bragging or inflating oneself—even in a playful or sarcastic way—an action that should be avoided. In many honor-shame cultures, behaviors like yelling or being overly loud in public are considered disrespectful because they draw unnecessary attention to oneself.

Principle 5: Relationship

At times, the impact of shame is more complex. For example, a team member might think it's funny to take a picture of what they consider to be unusual décor, food, clothing, or bathrooms and post it online. But if they pause to imagine the roles reversed—if guests took pictures of their own housing and circumstances and shared them online for others to laugh at, they would likely feel uncomfortable and disrespected. This simple act of laughing and making fun of differences can lead to feelings of humiliation and can harm relationships. Shaming others, even unintentionally, diminishes dignity and has the potential to damage connections and trust. Understanding the subtle ways that shame can appear helps teams navigate relationships with sensitivity and care, fostering a space of respect and mutual honor.

Site coordinators and leaders play a vital role in helping teams build meaningful relationships by preparing them to show proper cultural honor with respect and humility. Guests, especially those from the West—where individuality and equality are often emphasized—may need guidance in understanding who holds higher honor within the local culture. Teams should approach their role with a willingness to practice what the host culture deems honorable and avoid actions that could be seen as disrespectful or shameful.

It's essential for missions team members to remember that they are guests, stepping into relationships that belong first and foremost to those living and ministering there—the hosting team and site coordinator. Good guests honor these relationships by showing respect and extending dignity to everyone involved, ensuring they do not compromise ongoing ministries.

Dignity is the cornerstone of healthy relationships, transcending cultural differences. While its expression may vary from one culture to another, the call to honor and uphold dignity remains universal, shaping relationships with care, trust, and mutual respect.

Insider Perspective
Footprints of Concern

In a small village in the farmlands of South Asia lived a man who grew jackfruit to sell at the market. Solomon had a knack for growing jackfruit, and the townspeople always looked forward to harvest time. The garden was small but just the right size to support his family. When the jackfruit was ripe, Solomon hauled it to market, and his earnings were enough for his family to live off of until the next harvest.

One day, about the time the fruit was ready for harvest, Solomon went to his garden and saw, to his dismay, that the trees were mostly bare. The fruit had already been picked. Someone had taken it, and Solomon became worried. As he looked around, he noticed some footprints in the dirt. He followed the footprints, which led him directly to his neighbor, an older gentleman of modest means. It became obvious that his neighbor had stolen the fruit. Sadly, Solomon turned and went back home. He needed to decide what to do. He was worried and concerned.

Solomon returned to his garden and gathered up the remining fruit. There was enough to fill a small wheelbarrow. As he approached his neighbor's house, he knocked on the door. When the neighbor opened the door Solomon said, "My friend, you had a need and were too ashamed to ask me for help. I am so very sorry you felt you couldn't come to me when you had such a great need. Please forgive me and accept my apology." He then gave all the remaining fruit in the wheelbarrow to his neighbor in need.

Questions to Consider
Footprints of Concern

1. How does this story make you feel?

2. How was dignity shown?

3. Was the relationship between Solomon and his neighbor preserved?

4. What do you think will happen in the future?

Principle 5: Relationship

Discussion
Footprints of Concern

Solomon's solution to this difficult situation was influenced by the honor-shame culture they lived in. Solomon understood the shame of being in need. He knew the older gentleman would be uncomfortable asking him, his younger neighbor, for help. He also knew it was his responsibility to protect the honor of his older neighbor. This was important for their honor and social standing in the community. He also needed to make sure it never happened again.

Solomon's response didn't mean he thought the theft was okay. It probably also didn't mean he truly thought his neighbor had no other options than to take the jackfruit. It was surely a sacrifice for Solomon to give his neighbor that last wheelbarrow when he himself needed it—especially now that his garden was empty.

Covering shame doesn't mean a passive approach is taken. Solomon didn't overlook the insult. Rather, he confronted it head-on. It looked different than in much of the West because he handled it the way it's done in many honor-shame cultures. When establishing guilt isn't the priority, there is no need to vocalize blame. Restoration and honor were what the relationship needed, and a heated conflict filled with accusations would have hindered the healing process. If there was blame to be placed, it was taken by Solomon, for the greater cultural sin of the broken relationship. Solomon went so far as to offer his neighbor a motive for stealing that gave him dignity and honor. Even if it may not have been entirely true, it helped him save face in spite of being caught in the shameful act of stealing. The relationship was saved, honor was restored, and both of them knew it would never happen again.

For those from the West who might consider Solomon's conversation with his neighbor wrong, it might be good to put it into perspective this way: consider the feelings a husband might have while preparing to take his wife out for dinner if she asks, "Does this dress make me look fat?"

Setting aside for a moment the many problems surrounding such a question, and recognizing that cultural values and standards have shaped the very asking of it, we can put ourselves in the husband's shoes. Some husbands have learned the hard way that answering a certain way could ruin the evening and harm the marital relationship. The only response that will save the evening and preserve the relationship is, "Honey, you look fabulous!"

Wise husbands know that their wives and their marriage are far more valuable than assessing whether she looks "fat" in any given outfit. The deeper truth is that he loves her not for the size of her dress but for the beauty she holds in her heart—her role as his wife. The man sees the vulnerability of his wife wanting to be beautiful in his eyes and recognizes that she needs honor from him. In a culture that values thinness, she may feel the shame of having gained a few pounds, and he must offer her the honor of always being his favorite sweetheart. He covers her vulnerability with dignity, and together they are more convinced than ever that they belong to each other.

Just as dignity covers vulnerability, honor covers shame. The pointing of fingers, accusations, and blame may be seen as a means of problem solving in some cultures, but in much of the world it's viewed as harmful and leads to the more shameful problem of broken relationships.

✥✥✥

Preserving Relationships and Dignity through Love
1 Corinthians 13:1–13 (NLT)

If I could speak all the languages of earth and of angels, but didn't love others, I would only be a noisy gong or a clanging cymbal. If I had the gift of prophecy, and if I understood all of God's secret plans and possessed all knowledge, and if I had such faith that I could move mountains, but didn't love others, I would be nothing. If I gave everything I have to the poor and even sacrificed my body, I could boast about it; but if I didn't love others, I would have gained nothing.

Love is patient and kind. Love is not jealous or boastful or proud or rude. It does not demand its own way. It is not irritable, and it keeps no record of being wronged. It does

Principle 5: Relationship

not rejoice about injustice but rejoices whenever the truth wins out. Love never gives up, never loses faith, is always hopeful, and endures through every circumstance.

Prophecy and speaking in unknown languages and special knowledge will become useless. But love will last forever! Now our knowledge is partial and incomplete, and even the gift of prophecy reveals only part of the whole picture! But when the time of perfection comes, these partial things will become useless.

When I was a child, I spoke and thought and reasoned as a child. But when I grew up, I put away childish things. Now we see things imperfectly, like puzzling reflections in a mirror, but then we will see everything with perfect clarity. All that I know now is partial and incomplete, but then I will know everything completely, just as God now knows me completely.

Three things will last forever—faith, hope, and love—and the greatest of these is love.

Generosity through Relationship

Generosity can be a wonderful way to show care, but it's often most meaningful when it's done with the relationship in mind. Meaningful gifts allow the recipient to feel seen, and they receive the gift as a sign of friendship. Generosity falling outside of relationship has the real possibility of causing unnecessary burdens and painful hardships. It takes time to build relationships and learn what appropriate giving is within a culture. Short-term missions teams can depend on the existing relationships of the hosting community to guide the process. Site coordinators and hosts know the people, understand their needs, and comprehend the nature of things that may not be fully appreciated or understood by those visiting for such a short time. The site coordinator can offer good advice to teams who are willing to listen.

Generosity comes in all shapes and sizes. It's often thought of in terms of resources—in the form of money, gifts, or services rendered, such as medical or education. When the focus is solely on giving resources, it becomes easy to lose sight of relationships. Generosity in relationship offers team members another, possibly better, outlet that is not solely dependent on giving resources to satisfy the generous spirits. Generosity in the way of smiles, kind words, and joy will foster connection and help build the necessary relationships to support giving resources with dignity. This kind of generosity means team members might need to set the task down in order to pay attention to new friends. A generous spirit allows us to let go of our own comfortable position in order to try new experiences that foster connection. The spirit of generosity in relationship is a shared kindness that will be remembered. This kind of generosity should be appreciated and not be minimized by team members.

Generosity within relationships is beautiful. Gifts without relationship are transactions at best and, without understanding, can be a burdensome ordeal, like giving a white elephant. Through relationships, we understand what's needed and helpful, and communicate that we see and value each other. Teams arriving must depend on the relationships of the hosting community to understand what is appropriate and what isn't. "Giving a white elephant" refers to an origin story from Thailand. According to the story, an ancient king in the nation now known as Thailand would give white elephants as the ultimate passive-aggressive gift to his enemies and anyone else who displeased him. Why? Elephants of this rare and unusual color were considered sacred, and people were required to treat them with special care, feeding them expensive food and never using them for work. This imposed a particular burden on those who were unexpectedly charged with the care of a sacred white elephant. Recipients of the king's spiteful gift would suddenly be stuck with a hefty financial burden.

Today there are many so-called "white elephant" gifts sitting unused in homes, offices, and churches around the world. They may not have been given with the ill intentions of the Thai king but out of naïve and misplaced generosity. Copy machines have rested on counters, unused, for many years because buying new toner simply wasn't affordable or possible. Mattresses have been given to people who live in one-room houses and would rather sleep on a mat that can be rolled up in the morning in order to use the space for other things during the day. White elephants are burdens to those left to take care of them. They must keep the unsolicited gift and care for it out of respect to the giver, but it can be a costly inconvenience.

Without a relationship in place, gifts are often given to make the giver feel good, sometimes with little regard for the receiver. Without understanding, the giver might go home feeling great while the receiver is left to contend with the implications. Generosity outside of relationship can do unintentional harm without the giver ever understanding the impact of what they left behind. Relationships bring balance and understanding, leaving both giver and the receiver feeling good about the relationship and the gifts given or received.

Jesus shows us a beautiful way to channel our generosity. While others added to people's burdens, he was always about lightening the load, choosing to offer relief instead of rules. His gifts weren't white elephant gifts meant to weigh someone down; instead, his gifts were about lifting burdens. Jesus loved to remove what held people back—whether guilt, shame, fear, or physical hardship—setting them free and restoring their dignity.

But Jesus didn't stop with the individual. His restoration rippled through entire communities. When he healed the blind, it wasn't just sight restored—caregivers were freed from their burden too. When the lame could walk, it didn't just change one life; it gave families back a provider, and friends back a partner. Each time Jesus removed a burden, he restored dignity. It was a moment where God's glory broke through, blessing not only the person he healed but also everyone around them.

This is a great way for us to think about generosity as we serve in short-term missions. When we give in a way that removes burdens and restores dignity—not just to individuals but also to their whole community—it's a gift that can truly make a lasting impact. It's the kind of generosity that teams can pour their hearts into.

Insider Perspective
Dignity in the Rain

The missions team arrived during rainy season. They fell in love with Pastor Romeo and his ministry. He walked and lived among the people he served in an area where he was planting a church. He was a bivocational pastor and had a job in town where he earned enough to support his family and keep the ministry going. He rode the bus into town each day, as did his children, who attended a nearby school. They all stood together at the uncovered bus stop as they waited for their bus. This time of year, they often arrived at their destinations wet from the rain. The sight of this precious and godly man going to work wearing wet shoes and clothes bothered the missions team immensely.

The team loved the heart of Pastor Romeo and wanted to do something special for him and his family. They decided better transportation would solve the problem of his family getting wet on their way to work and school. Together they decided to buy him a car. Fortunately for the pastor, the missions team leader ran this great idea by the site coordinator first. What they didn't know was that Pastor Romeo had never driven. The site coordinator explained that fuel alone would be very expensive, almost prohibitive on the pastor's modest salary, and maintenance would become a worrisome burden too. Another important factor that the team needed to understand was that the pastor would possess one of very few cars in his community, and then everyone would depend on him to drive them places. The culture mandated it because he held a high position of honor; it would be his obligation. Not to mention that he would appear to others as wealthy, which would bring risks of its own. He didn't have the money, time, skills, or security to handle an extravagant gift of this nature.

The site coordinator suggested an alternative idea that would solve the problem for Pastor Romeo and his family while also blessing his community. Most people from his neighborhood used the unsheltered bus stop and had to endure the rain too. He suggested they build a covering over the bus stop so everyone who waited for the bus would be able to stay dry.

Principle 5: Relationship

The pastor and his family could then continue building relationships with those in the community as they waited for the bus together. Everyone's feet—not just the pastor's and his family's—would stay nice and dry. The gift wouldn't be burdensome to the pastor, socially or otherwise. In fact, his social standing in the community would benefit from what he and his friends did because the covered bus stop would belong to everyone. They all would be protected from the weather together.

The team decided to follow the advice of the site coordinator and constructed a roof over the bus stop. Generous hearts were redirected to remove a burden rather than adding one. This action brought relief and comfort to the community and brought honor to Pastor Romeo and made a positive impact on his ministry.

Questions to Consider
Dignity in the Rain

1. How would the team have felt buying the pastor a car?

2. How would the pastor, community, and other pastors in the area have felt?

3. Why do you think the missions team asked the opinion of the site coordinator before acting on their idea?

4. How did the site coordinator bring dignity to the situation?

5. What impact did the bus stop have on the pastor, the community, and the other pastors in the area?

6. What are some ways that you can channel gift giving from generous teams in your context?

Discussion
Dignity in the Rain

It's pretty common for teams to want to surprise their hosts with a gift at the end of their trip, though it's usually not something as extravagant as a car. In this case, the team had their hearts in the right place, and it is good they decided to check in with the site coordinator before making such a big purchase. Otherwise, the car might have sat unused or been difficult to care for. Additionally, it could've stirred up unintended jealousy among others in the area who knew how to drive and really needed a car.

Imagine the disappointment that could have occurred when the next missions team arrived and didn't leave behind something as fancy! The best part of this story isn't just that the team leader asked for the site coordinator's advice—it's that they actually listened and followed it. That made all the difference. Thankfully, the site coordinator was knowledgeable about the culture and had the wisdom to guide the team in a better direction. What is considered generous in one culture might be perceived as intrusive, disrespectful, or inappropriate in another. Good guidance helped the team give within the bounds of relationship to the benefit of the entire community. That missions team would be remembered by Pastor Romeo with love as he received something that honored him in the eyes of his community. If a white elephant had been given, he would remember them differently. He would feel a sense of burden and shame as he cared for the expensive car that he could barely manage rather than the joy he felt every time he was at the bus stop.

The site coordinator was able to leverage the power of social capital gained from the team and transfer it to the pastor and the church in his community. As the team traveled home, the pastor and his church were seen as the ones who brought the bus stop to the community. Pastor Romeo was seen as someone who cared about the community. This perception brought him good social standing, which allowed new connections to be formed, and because of all this, his church grew as the community was transformed.

Principle 5: Relationship

"True hospitality means accepting what is offered, adapting to unexpected changes, and trusting the leadership of those who have been rooted in the community long before we arrived."
—Marty Hoskins, Director of Missions Personnel and Partnerships

Transferring the Team's Social Capital

We can trust that the hosting team has been deeply invested in the local community, with ongoing ministries and relationships, since long before the missions team arrives. However, one of the greatest contributions a missions team brings to the project isn't just the work they accomplish—it's the fresh energy and encouragement they offer. Their arrival often brings renewed enthusiasm and a sense of excitement that can invigorate the local ministry, giving it a meaningful boost. With their presence comes a unique opportunity to strengthen relationships and amplify the impact of the work already being done—a moment full of potential to be embraced.

The social capital that missions teams bring is a powerful resource that can greatly benefit the ministry. Social capital represents the energy, enthusiasm, and goodwill they contribute. However, if this energy remains focused on the team, the credit for the project often goes home with them, leaving only fond memories behind. A more impactful approach, as demonstrated in the story above, is to intentionally transfer that social capital to the local church or ministry. By doing so, the positive momentum and recognition stay with the ministry leading the project, strengthening its presence and ongoing work in the community.

For social capital to be effectively transferred, it's essential for the community to see the ministries that the team is supporting—ministries that matter deeply to the local people. Engaging the team in activities where the community sees them working alongside these ministries helps shine a spotlight on the local leadership and their ongoing efforts. This could include serving meals in outreach areas, volunteering at medical clinics, singing at community events, meeting local leaders like the mayor, or even participating in a local parade. Such activities draw positive attention, not just to the team but also to the ministry hosting the team. Leveraging the excitement and energy a visiting team generates is a wonderful opportunity. When done thoughtfully, it directs recognition and encouragement to those leading the work, strengthening their connection with the community. Site coordinators and hosts are wise to use this social capital to amplify the impact of their ministries.

A missions team from Tennessee visited a mountainous region in southern Mexico. Several women from the team planned to do foot washings while on the trip as a beautiful act of worship. They brought all the needed supplies, beautiful-smelling soaps, foot scrubs, and nice big bowls for people to soak their feet in. They did a foot washing for all the women in the Mexican church, and they loved it. The women from the church had been doing an outreach Bible study with people from a nearby tribal community. They thought it would be fun to do a foot washing for these women too. Recognizing that connections would be strengthened if the locals were leading the foot-washing event, the leaders decided that the missions team would serve in the background. They made sure the women from the church had the necessary supplies and replenished the water as needed. They also prayed for the tribal women and the ministry of the church during the whole event. The relationships between the church and the tribe were strengthened because social capital was transferred from the team to the local leaders with the beautiful heart of dignity.

Transferring social capital is all about building strong relationships between local churches or ministries and their communities—connections that can continue long after the mission team heads home. For this to happen effectively, the hosts need to be actively involved and leading the way. It's important that they truly value the resources being offered and have the freedom to use them in a way that makes sense for their ministry. Local leaders should be the ones guiding the giving process, deciding how resources are distributed. As they lead the visiting team, they arrange how the team can best support their work in a way that truly helps the ministry. Since these leaders are already trusted and known in their community, it should be clear to everyone that the team is working under their direction. When done right, transferring social capital strengthens those ongoing relationships, bringing positive energy and creating a lasting impact even after the missions team has left.

Steve Corbett and Brian Fikkert share insights on this subject in their excellent book, *When Helping Hurts*. They tell us that bridging social capital changes the posture of the short-term missions team because it changes the question we ask. Rather than asking, "What's wrong with you, and how can I fix it?" they ask, "What's right with you, and how can we work together to be part of what God is doing in your ministry?" It takes superiority out of the equation, levels the playing field, and helps the hosting team maintain their position of leadership throughout the project.[2]

When missions team members give sermons or sing at church or community events, it's essential for local leaders to remain visible and active in their role as hosts. Their presence reinforces their leadership and maintains the community's connection to the ministry. By staying involved, local leaders ensure that the spotlight remains on the relationships and the trust they've built, helping to strengthen their role in the eyes of the community while celebrating the contributions of the visiting team. This balance honors the partnership and fosters deeper, lasting connections. Local hosts should be the ones to open and close services, make altar calls, and introduce their guests to the community. When the team serves in the community, church leaders are there to help make connections and handle introductions.

The more visible the missions team is, the more intentional their preparation must be. Representing the local ministry is a privilege that carries weight, so it's vital that team members embody

---

2. See Steve Corbett and Brian Fikkert, *When Helping Hurts: How to Alleviate Poverty without Hurting the Poor . . . and Yourself* (Chicago: Moody Publishers, 2014), 142–58.

Christlike character while remaining culturally sensitive. When social capital is effectively transferred, its impact can strengthen the ministry for years to come. Local leaders play a key role in guiding this process, ensuring that interactions leave a positive and lasting impression. A thoughtful approach can open doors and build trust, while a misguided approach can create challenges that linger long after the team has gone. For social capital to really make a difference, the team needs to be well prepared and humble enough to follow the guidelines set by the local ministry leaders. Thoughtful leadership can take the team's social capital and use it to bring lasting, eternal value to the project, creating the kind of impact everyone hopes for.

Insider Perspective
Global Politics, War, and Ministry Relationships

The rich aroma of coffee filled the air as Daniel sat down with his new friend Rocco. He was looking forward to another lively conversation, and today he had a few cultural questions he hoped Rocco could help answer. Daniel was spending his summer in Serbia, a small country in Eastern Europe, as part of a missionary internship. The people of Serbia had been incredibly friendly—welcoming, curious, and genuinely interested in getting to know him. They often asked where he was from.

Daniel's family had emigrated from Mexico to the United States, and he held dual citizenship. Sometimes, to keep it simple, he'd say he was from Mexico; other times, he said he was from the U.S. But he started to notice something interesting. When he said he was from Mexico, people would lean in, smile warmly, and say, "Sit down, tell me more about yourself!" But when he mentioned he was from the U.S., their reaction was different. People would step back, cross their arms, and sometimes even scowl. Daniel was curious to know why.

Feeling comfortable with Rocco, Daniel asked him about the two different reactions. Rocco suggested they finish their coffee and take a walk. They left the café and headed to another part of the city. Rocco led Daniel to an area that was in ruins. One building

Principle 5: Relationship

had once been a hospital, another an orphanage, but now they stood as crumbling skeletons. "These buildings," Rocco explained, "were bombed by the Americans. This is part of our history. It's hard for us to forget."

In Manila, Philippines, Asia Pacific Nazarene Theological Seminary (APNTS) had always been led by a North American president—until 2003, when Dr. Hitoshi "Paul" Fukue took the helm. It was an exciting moment for the school because Dr. Fukue was the first president from that general geographical region. A highly qualified leader from Japan with a deep heart for Christ, he and his wife, Mitsuko, became shining examples to the students, missionaries, and the entire Nazarene community.

Whenever they met someone new in the Philippines, the Fukues had a unique way of greeting them. Whether addressing a single person or speaking to a group from the podium, they always began with a sincere apology. They would humbly bow their heads, look down, then lift their eyes to meet those in front of them, offering a heartfelt apology for what their country did in the Philippines during World War II. Although the war had ended nearly sixty years earlier, they understood that its painful impact still lingered in the hearts of the Filipino people. By offering this long-overdue apology, the Fukues brought a sense of healing. Their humility and sincerity opened doors for them to serve in the name of Jesus, building relationships rooted in love and reconciliation.

In Thailand, a young woman on vacation was strolling through the streets, taking in the sights, when a man approached her with a warm smile and asked if he could shake her hand. Surprised, she hesitated for a moment—after all, she didn't know him—but quickly said, "Yes, of course!"

The man explained that he had learned to speak English while studying to become a dentist. Then, with a curious smile, he asked, "Are you American?" She nodded, and what he said next completely caught her off guard.

"Thank you," he said with sincerity in his voice. "Your country gave our country a generous loan, and I've always wanted to personally thank someone from America. I'm so glad to see you here."

She smiled back, touched by his gratitude, and replied, "It was our pleasure. Your people are so kind, and we were happy to help."

The man walked away beaming, and she was left feeling both delighted and amazed at the unexpected encounter. She had just learned, in the most heartfelt way, about the loan between their two countries.

Questions to Consider
Global Politics, War,
and Ministry Relationships

1. Why is it important to know how one country is perceived by another?

2. Why was it important for the Japanese couple to understand their home country's political relationship with the Filipino people?

3. What should teams learn about a country's history before visiting?

4. What should teams know about current political situations in a country they are visiting?

5. How do historical relationships impact social capital brought by the team?

6. What specific political or cultural concerns are present in your context?

Principle 5: Relationship

Discussion
Global Politics, War, and Ministry Relationships

World history impacts how we will be perceived in cultures and countries across the globe. Stories are told and retold, passed down from one generation to the next about the relational history between two countries. Those accounts shape how the culture views visitors long before we arrive. Sometimes it's to our benefit and sometimes not. Current political issues can also add a layer of complication to the equation.

It's best when teams refrain from talking about politics from their home country, politics from the country they are visiting, and any current or historical political events involving either country. Teams are there to be the light of Christ, not to give their opinions on political issues. A good practice for team leaders is to guide teams to remain neutral and not discuss political issues at all.

Considering how the team is viewed both politically and culturally gives leaders the ability to gauge the impact the team will have on their ministry, what dangers it might bring, and the possibilities of social capital being leveraged to their benefit. Teams must be prepared to handle the conversations skillfully and delicately when needed. Gaining political understanding isn't for teams to form their own opinions but to prepare them to encounter the culture with dignity.

> "Plan for relationship building during the project."
> —Site Coordinators Everywhere

Another reason team members should be encouraged to refrain from all political discussion is that it helps maintain focus on the mission's purpose—serving with humility and building relationships. Politics can be divisive, even unintentionally, and when we carelessly share our own opinions, we risk overshadowing the work of Christ that the team is there to support. By steering clear of political topics, teams can ensure that their presence brings peace, unity, and encouragement to the ministry and its community, fostering trust and leaving a positive impact.

Making Decisions Together

When we embark on short-term missions, we often find ourselves making decisions with people we don't yet know well. Our goal is always to collaborate effectively to benefit the project and everyone involved. However, the dynamics of power within these relationships can sometimes be unexpectedly complex. Power dynamics shape how decisions are made and who has the most influence. This power can stem from various sources—leadership roles, financial resources, education, language skills, or even one's background. Often, those with more perceived power have a stronger voice in decision making, while those with less may feel compelled to accept decisions, even if they have concerns. This imbalance can affect how well a project is executed and how respected everyone feels.

Sarah Lanier, a thoughtful author and speaker, explained in a 2021 Work & Witness conference workshop that each person holds a certain number of "power points." These points represent advantages or resources that impact their influence. For example, having financial resources, speaking multiple languages, or holding a valid passport can all be power points. The more power points someone has, the more influence they wield. Conversely, those with fewer power points might face challenges in accessing opportunities or being heard. Those holding the most power points often don't realize it. They may have never thought of it that way before, or they may feel quite ordinary because in their own context they are neither wealthy nor someone of a high social position. Just because they don't recognize it doesn't mean that everyone else doesn't.

When bringing together diverse cultures, it's vital to understand power dynamics. Countries with abundant resources and opportunities are often perceived as powerful. If a team from a high-power country is unaware of these dynamics, they might unintentionally make decisions that others feel they must accept, even if those decisions aren't the most effective. This can diminish the dignity of the project and its participants.

It's crucial for teams and leaders to recognize their own power and use it thoughtfully. Those with more power must be mindful and willing to use their power to empower others, ensuring that everyone has an opportunity to contribute and be valued. Leaders from both the hosting and missions teams must be attuned to these dynamics and work together to honor each person's voice. By doing so, we can foster a respectful and balanced environment, allowing our projects to thrive and benefit everyone involved.

> "As we engage in this journey, maintaining dignity, spiritual awareness, and flexibility will shape not only our experience but also the impact we leave behind."
> —Marty Hoskins, Director of Missions Personnel and Partnerships

Insider Perspective
When the Lion Enters

The director of the mission, Eddie, had been serving in this part of the world for many years. He was gentle, humble, and Christ-like in every way. He learned to understand culture from those he served. He was loved by the people, and he loved them in return. He was an excellent director.

Eddie was invited to an international conference in Southeast Asia that was attended by many mission directors and leaders from many denominations. It was a time for them to come together, to share ideas, to learn from each other, and to strategize new ways to reach people in the Asian context. The majority of the leaders were from Asian countries. They were highly educated. Eddie was eager to get to know them and to learn from them.

Eddie was from the West. He was tall, had light skin, blue eyes, and spoke perfect English. He had many years of experience in the East as a missionary. He had spent more of his life overseas than in his home country. He began his early years completely immersed in a new culture and developed healthy missiology practices in the process. His heart always remained open to new concepts and ideas. He often expressed that everyone you come in contact with has experiences and expertise from which you can learn. He was willing to hold the posture of a learner.

When a topic of interest was being discussed at the conference, one of the Asian leaders asked if he could interrupt to share a perspective from the Asian leaders. He shared a story in order to illustrate what it was like working alongside Westerners from powerful countries: "There is a large cage full of mice. There are many mice living in the cage. They are friendly mice, doing normal mice things to help themselves enjoy life the best they can in their happy home. All is well until one day, a large, beautiful, majestic lion enters the cage. The mice have no option but to pay attention to the lion. When the lion turns his head, the air flowing off his mane can be felt by all the mice in the cage. It's strong enough to knock them off balance. Heaven forbid he take a step! The whole cage would be disrupted."

The leader turned and spoke to the Western directors: "My friends, you are the lion, and we are the mice. When you speak, your gentle words are a roar to us. We want you here, and we want your input, but you should know that we are mere mice in your presence."

Even though Eddie had lived in this part of the world for many years and understood honor-shame cultures better than most, he still experienced the difficulty of meeting new people who had a hard time seeing beyond the initial external power points he carried. His height, light skin, and blue eyes revealed his Western origins, making it easy for them to assume wealth, since he had also traveled to get there carrying a coveted passport and speaking the English language flawlessly. With all of Eddie's best and most humble qualities, the first impression outsiders had of him was of the powerful nation he was from.

Questions to Consider
When the Lion Enters

1. Why was the Eddie seen as a lion?

2. Did Eddie desire this, or bring this treatment on himself by his actions?

3. Why is it important for Eddie to be aware of how others perceive him?

4. How might this insight change our comments and opinions as we serve cross culturally?

5. What power points might be brought by a visiting team?

6. What perceived power imbalances are exemplified in your context?

Discussion
When the Lion Enters

This story gives an image of what it is like to be seen as a lion. It's doubtful that many serving in missions enjoy being perceived that way. However humbling it is to be aware of this viewpoint, it is very important that we understand it. A thoughtless, flippant comment from a lion will thunder across a room. Sarcasm, idioms, and other words that don't translate well or aren't easily understood can have an unintended impact. Suggesting a plan that isn't well thought through can have the same effect. Suggestions and biblical interpretations should be offered with great care. The volume of the opinion is heard much louder than you may think.

Power isn't bad. How it's used is what matters. Think about a high-intensity speaker with a lot of volume. If the words are good and the tone is nice, it can be a wonderful thing. However, when the opposite is true, it can be painful to the ears of many. Knowing the power we bring into a situation is helpful as we engage in decision making. Power gives us influence we may not have otherwise. To walk in the way of Christ is to walk in meekness—we restrain our own power and allow others to act and make decisions on their own behalf. We must understand that our mere presence has an impact, and sometimes we might need to take a backseat, or step out of the room when important decisions need to be made.

Some of the power points we carry are easily perceived by those we meet while others are less visible. Some power points we may not even recognize as power points, but that won't stop others from seeing them. People serving on missions teams will be watched closely and carefully by those they serve. In many contexts team members will be perceived as missionaries representing the Church of the Nazarene. Humility and meekness will communicate the spirit of Christ in all cultural contexts.

The Relationship of the Global Church

To serve in short-term missions with the Church of the Nazarene is to be invited into a global relationship. Missions teams are welcomed into ongoing ministries and relationships throughout the world. Teams don't arrive at a project greeted by a one-size-fits-all program or a cumbersome spreadsheet with a list of do's and don'ts. They arrive to a relationship of fellow Nazarenes who receive them with open arms.

Giving is always best when done inside relationship. Working within a global structure offers the necessary relationship for churches to give generously while maintaining the health and longevity of their short-term missions ministries. Both missions and hosting teams are protected from the many hazards that get en-

Principle 5: Relationship

tangled in a project when too much generosity is given outside the bounds of healthy relationship. Our global structure is a pathway paved with relationships, connecting us to our brothers and sisters a whole world away. Short-term missions ministries stand on the shoulders of giants. As much as we have learned from the past, we depend on today's leaders bringing global perspectives to guide this holy ministry forward. The church offers us a network of trusted relationships that we can depend on. Churches venturing into projects outside their home cultures can depend on the wisdom coming from those serving the global church.

Relationship Action Plan

1. Developing Long-Term Relationships
What steps can the missions team take to ensure the project is rooted in sustainable relationships, honoring both local leaders and the mission organization's structures?

2. Building Trust through Financial Sensitivity
How will financial exchanges—such as hospitality costs, resources, or gifts—impact relationships, and what boundaries need to be in place to ensure trust and dignity?

3. Identifying Strengths and Needs
What are the strengths of the hosting team, and what do they truly need or desire from the missions team to ensure the partnership is balanced and respectful?

4. Preventing Dependency
What measures can be taken to ensure that the support of the missions team empowers the hosting team without creating unhealthy dependencies?

5. Guiding Generous Hearts Wisely
How can team members give in ways that align with local customs and community needs, avoiding burdensome or culturally inappropriate gifts?

6. Navigating Honor-Shame Dynamics
How do concepts of shame and honor impact relationships, and what do both teams need to know to show mutual respect and preserve dignity?

7. Addressing Cultural Misunderstandings
What cultural norms—such as showing respect, communicating problems, or receiving help—need to be understood to prevent relational strain?

8. Leveraging Social Capital
How can the missions team engage thoughtfully with the hosting community to enhance the ministry's social capital without unintentionally reinforcing stereotypes?

9. Respecting Political and Historical Contexts
What political, social, or historical dynamics between the cultures need to be understood, and how can the missions team honor those perspectives during their work?

10. Balancing Power Dynamics
What power dynamics (real or perceived) exist between the teams, and how can overlooked voices be included in decision making to ensure mutual respect?

11. Honoring Local Resources
How can the missions team prioritize and utilize local resources—skills, materials, or knowledge—so that their presence strengthens the community rather than replacing what already exists?

Principle 6: Expectations

We have different gifts, according to the grace given to each of us. If your gift is prophesying, then prophesy in accordance with your faith; if it is serving, then serve; if it is teaching, then teach; if it is to encourage, then give encouragement; if it is giving, then give generously; if it is to lead, do it diligently; if it is to show mercy, do it cheerfully.
—Romans 12:6–8

Key Definitions

✦ **Expectations**: The strong belief that something will happen in the future. Planning that someone will or should achieve something.

✦ **Flexibility**: A person or object having the ability to change or be changed easily according to the situation.

✦ **Global Missions**: The missions department in the Church of the Nazarene is led by the Global Missions director. The Global Missions office is located at the Church of the Nazarene's Global Ministry Center in Lenexa, Kansas, USA. They support the mission of the church by working with the regional and field leaders. They work to expand the church globally through Nazarene Ministries. An important role of Global Missions is to appoint and place missionaries in locations that are strategic to the global church.

✦ **High-Context Culture**: Communication is often indirect, and much is conveyed through nonverbal cues such as body language, facial expressions, and tone of voice. People may assume a shared understanding based on their shared cultural context.

✦ **Leader**: Effective leaders prioritize the well-being and success of their team members by enabling them to accomplish tasks with dignity and foster a sense of trust and collaboration.

✦ **Low-Context Culture**: Communication tends to be more direct, and people may rely on verbal expressions rather than nonverbal cues. The emphasis is on clarity and precision in conveying the message.

✦ **Per Diem**: The daily allowance for each person's expected expenses while working on the project, including meals, lodging, and incidentals.

✦ **Roles**: There are many roles in a project. Each role is filled by a person who will accomplish tasks and duties specific to their assigned role. The roles align harmoniously to complete the overall project.

Guiding Principle #6: Expectations

Site coordinators and team leaders attribute their ability to create outstanding, life-changing experiences in short-term missions to the seven principles outlined in *Following Dignity*. They emphasize that one principle in particular—aligning and managing expectations—is foundational to ensuring dignity for every participant. When expectations are aligned, participants are more likely to feel successful. Success, in this context, is defined by whether a person feels their expectations have been adequately met. When they are, it's considered a success; when they aren't, disappointment follows. Therefore, it is of utmost importance for leaders to bring expectations into alignment. Leaders who prioritize aligning and meeting expectations will see their projects deemed an overwhelming success. Those who don't, risk leaving their teams grumbling in disappointment.

The phrase "clear is kind" is a common refrain around the tables at the Global Missions office. We can trust that those serving the Lord genuinely want to do the right thing—God's people typically aim to meet and even exceed the expectations set before them. However, they can only do so if they clearly understand what those expectations are and, more specifically, what is expected of them individually. People feel disappointed not only when their own expectations aren't met but also when they let others down by failing to meet what others expected of them. Emphasizing "clear is kind" is especially helpful when working with people from diverse backgrounds, where assumptions and unspoken expectations can easily lead to confusion.

The cultural backgrounds and worldviews of participants will inevitably shape their perceptions of what a successful project looks like. Success is likely to be viewed from various angles. As a result, conflicting expectations are bound to arise, and it falls to the leaders to bring these expectations into alignment. To do so, leaders must have a clear vision of both the project's objectives and the roles of the teams and their participants. Clear communication of goals, roles, and expectations is essential for achieving a positive outcome. Let's explore how we can align and meet the expectations of those we are serving.

Minding the Gap

Numerous studies have shown that our happiness and disappointments hinge on the gap between our expectations and reality. Happiness resides on one side of this gap while disappointment lies on the other. When we set an expectation, we hold a strong belief that something will happen. Once that expectation is established, the outcome can fall into one of three possibilities: it can be met exactly as anticipated, fall short of what we hoped, or exceed our expectations entirely. When expectations are met, we feel a sense of calm, as if everything is right with the world. But when things fall short, we experience disappointment and the accompanying pain. On the upside, when our expectations are exceeded, we experience joy and the pleasant surprise of things turning out better than expected. Ultimately, our happiness and disappointments are shaped by the gaps surrounding our expectations.

Researcher and storyteller Brené Brown reminds us of the importance of taking our expectations seriously. In *Rising Strong*, she writes that "expectations are resentments waiting to happen."¹ The more significant the expectation, the more profound the disappointment when it isn't met. A short-term mission trip is a significant journey in the life of a Christian, and it is often laden with many expectations. Therefore, managing and aligning expectations is essential to preserving the dignity of those we are serving.

Australian-born researcher and social entrepreneur Nat Ware highlights the areas where we are most vulnerable to letting our expectations get the best of us. He identifies these as the gaps of imagination, comparison, and past experience.[2] When people walk away from a short-term mission project disappointed due to unmet expectations, it's often because they've fallen into one of these three gaps. The unarticulated thoughts we carry in our minds—our imaginations, comparisons, and past experiences—quietly but inevitably turn into expectations that are sometimes so large that our actual experiences pale in comparison.

The Imagination Gap

We find ourselves in the imagination gap when our experiences fail to align with the grand visions our minds have conjured up. This happens when our expectations grow to unreasonable proportions, making them nearly impossible to fulfill. For instance, a team member might hear stories of people coming to know the Lord on mission trips and believe that will be their experience too. They might even bring along a wayward child, certain they will find the Lord during the trip. When things don't turn out as expected, they return home full of disappointment. Others might romanticize the project in their mind, having been sold an idea and promised many things. They prepare for the project with inflated expectations that are bound to come crashing down when reality doesn't measure up. Enthusiastic leaders must be careful not to oversell the experience with empty promises that can create unrealistic expectations and crush spirits.

---

1. Brené Brown, *Rising Strong: How the Ability to Reset Transforms the Way We Live, Love, Parent, and Lead* (New York: Random House, 2017), 140.
2. Nat Ware, TEDxKlagenfurt, "Why We're Unhappy: The Expectation Gap," 2015, https://www.youtube.com/watch?v=9KiUq8i9pbE.

Before the project begins, leaders are often met with a barrage of questions. While they may have plans in place, they can't be expected to know every detail of what the team will face on-site. However, it's crucial for leaders to remember that whatever they share with the team will likely become the team's expectation. Once the team arrives, leaders must work diligently to fulfill any promises made beforehand. Leaders who manage to align expectations without raising them too high will find it easier to meet those expectations, resulting in a better experience for everyone involved—especially the leader.

The Comparison Gap

Both hosting and missions teams are particularly vulnerable to the comparison gap. Hosting teams may see the successes of other churches—the projects they've completed, the growth they've experienced—and expect similar results. The tendency to compare creates expectations based on external factors, often distracting us from what God has planned for us and stealing our joy in the process.

Team members on a project are also susceptible to the comparison gap when they compare themselves to one another. For example, if one team member receives a special privilege—like a better room, an exclusive outing, or a unique gift—the comparisons begin. Those left behind hear stories of the fancy room, the exciting adventure, or the unique gift, leading to feelings of exclusion and disappointment.

Comparisons can breed expectations among the rest of the team—perhaps they think they should have an outing of their own or expect to receive a similar gift. When these expectations aren't met, even if unspoken, feelings need to be managed. As social creatures, we often carry the vulnerabilities of childhood into our adult lives. While we may pretend not to care, inclusion is a fundamental human need and a component of dignity that most of us still value deeply.

The great news is that site coordinators and hosting leaders can turn the comparison gap into a valuable tool. When a team arrives to work on a project, other churches and ministries in the area will naturally take notice. This is a golden opportunity for leaders to model the kind of collaboration and generosity they hope to see replicated. By practicing good missiology from the very beginning, they can set the tone for what future hosts should strive for. Whether it's tithing part of the project to another church, inviting the missions team to assist with a ministry at a neighboring congregation, or creating opportunities for multiple churches to be part of the experience, leaders are laying the groundwork for shared expectations. This kind of intentionality not only strengthens relationships in the community but also ensures that when other churches step into the hosting role, they'll follow the positive example that's already been set.

Another opportunity for site coordinators to leverage the comparison gap is by creating positive gaps as they organize the team's schedule. Team members know things will be different, and as they arrive and soak in their new surroundings, their expectations naturally begin to take shape. Knowing that happiness often comes from exceeding expectations, leaders can design the schedule to improve steadily so that each experience is a little better than the one before. If there are multiple restaurants, shopping experiences, hotels, ministries, or church events, leaders can arrange these experiences in a crescendo, creating a continual positive expectation gap, starting with the most rustic or ordinary experiences and gradually building to a final, meaningful event. Of course, team members shouldn't be in on the crescendo plan—it's all about managing expectations behind the scenes. If they knew what was coming, the surprise and joy of surpassing their expectations would lose its wonder.

Playing with expectation gaps can add a dose of fun to the planning process. Cultures vary in delightful ways, even when it comes to something as simple as how drinks are served. In some places, sodas are enjoyed at room temperature, while in others, a frosty glass with plenty of ice is the norm. Imagine a team arriving from a country where drinks are always served cold, only to find themselves in a place where ice isn't a staple. Leaders getting ice every day might be a bit of a challenge, but finding ice is not impossible. Here's where a little creative planning can add a touch of charm. If no ice is expected throughout the trip and then, toward the end of the project, it suddenly appears—what a treat! But imagine if ice were offered in abundance those first few days and then suddenly disappeared. Team members might feel let down every time a drink came without that familiar chill. By holding off and introducing the treat in the final days, leaders can create a moment of joy—a small but memorable surprise that leaves everyone smiling. Sometimes a little planning and timing can turn an ordinary detail into a highlight of the trip.

As leaders plan their schedules, they should be thoughtful about the expectations that naturally come from comparisons. Seeing what others are receiving or experiencing can shape how teams, churches, and districts view their own involvement. By treating everyone fairly, leaders can help minimize feelings of jealousy or unrealistic expectations. When approached wisely, comparisons can actually be a helpful tool to set expectations that support long-term goals for the ministry. And when used thoughtfully, the gap between expectations and reality can even spark moments of unexpected joy for those being served.

The Past Experience Gap

People caught in the gap of past experience believe that what happened before is better than what's happening now. For them, the "good old days" are untouchable glory days, and nothing in the present ever measures up. They often think that for an experience to be meaningful, it must mirror a cherished memory from years gone by—a nearly impossible standard since those memories are colored by nostalgia and imagination.

Leaders might hear glowing descriptions of a past trip, complete with specific details, and be asked to replicate the magic of that moment. But chasing down an experience from twenty or thirty years ago is an uphill battle. Even if a site coordinator tries their best to re-create it, disappointment often follows because the gap between the memory and today's reality will simply be too wide. Time has changed so much—the people, the places, and even the way things are done. Memories grow grander with age, and even a perfect re-creation rarely measures up to what the team member remembers in their heart.

Some projects require more than one team to complete, and it's important for hosting teams to approach each new group with fresh eyes. Expecting the arriving team to behave just like the one before them can set the stage for disappointment. Every team is unique, bringing its own personality, strengths, and dynamics. Even if the project is similar, this is a whole new experience.

Placing a team in the shadow of past experiences isn't fair—it limits their potential and almost guarantees they'll fall short of the hosts' memories. Dignity calls for giving each team the freedom to be themselves, allowing them to contribute in their own way without being measured against what came before. This mindset creates space for both teams and hosts to enjoy the beauty of what unfolds in the present.

While sharing great stories about past trips is wonderful, and recounting past experiences makes for good conversation, creating expectations based on memories or trying to relive old stories should be approached with caution. Every group of people and every situation is different. God works in the present, often in new and unexpected ways. Letting go of the tendency to compare this experience with past ones will lead to embracing what God is doing here and now.

Managing Expectations

Great teams arrive with expectations that are well managed and aligned to meet the goals of the project with grace and flexibility. Exceptional team leaders and site coordinators ensure that their teams feel special by treating each project and team as a distinct and unique experience. Team leaders avoid making participants feel like they're just collecting another stamp in their passports, while site coordinators don't complain about how busy they are with all the projects and teams they oversee. Instead, they show up fully present, set aside comparisons, and recognize that this is a one-of-a-kind experience. They honor everyone involved by being attentive and respectful, working within their team's dynamics to ensure fairness and avoid creating comparison gaps among team members.

Most importantly, these leaders take the task of aligning expectations seriously. The gap between meeting and exceeding expectations doesn't need to be large to create a joyful experience. In fact, too wide a gap can make some people uncomfortable because it shifts the nature of the expectation. Wise leaders set realistic expectations, leaving just enough room for them to be pleasantly exceeded. They understand that this small, beautiful space where expectations are surpassed is key to creating happy, satisfied teams.

> "Expectations not being met are the greatest source of conflict."
> —Site Coordinators Everywhere

Empowering Leadership: Cultivating Trust and Dignity

Site coordinators and hosting leaders share a special partnership, working together to shape the vision and goals for each project. Once the site coordinator fully understands the outcomes the hosts are hoping for, and how the visiting missions team will contribute, they also take into account how the experience will benefit the visiting team itself. With confidence in this mutual exchange, the site coordinator can then evaluate whether bringing a team onsite is truly feasible.

It's essential for site coordinators to ensure that hosts are ready—both in spirit and in practical ways—not just to meet their own goals but also to extend hospitality and support to the visiting team. Preparing hearts and minds for the journey ahead fosters a strong foundation for the work to come.

Once everyone is aligned, it's time for the site coordinator to craft a clear and thoughtful plan. The plan should outline roles and set realistic expectations that are all tied to the shared vision of the project. Special care is taken in selecting the right people for key responsibilities, equipping them with the tools and preparation they need to succeed. With everyone on the same page and ready to contribute, the stage is set for a collaborative and meaningful experience.

Site coordinators don't micromanage every detail themselves. Instead, they focus on the bigger picture, empowering their teams and leaders to take responsibility. This allows them to keep an eye on the project's progress without being bogged down by the daily tasks. Clear and open communication about goals, roles, and expectations keeps things running smoothly. Because site coordinators often live locally, they have a deep understanding of potential challenges and can ensure that the team is equipped with the right skills and resources. They also know that hosts are often in the best position to handle certain responsibilities, thanks to their local expertise and long-standing relationships. This cultural insight is key to making sure everything flows toward the project's goals. Throughout the project, site coordinators stay connected, offering support, checking in regularly, and ensuring accountability. This steady guidance helps keep everything on track.

Simon Sinek, a bestselling author and founder of The Optimist Company, reminds us that great leadership is not about being in charge. It's about taking care of those in your charge. Leaders don't need to manage every detail themselves; they take care of the team, ensuring everyone has what they need to succeed. This behavior creates trust, which flows in both directions. When leaders trust their teams, team members rise to the occasion, eager to learn and meet the expectations set before them. They know that their work is valued and that they are part of something bigger than themselves.[3]

Leaders know that everyone involved is making a sacrifice, big or small, and each contribution is a precious thread in the fabric of the mission. Every act matters and deserves to be seen. Leaders also understand that those who come to serve don't come alone—behind each team member are families, friends, coworkers, and church members who've stepped up to cover responsibilities, allowing their loved ones to fully immerse themselves in the project. With this in mind, leaders go the extra mile to express their gratitude—not just to the participants but also to their amazing

---

3. Simon Sinek, *Leaders Eat Last: Why Some Teams Pull Together and Others Don't* (New York: Penguin Random House, 2014), 20–25.

supporters as well. Whether through heartfelt notes, shopping excursions so team members can take home souvenirs, little tokens of appreciation, or simple and sincere words of praise, they make sure everyone feels the warmth of being truly valued.

In the end, meeting expectations isn't just about getting tasks done; it's about honoring the hearts and sacrifices of everyone who has contributed to the project's success.

> "The more you collaborate on ministry ideas with your hosting team, the better; this will truly benefit the goals and vision of the field."
> —Josh Herndon, Missionary, Eurasia

Communication in Context: Setting the Stage for Success

Anthropologist Edward T. Hall introduced the concept of "context cultures" in the 1970s in his book *Beyond Culture*, identifying two distinct styles of communication: high context and low context. Understanding this concept offers insights for those navigating the nuanced conversations that arise in cross-cultural ministry. High-context cultures tend to rely on implicit communication, where much is understood through shared background knowledge and contextual cues. In contrast, low-context cultures are more likely to depend on explicit verbal communication, where information is conveyed directly and clearly.

In high-context cultures, much of the communication is embedded within the situation itself. People in these cultures often understand each other with minimal verbal explanation because they share a common history and set of experiences. Countries with long histories—such as those in the Middle East, China, Korea, Greece, and India—are typically considered high context. In these cultures, direct communication may be seen as redundant since so much is already implied by the context.

On the other hand, low-context cultures are often younger or have undergone significant social changes, leading to a communication style that prioritizes clear, explicit verbal exchanges. Countries like Switzerland, Australia, New Zealand, Germany, and the United States are considered low context. In these settings, people tend to express expectations directly, and communication may be more straightforward because there is less shared context to rely on.

While every culture has context, the degree to which it influences communication varies. In low-context cultures, people often articulate expectations directly, using clear language. However, even within low-context settings, there are pockets of higher context, such as long-established communities where unspoken cues and shared history play a larger role in communication. Imagine attending a birthday party. Every culture has certain norms around these events. In your own culture, you know the rules without needing them spelled out. No one has to explain the cake, the gifts, or what's expected. Now, imagine someone standing over your shoulder, describing every detail, explaining not just *what's* happening but also *why* it's happening and what will happen next. It would feel redundant because everyone already knows the script. We've all experienced birthdays, so the context is obvious. That's the power of context. High-context cultures understand what's going on in any given situation and share ideas without needing direct language. They're adept at "reading the room," so to speak.

However, if this were your first birthday party, you might appreciate some guidance—like why there are fiery candles on a cake. Working with short-term missions is similar; you're dealing with people who are often in an unfamiliar context, and they'll need more explicit information to fully grasp what's happening. This means that when making plans and setting expectations, leaders will need to adopt a low-context approach to ensure clear communication. Remembering that "clear is kind," leaders should share expectations using a more direct language style. For site coordinators working in cross-cultural settings, it's important to recognize that short-term missions teams often find themselves in unfamiliar contexts. These teams will require clear, explicit information to understand what's happening around them. Leaders should adopt a low-context approach when making plans and setting expectations, ensuring that communication is as clear and detailed as possible, which will help prevent misunderstandings and unmet expectations.

To communicate effectively in a low-context style, leaders need to replace assumptions and implicit cues with explicit, detailed information. Establishing a collaborative environment where questions are encouraged helps lay the groundwork for clear communication. Leaders and coordinators should outline tasks together, set deadlines, and follow up with written communication tailored to the needs of those responsible for each task. Providing enough background information helps bridge the gap between explicit and implicit communication, making the reasoning behind expectations clear.

> "Communication is key in helping teams manage expectations."
> —Sam Senica, Missionary, Mesoamerica

To communicate explicitly, cues and assumptions need to be replaced with detailed information. Establishing a collaborative environment where questions are encouraged lays the groundwork for clearly defined outcomes. Leaders and coordinators might outline tasks together and set deadlines. Once expectations are set, they should be reinforced with written communication in the format most accessible to those responsible. Providing enough background information helps bridge the gap between explicit and implicit communication styles, fostering clarity.

Site coordinators can create comprehensive checklists covering the essential details teams need to know—like electrical voltage, currency exchange procedures, and airport information. Hosts should have their own checklists too, covering the importance of clean drinking water, safety reminders, and other routine tasks necessary to care for the team. Keeping detailed notes and checklists helps ensure everything stays on track.

Expectations: Money & Finances

The thread of dignity extends into the financial aspects of short-term missions as well. Transparency in finances isn't just a good practice—it's essential. Every penny given to the church belongs to the Lord and is set apart for his purposes, including funds for projects and per diems. Managing finances with clarity and openness is key, so a low-context cultural approach works best. Everything should be neatly documented with clear records of purchases, prices, and dates. Whenever possible, receipts or invoices should accompany each purchase. To ensure everyone is on the same page, the site coordinator should provide the missions team leader with a hard copy of the per diem expense report before they depart, ensuring transparency and accountability every step of the way.

The per diem funds belong to the team. As the trip nears its end, if the site coordinator realizes there will be leftover funds, they can collaborate with the team leader to plan something extra for the team, such as a nice dinner or an excursion as a reward for their hard work, or the remaining funds can be used to cover additional, unexpected team expenses, such as luggage fees.

If the team prefers not to use the leftover funds and chooses to leave them on the field, the site coordinator and team leader must work together to determine how the funds should be designated. If there is an additional need within the project, the funds can be donated there. The district superintendent must approve any donations, and once approved, the funds should go to the district office to be disbursed through the local church or pastor toward the project. Global tax laws vary and should be considered when determining the appropriate use of leftover funds.

When the team chooses to give remaining per diem money or any other funds to a project or ministry, to preserve the dignity of everyone involved, money should never be given directly to a local church member or pastor. Instead, it should be directed to the project or ministry through the proper channels. Any offerings to the coordinator or other hosts should be documented with a receipt and included in the final report.

Principle 6: Expectations

Flexibility—A Treasure of Gold

A common saying among overseas workers and missionaries is the old adage "Blessed are the flexible, for they shall bend and not break." While it's not in the Bible, it is the golden rule when it comes to short-term missions. Even with well-aligned expectations, flexibility remains crucial. It's an essential expectation that everyone relies on. Flexibility fosters collaboration, allowing us to embrace and be open to new ideas from diverse perspectives. It helps team members work together cohesively and adapt effectively when faced with emerging needs.

Everyone working on the project has a flexibility muscle. Some are stronger than others. We can be certain that everyone's flexibility muscle has been stretching long before they arrive to the project. After they arrive, team members will continue to bend and stretch. When faced with something new and unusual they will be stretched. Eating new foods, sleeping in new places, and finding themselves in awkward situations—sometimes with peculiar new people—are all stretching activities. Their faith will be stretched as they discover new ways to see and experience God's world. Expect that everyone's flexibility muscle will be in full use.

Flexibility is expected, but it isn't free. It costs the team something, and it's a gift we ask them to bring to the project. We must remember that flexibility from others is always theirs to offer—we don't take it from them; they give it. They give up control of what they thought might happen and then bend to accommodate us. It costs team members something every time we ask them to shift their expectations. We must consider how failing to meet preset expectations due to poor planning impacts a team's dignity—it adds to their existing burden. Flexibility is a gift of the heart that leaders need to handle with care and awareness. When people get stretched too far, it can be an uncomfortable experience for everyone.

Aligning expectations, on the other hand, brings much comfort to everyone and is essential to the success of the project, but we must also approach our expectations with a dose of flexibility. Teams thrive when site coordinators not only align expectations but also hold them loosely. Just as a rider guides a horse with soft reins, a leader should manage expectations without rigid control. If the reins are held too tightly, the horse becomes restless, and the journey turns rigid and uncomfortable. Holding expectations lightly allows for necessary flexibility. Sometimes leaders may find that the sheer number of expectations overwhelms the team—not because any expectation is wrong but because the weight of too many can exhaust their flexibility. Leaders should strive to meet expectations while being prepared to adjust or set them aside if they become too burdensome.

Flexibility serves the project best when it's seen as a gift and applied when it becomes necessary to pivot. Plans will surely change, and flexibility from teams and leaders is sure to keep dignity up front where it belongs.

"Remember: I am not the exception."
—Brian Becker, Point Loma Nazarene University

Insider Perspective
When Fast Food Is King

The site coordinator had some training, but clearly not enough, which became apparent with the arrival of a difficult team. They were not difficult because they were doing anything wrong but because they were merely human.

The team had been preparing for more than a year, saving and raising money for the project. They had raised more money than they even thought possible. They gathered the right people for the project. They were going to paint the inside and outside of a new outreach center for children at a rural church in a remote coastal village. Many people donated paintbrushes and other supplies. Donations were gathered to fund a young artist to go who would paint a mural for the children on one of the walls in the building. God was doing so many amazing things. Most people on the team used their paid time off work and were ready for God to do something great.

Principle 6: Expectations

There were difficulties on the way to the destination. They were excited, but they had been overnight in one airport and delayed in another, and then they had more delays with immigration. They had several unexpected expenses because of immigration hassles. They had been traveling almost forty hours, with not enough rest, food, or even water. When they finally arrived, the arranged transportation wasn't sufficient. There were not enough seats for everyone during this final leg of the journey. They crammed everyone in, sitting on laps and on floorboards, they rolled down the windows, they breathed in the steamy tropical air, and they made do.

Everyone on the team was relieved to finally arrive. They had two rooms—one for the men and another for the women. As they settled in their rooms, they realized they had a bit of a dilemma on their hands. Some wanted the windows open because the rooms were stifling hot. Others wanted them closed because of the lack of screens on the windows. They were more concerned about the bugs, mosquitos, and other creepy things that would come in. Either choice made sleep nearly impossible.

After another night without enough sleep, they came together for their orientation. They were served cereal with warm, boxed milk. They were excited to start the project, but then they learned that the project was delayed. Additionally, instead of painting, they would be pouring a concrete floor. All the supplies and expert painters they'd brought with them were now unnecessary. They were also made aware that the national church where they were working would be holding a training seminar. There were more than a hundred local pastors who would be attending meetings while the team was working on the project. It wasn't what they expected, but they were prepared to be flexible.

All morning, church ladies prepared a feast for the guests. It smelled amazing, and the team was excited to try the local food they'd heard about. Just as the national pastors were breaking to eat, a motorcycle arrived carrying a delivery from McDonald's. There were cheeseburgers, French fries, and Cokes for everyone on the missions team. They weren't eating with the locals. Again, for dinner, they were separate—not McDonald's this time but pizza. The next day, fast food again, chicken. Every day on the trip fast food was served to them, usually twice a day. No vegetables, no fruit, and more soda than water.

Often the team couldn't work because they needed to be quiet during the meetings. Other times when they could work, the area was small, and only a few could work at a time. There was never enough water to drink. They were thirsty and stood around and waited a majority of the time.

While the nationals ate together, the team ate together. Separate. Separate food, separate tables. The nationals had the local cuisine. The team ate the international fast food. The team never knew whose idea this was or why it was this way. The trip was harder than expected, and people grumbled.

Questions to Consider When Fast Food Is King

1. Why do you think the people were grumbling?

2. Do you think this is what biblical hospitality looks like? Why or why not?

3. Do you think the team felt that they were seen?

4. What assumptions do you think were made?

5. How did those who were unprepared take advantage of the team's flexibility?

6. How does this story relate to your ministry experience?

Discussion
When Fast Food Is King

Underneath it all, we are all just human. This team, despite being well prepared and ready to embrace the rough conditions, found themselves disillusioned. They had come with open hearts, planning to be gracious guests and accept whatever was offered, even if that meant roughing it. However, from the start, the spirit of hospitality was absent. Poor sleeping arrangements and insufficient hydration left them tired and thirsty. They found themselves with too little work and felt that their sacrificial preparations had simply been dismissed. The connection they expected and the project plans they were given did not align with the reality they encountered. They felt unseen, unwanted, and misled, with some members questioning whether the hosting team was more interested in the money they brought than in their presence and labor.

Unmet expectations on the project led to a disheartening experience for the team, causing further disappointment upon their return home. Rather than writing thank-you notes to their donors, they had to explain why the painting supplies had been unnecessary. They also needed to account to those who had funded the artist, explaining why there were no pictures of the mural she was supposed to paint. Setting and meeting clear expectations honors not just the team but also those who supported the project and the church family that sent them.

Team leaders, site coordinators, and hosting teams should always collaborate to make the best arrangements for the team's care. This doesn't mean providing fancy or expensive accommodations, but it does mean addressing and meeting basic human needs while the team serves. Teams should expect to have clean drinking water available whenever they need it, food that is properly handled to avoid illness, and a safe place to sleep. Showers, restrooms, and laundry facilities are also necessary and should be planned for by the hospitality team. While teams arrive prepared to be flexible and understand that their needs might be met in new and interesting ways, it's crucial that these needs are still addressed. Team leaders rely on their hosts to meet the team's hospitality needs with dignity.

If these needs aren't being met, effective communication with the site coordinator is essential to resolve the situation.

Flexibility is an essential element of short-term missions. Teams that have been well prepared arrive with the understanding that things often change and that flexibility is expected. Unpredictable situations are sure to occur. However, the burden of poor planning and disorganization by the hosting team should never be placed on the shoulders of the missions team. Site coordinators and hosts must work together to meet the expectations that they set ahead of time in order to serve everyone who participates on the project with the dignity they deserve. Taking advantage of a team's flexibility by being unprepared is unacceptable on all accounts.

> "Preparation, preparation, preparation.
> And lots of water."
> —Roger Kellogg, Missionary, Mesoamerica

Expectations and Biblical Hospitality

Biblical hospitality can be experienced in as many ways as there are cultures. Sometimes teams depend entirely on their hosts to prepare all the meals. Other times, teams are given a kitchen to use and prepare their own food. Some teams only eat local cuisine; others bring a few goodies from home. In whatever way that meals are prepared, hospitality is best shared around the table. Food is a cultural experience, and we can depend on it to bridge teams together in a meaningful way. Leaders should be flexible as they creatively organize meal plans that are practical to implement and acceptable for both hosting and missions teams.

Most visiting teams have something that hosts need to be aware of beforehand. Whether it is food allergies or simply a preference to have rice served at every meal, the hosting team should be aware of these needs before the team arrives. Gathering information beforehand about the unique needs and desires of the team helps leaders put a good plan in place. Teams may have a prefer-

Principle 6: Expectations

ence about how much of the local food will they like. Some want to try just a few things; others want to eat it every day and may want to join in preparation so they can learn something. Usually, a good balance of local fare along with a few staples from home will make everyone happy. In order to take care of the team, the hosts need good information well before the team arrives to make a great plan that will serve them well.

Teams arrive expecting to eat food that is different. Most importantly, they are trusting that it will be prepared properly so they won't get sick. Teams coming from countries where the food is different may have digestive troubles when they experience a sudden change in their diet. Even the water they drink can affect their digestive systems. Those cooking for teams from other countries will need to be careful about the water used for food preparations. The indignity of getting sick because the food served hasn't been prepared well may cause visiting teams to lose trust and not want to eat anything for the rest of their visit. Locals preparing meals may need some need training in order to cook meals that the missions team can safely eat. The site coordinator works with those preparing meals for the team well in advance of their arrival. They will need help choosing meals that the team will like while being assured they can safely eat what's offered to them.

Site coordinators and hosts should thoughtfully consider whether dining in restaurants is the right choice for the team. If so, it's important to choose restaurants that can comfortably accommodate the group, making sure the food and water are prepared safely for everyone's well-being. At the same time, they'll want to keep an eye on the team's per diem budget, ensuring that the choice aligns with both the team's needs and financial expectations. Thoughtful planning can make the dining experience enjoyable and worry-free for everyone.

The global spread of American fast-food chains has certainly made its mark in many areas where the Church of the Nazarene is active. While these familiar spots might appeal to missions teams, it's best to avoid relying solely on fast food. A thoughtful balance of familiar foods and local dining options not only offers variety but also ensures a healthier and more culturally immersive experience.

By carefully considering the options, team leaders and site coordinators can create a plan that blends comfort with adventure, all while ensuring everyone's well-being.

The Power of Clarity

For smooth operations and to minimize conflict, it's good when everyone understands not only their own roles and responsibilities but also those of others and how everybody's role fits into the larger picture. When team members are clear on these aspects, it fosters harmony and reduces the risk of duplication of efforts. Few things are as frustrating as pouring your time and energy into a task only to find out it's already been done—sometimes at great expense. It can feel discouraging, and, worse, it means other important tasks may have been overlooked while efforts were unknowingly duplicated. That's why thoughtful coordination is important. When everyone's contributions are aligned and purposeful, it not only avoids wasted effort but also ensures that every need is met and every hand plays a meaningful role. When everyone's roles and expectations are clearly understood, it creates a smooth path forward—saving time, money, and energy while keeping frustration at bay. For things to run smoothly, site coordinators and team leaders need to work closely, each focusing on supporting their own teams. The team leader will be the main point of contact for the missions team while the site coordinator connects with the hosting team leaders. When both teams collaborate well, everyone works together toward the project's goals.

If any challenges or concerns come up along the way, it's important for missions team members to bring them to their team leader and for the hosting team to do the same with their own leader or the site coordinator. Each team works best when they communicate within their group and trust their leaders to address issues, rather than going directly to someone from the other team. This way, leaders can communicate and make sure everyone stays on the same page.

Site coordinators, team leaders, and hosting leaders must educate their teams on the importance of this communication process. The hosting team should understand that any suggestions for outings should be directed to their hosting leader, who will relay

Principle 6: Expectations

them to the site coordinator. Similarly, missions team members should not be taken out on their own without prior permission from both the site coordinator and team leader.

Insider Perspective
A Clear Vision

A kind woman named Susan was part of a missions team visiting a country for the first time on a bustling church project. One sunny afternoon, as Susan chatted with a friendly person at the project site, she casually mentioned that her eyeglasses had just broken. With the best of intentions, the friendly woman from the neighborhood offered to take Susan to the local glasses store to help her out. Susan, being ever so trusting, agreed and set off with her new friend, unaware of where she was going or when she might return. The team leader, the site coordinator, the hosting leader, and everyone else were left in the dark about Susan's sudden adventure.

When Susan finally made it back, she was wearing a pair of stunning, budget-friendly glasses that caught the eye of another team member. This team member, impressed by Susan's new look, decided she also wanted a pair. So, off she went to the glasses store and came back with a beautiful new pair herself. Meanwhile, another team member, Gary, heard about the glasses and was also eager to get a pair for himself. But alas, the team was scheduled for a day of rest and relaxation, and Gary missed his chance. Feeling left out and disappointed, he sulked around, wishing he had stayed behind instead.

If only the site coordinator had known about this fantastic opportunity! He could have informed the team leader, who could then have organized a special trip to the glasses store for anyone interested. That way, everyone would have had a chance to grab a stylish pair of glasses at a discount, and no one would have felt left out.

Questions to Consider
A Clear Vision

1. Why do you think Susan decided to go to the glasses store?

2. What potential problems could have arisen other than scheduling issues?

3. What is going to be one of Gary's most memorable experiences of the trip? Why?

4. How could the site coordinator have helped?

5. What can leaders do to prepare better next time?

Discussion
A Clear Vision

Church projects often attract a mix of community members—some actively helping, some just observing, and others merely curious about the new faces and what they're up to. Missions teams naturally stir up a lot of excitement.

Susan, with her trusting nature, found herself in a tricky situation. She agreed to go with a local woman who offered to help her get a new pair of glasses without informing her team leader. Unbeknownst to Susan, this woman had not notified anyone about their outing either, leaving Susan's whereabouts unknown. The woman's intentions could have been anything. Susan's disappearance for several hours caused undue panic and concern among the team, highlighting the importance of communication and safety. And then there's Gary. Poor Gary felt left out. On a day meant for enjoying the sights and sounds, he found himself grappling with disappointment over missed opportunities.

Site coordinators and leaders establish rules and expectations not to control people but to ensure the safety and well-being of everyone involved. In some regions, a local church member taking an international guest to unfamiliar or potentially risky areas could pose certain dangers. These guidelines are in place to protect, not to intimidate or burden team members. Leaders are also mindful of the impact on team morale when some members receive opportunities that others do not. Their goal is to plan for success in every aspect of the project, ensuring that all team members are safe, informed, and included.

Teams should trust the host even when they don't understand. There are dynamics that are beyond their view and comprehension.

> "Trust that your host and your team leader are working in your best interest."
> —Brian Becker, Point Loma Nazarene University

Code of Conduct, Orientation, and Checklists

Site coordinators and team leaders should work together to develop a code of conduct for their teams. It's important to remember that not everyone on the team may be familiar with the host culture or its sensitivities. Some may not be Christians, or this might be their very first service project. Even well-meaning team members might need a bit of guidance, so creating a code of conduct is a great way to foster a positive and productive environment.

This code should align with the values and expectations of the Church of the Nazarene while also reflecting the specific behavior needed for the project at hand. Site coordinators can include important cultural elements and project-specific details in the code. It's helpful to frame this code around the seven guiding principles outlined in *Following Dignity*, adapting them to fit the local context.

Site coordinators should prepare the visiting team with these cultural insights and work closely with the hosting team to ensure they understand the specific context of the project. Knowing potential issues in advance will help address them effectively.

Checklists are invaluable tools for site coordinators and team leaders. They help keep track of essential tasks and ensure that roles and expectations are clearly communicated. By using each chapter's Action Plan, leaders can create checklists that include roles, timelines, and other important details. A reliable system, like a notebook or spreadsheet, will help ensure that all necessary tasks are completed before, during, and after the project, preventing oversights and maintaining a systematic approach.

For ongoing ministry, the checklist should be a dynamic document that evolves with each project. Leaders should review and update their checklists before and after every trip, adding new questions or insights relevant to their context. Keeping the checklist up to date ensures that each new team has the best experience possible, improving with each iteration.

When teams arrive, a thorough orientation from the site coordinator is key to setting them up for success. Orientation should cover essentials like cultural engagement, roles and expectations, schedule details, hospitality, and safety issues. It's also important to allow time for questions so that teams feel fully prepared.

The team leader also plays a crucial role in orientation. They should gather the team upon arrival and set the tone with a focus on spiritual growth and seeking the Lord. Team leaders should review personal goals, the code of conduct, and encourage adherence to the guidelines set by the site coordinator. Checking in with each team member to ensure they have what they need and addressing any questions is also essential.

Key Roles and Responsibilities

The site coordinator and the team leader are the heart of the project, working together as key connections before, during, and after the mission. The site coordinator will coordinate with the hosting team while the team leader manages the missions team.

If the missions team has any questions or concerns, they should reach out directly to their team leader. The team leader will

Principle 6: Expectations

then bring those concerns to the site coordinator, who will help find solutions by connecting with the appropriate hosting team member. The site coordinator acts as the go-between for both teams, and it's important for the missions team to respect this communication channel because the site coordinator will continue managing these relationships even after the team has left.

For the hosting team, any concerns, ideas for outings, or suggestions should first be shared with the hosting team leader. It's essential for everyone to remember that each team is guided by their own leader. Team members should work through their team leaders when presenting ideas or suggestions, rather than bypassing them. Missions team members should not be approached individually for special opportunities, extra offerings, or side project needs. Similarly, they should not propose new projects or offer additional resources or funding directly to members of the hosting team. All ideas, suggestions, and concerns should be channeled through their respective team leaders. It's also important to remember that accepting or asking for money from members of the other team is not acceptable.

Both the hosting team and the missions team have the full support of their home church families. Brothers and sisters in Christ are praying for them and taking care of their duties while they're away. The churches, districts, fields, regions, and global church are all standing with them, ready to step in if needed. The team is never alone; they have the entire church community cheering them on.

The Role of the Equipped Site Coordinator

In short-term missions, the site coordinator plays a vital role that blends both project management and cultural liaising. Think of them as the key player who ensures everything runs smoothly while building bridges between teams and local communities. The site coordinator is more than just a project manager—they're also a cultural bridge. They help navigate the cultural nuances that arise when visitors and local hosts come together. Ideally, they live near the community they serve, understand local customs, and have strong relationships with local leaders. They ensure that both teams feel respected and understood while aligning the project with both field goals and Global Missions guidelines. Their role is all about fostering mutual respect and understanding. They make sure that the missions team not only contributes resources but also gains valuable insights from their experience, creating a true spirit of family and camaraderie.

As a cultural translator and project manager, the site coordinator handles everything needed to organize the project. They set clear expectations, align roles, and make sure that both teams achieve their goals. Just as a translator bridges two languages, the site coordinator bridges the cultures of both teams while managing project logistics. They're well acquainted with local resources and are prepared to help team members adjust to culture shock. From organizing supplies and interpreters to ensuring clean drinking water, they balance the needs of the missions team with local cultural expectations.

Throughout the project, the site coordinator supports both the hosts and the visiting team, staying involved from arrival to departure. They work closely with the team leader to orient the team, answer questions, and manage daily briefings. They continue to act as a liaison, ensuring smooth communication and coordination between both teams.

Additionally, site coordinators inspire and encourage those who feel called to missions. By sharing stories and expanding the team's understanding of what God is doing globally, they fuel the team's passion for missions. After the project, the site coordinator wraps up everything according to expectations, from gathering additional resources to sending heartfelt thank yous. They follow up with both teams, sharing updates on the project's success and impact.

In summary, the site coordinator is a blessing to everyone involved. Their combination of organizational skills, cultural insight, and commitment to dignity makes them an invaluable and trusted leader for both teams.

The Role of a Thoughtful Team Leader

A great leader is thoughtful and intentional in everything they do. They understand the value of clear communication, but they also keep a humble and teachable spirit. With prayerful consideration, they gather their team and choose a project that feels led by

Principle 6: Expectations

the Lord. The local church plays an important role too, offering their support, prayers, and sending the team off with a sense of shared purpose.

The team leader acts as a bridge between the missions team and the site coordinator, keeping the church connected and encouraging everyone's involvement. When selecting a project, the team leader works closely with the site coordinator to understand what's needed—whether it's the project's scope, hospitality expectations, or resources. Then the team leader helps prepare the team to meet those needs, covering everything in prayer and making sure all the practical details are handled. The team leader gathers and shares key information with both the team and the church.

Before the trip, it's important to bring the team together regularly. These meetings are a time to set a positive tone, build unity, and get everyone ready. You'll talk about teamwork, go over the code of conduct, and handle logistics like finances, roles, and travel plans. You also help the team prepare spiritually and culturally, and make sure all the registration and protocols with Global Missions are in place.

The team leader shapes the team's overall experience, guiding them through every step—navigating details with the site coordinator, adapting to the project, and building strong relationships along the way.

When the team arrives at the project site, it's time for the team leader to model embracing the role of a guest. Encouraging the team to let go of ownership and allow the hosts to offer their hospitality is key. The site coordinator will help everyone adjust to the cultural aspects of being gracious guests, and the team leader gently guides the team to follow their lead.

At the project site, the team leader also helps assign tasks based on each person's strengths, making sure everyone has a chance to contribute. You'll handle briefings and debriefings, oversee project needs, and take care of any personal concerns that come up. Throughout the trip, you keep the team focused on healthy engagement, spiritually and otherwise. Encouraging daily devotions, both individually and as a group, helps build unity and strengthens the team's spiritual journey.

> "Team leaders must give leadership and set plans for devotionals, team meetings, and debriefings. They should know when to talk to the team apart from the hosts and also know when to invite hosts into their meetings."
> —Brain Becker, Point Loma Nazarene University

Insider Perspective
What a Candid Photo Taught Me about Human Dignity[4]

Have you ever done something on a mission trip that, upon looking back, makes you feel sick to your stomach? Sometimes our best intentions result in actions that make us cringe in hindsight.

I once led a short-term mission trip to southern India where we went door to door with local pastors sharing the gospel. We rolled up five Americans deep with one local guide and translator, carrying a bag of food and other hygiene supplies for families in need. It's worth asking whether we needed so many foreign arms to carry this donation or if most of us functioned primarily as onlookers, curious to peer into homes that look very different than our own. But that's a topic for another time.

This story is about my blunder. During one of our village tours, we visited the home of an elderly woman suffering from cancer and chatted with her after giving out the supplies. As we were turning to leave, I reached into my Patagonia bag, pulled out my iPhone and pushed the shutter button to get a quick picture of the woman. That

---

4. Kylie Nguyen, "What a Candid Photo Taught Me about Human Dignity," Center for Faith and Culture, November 3, 2020, https://cfc.sebts.edu/faith-and-economics/what-a-candid-photo-taught-me-about-human-dignity/.

Principle 6: Expectations

night as an update to our church at home, I captioned what looked like a *National Geographic* candid photograph with these words: "Today we gave out end-of-life care buckets to HIV and cancer patients and shared the gospel. This lady received a bucket and heard for the first time about the Father who has loved her all along."

Cringe.

Years later, I'd like to share three reasons why this moment stands out as a worthy candidate for a rewind and do-over.

First, I'm embarrassed that I took her photo at all. By not asking her permission, it could look like I assumed I deserved a photographic souvenir of my charitable act. I never gave her the chance to fix her hair or to smooth her clothes or even to smile—things I always do before someone takes my photo. I valued the "raw moment" more than treating her the way I expect to be treated.

When I think back, I put myself in her shoes. If I were the recipient of a bag of food because I was struggling through a really difficult season, would I feel empowered or humiliated to have my picture taken at such a vulnerable moment?

Second, I posted her photo as if I had a right to broadcast her and the inside of her home to my followers. I try to imagine if I would have done that to someone in America. I probably would've been worried they might log on and see it, but almost everyone in the world has a smartphone and the capability to access the internet now. Would I want someone in another country putting a similar picture of my family member on their account? Or would I assume we have some right to privacy that I denied this woman?

Third, I wrote the caption as if our short-term team was the hero. I made no mention of the local pastor who works in that village, arrogantly assuming he'd never told her about Jesus even though he arranged our visit to her. I cast us as swooping in to be the solution to her problem when I actually had no relational context to understand her needs at all. Imagine for a moment all the elements of the story that might be missing—the years this woman labored in the fields to provide for her family, children and neighbors who have sacrificially contributed to her needs in old age, a humor and quick wit with which she still brightens conversations. In that moment, a person with a lifetime of stories was transformed into my single snapshot prop. I was content with a story that kept me at the center, minimizing or neglecting the worth of the person in front of me and the contribution of the community who supported her before and after our visit.

Coming to terms with past mistakes is hard, but I recognize that humility is the only way forward. Repenting of ways that I've unintentionally caused harm and striving to do better for the sake of the global church is a worthy cause. Now I ask proactively as I take photos, "What story is this image really telling?" I think about how my followers who will never visit India might stereotype all of the country in light of the content I post. I consider how a simple click could undermine human dignity or how a caption might elevate myself over others. I look for ways to build up the community with my camera and to make much of local leaders who are doing gospel work there. I believe we are called to a higher standard, even if it means I miss getting the picture altogether. I'm committed to dismantling these attitudes in myself, and I believe that these efforts both help me to live as a thoughtful, global Christian and honor the name of Jesus in the spaces he's given me to serve.

Questions to Consider
What a Candid Photo
Taught Me about Human Dignity

1. How was dignity compromised in this story?

2. What do team members need to know about picture taking?

3. What impact did the cultural difference have on taking this picture?

4. How should this potential impact be communicated to team members?

Principle 6: Expectations

5. What other factors should be considered about this story?

6. What guidelines should be in place for your teams as they approach vulnerable ministry contexts?

Discussion
What a Candid Photo Taught Me about Human Dignity

Team members and leaders alike strive to capture their experiences and share their stories. It is clear that the writer in this story felt honored to be part of her short-term mission trip and simply wanted to share her experience. She thought capturing a moment on camera would feel good and help her remember her good deed. But that good feeling did not last. She realized later that the story was far more than just hers to share. It was someone else's story, and it carried its own vulnerability. Snapping the photo and sharing about it on her social media meant she didn't handle that situation's vulnerability with the dignity it deserved, shaming both the subject of the photo and the heart of the photographer.

As we witness the incredible story of God's love and work here on earth, it's important not to keep it to ourselves. Dignity is all about finding the right balance. Teams involved in cross-cultural ministry need clear guidelines for taking photos and, even more importantly, for sharing them on social media. In many countries, posting pictures of other people's children can be against the law. Teams should be well prepared to honor and protect the dignity of the vulnerable in their photographs and online posts.

Sadly, many potential abuses can occur from media getting into the wrong hands. Seemingly innocent photos and videos of children and adults have put people at risk of sexual exploitation, abuse, and trauma of various kinds. Even with good intentions, you can accidentally dishonor and disrespect someone by posing a photo before understanding cultural and societal norms. For the safety and dignity of those we are serving with, it's important to consider whether the story or image is being safely shared, is dignifying, and honors that person. As site coordinators and leaders set policies and structures, it's imperative that dignity be considered from all angles.

The Role of a Well-Prepared Hosting Team

Field and district leadership are excited about the project and warmly welcome the missions team's involvement. It's important to align with the expectations of the hosting team, who might sometimes find their voice overshadowed in a gentle, non-dominant culture. That's where the site coordinator plays a crucial role to ensure that the hosting team's goals and needs are clearly communicated and respected throughout the project. If the hosts feel their needs aren't being fully understood, they should reach out to the site coordinator so adjustments can be made.

Hospitality is at the heart of this experience, and the hosting team is encouraged to embrace it with open arms. The site coordinator will work closely with them to arrange lodging, meals, and transportation. As the local experts, hosts will offer valuable suggestions for local support and collaborate with the site coordinator to set clear expectations for the missions team. They'll also coordinate on ministry options, special outings, budget plans, safety concerns, food handling, and emergency plans. This partnership will ensure that the missions team receives excellent care, showcasing God's love and work through genuine hospitality.

Additionally, the site coordinator helps the hosting team prepare to welcome the missions team with warmth and kindness, fostering meaningful connections and mutual understanding. Everyone involved should remember they are representing the hosts within the community and approach their roles with grace and the dignity of true hospitality.

The Role of a Great Team Member

Serving in cross-cultural settings is a wonderful opportunity and a cherished responsibility. Team members come with the openness to set aside personal preferences, follow directions, and work together with a spirit of cooperation. Engaging sincerely and respectfully in all activities—before, during, and after the trip—is crucial. Keeping in touch with the team leader and following the site coordinator's guidance ensures everything runs smoothly.

It's important to remember that the project is a collaborative effort led by the hosting team. Team members are there to support and enhance the work of those who have established long-term connections in the community, not to take the spotlight. Embracing differences and unfamiliar practices with an open and non-judgmental mindset shows respect for the hosting team's culture.

Being a gracious guest throughout the trip is key. Whether at airports, hotels, markets, or in local neighborhoods, acting with respect and adapting to local customs is essential. Trying new foods and accepting hospitality with gratitude are part of being a considerate guest. It's natural for team members to feel unsure about some cultural nuances, so trusting the guidance of leaders, even when it feels uncomfortable, is important. Every part of the mission trip is an opportunity to be a respectful and appreciative guest.

> "The missions team's purpose is to serve, not to save."
> —Robin Radi, Missionary, South America

Success and Expectations

The most impactful interactions will be between the site coordinator and the team leader. Effective communication and clear expectations between these two key roles are crucial for the success of the project. They will often work cross culturally and must use a low-context style of communication to ensure clarity.

Team members will observe their leaders' actions and character long before the project begins and well after it ends. They will also see one another's social media posts. Everyone involved should be mindful of their behavior and online presence. Christian dignity is not something we adopt only during the project. It's a continuous part of our Christian journey, beginning long before the project starts and extending well beyond its completion.

Managing expectations and achieving success go hand in hand. When expectations are met, we experience a profound sense of calm and satisfaction, as if everything is perfectly in place. Conversely, when things fall short, we face disappointment and discomfort. By working together and aligning our expectations with a spirit of flexibility, we can navigate these challenges more gracefully. Above all, maintaining dignity in every interaction—respecting ourselves, one another, and the culture we are part of—ensures that our efforts are not only successful but also meaningful and respectful. Dignity is the key to harmonizing expectations and celebrating success.

Principle 6: Expectations

Expectations Action Plan

1. Clarifying the Vision
What are the goals of the project, and how can the missions team best contribute to achieving the vision in ways that align with the hosting team's expectations?

2. Defining Success Together
How does my view of success differ from that of the hosting team or missions team, and what steps can I take to align these perspectives for a shared outcome?

3. Managing Expectation Gaps
What gaps in expectations might exist between the hosting team, the missions team, and onlooking churches, and how can I create positive opportunities to close those gaps?

4. Communicating Expectations Clearly
What is the best way to communicate expectations to both teams, ensuring clarity while respecting high- or low-context communication styles?

5. Preparing for Flexibility
How will I help both the hosting and missions teams hold expectations loosely and embrace changes with flexibility, grace, and dignity?

6. Identifying Roles and Responsibilities
What specific roles need to be filled, and how can I prepare each team member to successfully meet the expectations of their role?

7. Honoring Local Leaders and Resources
What strengths, skills, and resources do the local leaders and hosting team bring to the project, and how can I match them with roles that highlight their gifts?

8. Acknowledging Everyone's Contributions
How will I recognize and appreciate both visible and behind-the-scenes contributions to the project so that everyone feels valued?

9. Setting Healthy Financial Expectations
How will finances be managed transparently, and what boundaries need to be communicated to protect relationships?

10. Modeling Healthy Communication
What changes do I need to make in my communication style to ensure expectations are understood, documented, and followed up on in culturally appropriate ways?

11. Ensuring Alignment Between Vision and Execution
How can I continually evaluate whether the team's actions, roles, and attitudes are aligned with the project's overall vision while maintaining respect for the hosting team's leadership?

Principle 7: Spirituality

Therefore, I urge you, brothers and sisters, in view of God's mercy, to offer your bodies as a living sacrifice, holy and pleasing to God— this is your true and proper worship.
—Romans 12:1

Key Definitions

✦ **Bear Witness**: A witness shares their experience or firsthand knowledge as a testimony. In the Christian sense, they share the goodness of God as they have witnessed it.

✦ **Call**: A deep knowing felt in the soul of a person when they are invited to join God's work in a particular way. A call is accompanied by faith and compels movement or direction.

✦ **Ethnocentric**: The belief that one's own culture, ethnicity, or way of life is superior to others. People with an ethnocentric perspective tend to evaluate other cultures based on the standards and values of their own.

✦ *Light for the Path*: A devotional book for short-term missions presented by the Church of the Nazarene, designed to guide the team to approach their mission with a focus on dignity.

✦ **Poverty**: A multifaceted condition characterized by lack of essential resources and opportunities necessary for individuals to lead a basic and dignified life, regardless of the prevailing level of wealth in their society.

✦ **Prevenient Grace:** The divine influence that precedes and enables human response, offering grace that draws us deeper into our relationship with God. It is grace that goes before us, preparing both missionaries and those they serve by fostering openness, understanding, and readiness for transformation.

✦ **Spirituality:** Christian spirituality consists primarily of living in the Spirit. When you turn to God and receive salvation, God's Holy Spirit comes to live within you. Your spirit comes alive, and you have a spiritual relationship with God that you could not have had otherwise.

✦ **Witness:** To observe, experience, or have firsthand knowledge of. To be a witness is to have information gained from personal observation or experience.

Guiding Principle #7: Spirituality

The first six guiding principles of short-term missions focus on *how* we accomplish projects. The spirituality principle explores *why* we do them. It is the heart of the matter. Without this crucial principle, our efforts in short-term missions would simply become social work—valuable and helpful but not the work of Jesus Christ.

Following the path of dignity leads us to a deeper spiritual connection with one another and with Christ. Scripture assures us that we are all created in the image and likeness of God. Recognizing this inherent dignity in ourselves and others helps us see each person as a reflection of God's image and presence. Appreciating the dignity of others fosters a sense of unity and interconnectedness, reinforcing the holy idea that together we are all part of God's kingdom.

Mission projects are not always easy, and those with experience know that things don't always go as planned. Leaders far and wide attest to the difference a Spirit-filled team makes; they recognize its presence and feel its absence. Walking in dignity is a spiritual practice modeled by Jesus, guiding us to follow in his footsteps and reflect his love and compassion. Teams with hearts set on things above are more resilient, trusting, and find a sense of purpose beyond themselves. Teams centered on Christ bring a peaceful perspective even when things don't go as expected. They grow in their relationships with the Lord and with each other, return home with new insights, and leave everyone they worked with filled with the joy of having been with them.

We don't extend dignity only to one another; it's a necessary part of our relationship with Christ as well. We trust in God's prevenient grace and recognize that he is our ultimate host, has already prepared the way and welcomes us, and that it's our honor to arrive as his guests, giving him dignity as leader of the great banquet. If a team were to show up with a plan that doesn't include God, taking the lead and excluding our royal host, that's hurtful and is no way to treat the Savior of our souls. Giving Christ the dignity of including him and inviting his presence to be with us offers everyone on the team the opportunity to experience and witness the goodness of God in new and profound ways.

Short-term missions should always be recognized first and foremost as a spiritual journey, a sacred adventure where Christ's presence is sought and warmly welcomed throughout the entirety of the project. Faith-building opportunities have a beautiful and significant place in all short-term missions ministries. Jesus is at work all over the world, and he is doing it through his people, and that is great news because *we* are his people!

Insider Perspective
Anticipations and Expectations

John is an experienced team member. He has been to several countries serving on Work & Witness trips with his church, he has done a variety of projects, and he always enjoys being part of the team. He is an esteemed member of his community, a vital part of his church, and a trusted member of the church board. After returning from his latest trip, he stood before the congregation to share his experience:

"The theme of this trip was 'Nothing went exactly as anticipated but exactly as expected.' I learned that working according to my own plan didn't make things happen. My own strength and brain power weren't enough. But when I let go and saw that God was planning something different, things started to happen.

"Before we left, I wasn't sure what I was going to do on this trip—and then the team leader asked me and our pastor to facilitate some training. I thought, *Sure. I'm open to that.* Then I learned it's on church planting for pastors and leaders in the area. Let's see, it's in Central America, on a topic I know nothing about, for people whose language I don't know. What could go wrong? So, I went through the training that was provided—it was just a half a day, and I didn't feel ready. I needed more time, so I worked with the materials for a couple more weeks. The materials are good, and I learned that it's been successful in the past. It seems to take a lot of relationship building, which would be critical for this to work.

"Because of delays, it took us a couple days to get there, with little to no sleep. We arrived in Honduras and were exhausted. I was pretty much brain dead by then. Finally, we head over to the town—a 'little village,' they called it, but it had over a million people. We were in the industrial section, with security all around, and we finally made it to the training center at the church, where professional trainers were already there working. I watched one trainer, and he was doing great. He knew the language and the people. There were about seventy-five of them in the room, and everything was going very, very well. My pastor and I looked at each other, and I thought, *Well, what are we going to do?*

"We had dinner, we were tired, and I was ready to go to the hostel to get some rest. Then they asked us to come and share how we do these things back home, and I'm thinking, *I can't really tell you that—because I have never done it before.* I finally realized that God had laid a message on my heart for them, so I went up and shared, 'We have been praying for you. This material is excellent, and it's been successful in hundreds of thousands of churches. Home churches have been launched. The principles are great, and the teachers here are really effective.' And then I felt God prompt me to say, 'You are going to come away with a lot of knowledge, but people don't really care about what you know.' The guy interpreting looked at me like, *What?* And then I went on, 'Until they know how much you care. This is only going to work if you create the relationships needed before you share this important information.'

That's it. That's all I did. All the planning and prep I did beforehand had been unnecessary.

"Then the pastor and I left to join the others on our team doing the Work & Witness project in a small town just across the border in Guatemala. The church wasn't in town like we expected; it was in the middle of the jungle. You could see that part of the project had washed away down the hillside. It was not what we expected, planned for, or anticipated, but we jumped in and started working. The leaders kept changing their minds, and we had to do things over and over again, so that was kind of interesting. We poured the concrete from wheelbarrows to set the footings for the roof. Things certainly weren't done the way we did them back home. As we got the roof on, I thought, *Too bad we couldn't have been here to do this because this is what we came for.* The pastor was a professional roofer, and I have helped put plenty of them on, and we could have finished that building in no time.

"But then I realized, it's what God wanted to happen all along because, the next day, they came to have church. They set up their chairs on that clay dirt under the roof we just put on, and they had church. Then it started raining, and I thought, *Wow, they have a roof.* I went down and sat in one of those chairs, and I felt this presence behind me. A child from the church came up behind me. I took a picture, and I heard the people worshiping in the background."

With tears running down his cheeks, John said, "I looked at that picture and felt God saying, 'The building is important, but it's the people I care most about. That's why you're here, building a place where they can see Jesus.' I've heard it said before that a team is charged with 'taking' Jesus there. Our team went to train pastors and to build a church—to somehow 'take' God to a remote part of the world. However, it was easy to see that God was already there, fully alive and at work in his people.

"In the past, I have struggled with anxiety. I tend to worry about the future. On this trip, I was able to focus on knowing that God is already there and that, because I don't have to take him anywhere, I can also trust that he's in the future. He's in my future, and he's in yours too, ready to meet us there. This has given me a newfound peace in my life.

"Again, nothing as I anticipated or planned. But it was exactly something God would do, as I should have expected all along. If you haven't gone, you have to go because it's life changing."

Questions to Consider
Anticipation and Expectations

1. How many times did John experience unmet expectations?

2. Should things have been done differently by the leaders?

3. Why was John's attitude so remarkable?

4. How do you think John's go-with-the-flow attitude impacted the rest of his team?

5. How did this experience grow John's faith?

6. What can you learn from this experience?

Discussion
Anticipation and Expectations

Serving in short-term missions is not always easy. Unpredictability is common, and misunderstandings can add confusion to already stressful situations. John faced several uncomfortable scenarios that could have been handled better by the hosting team. Unmet expectations often lead to frustration. It can be disheartening when we're told one thing and experience something entirely different. John spent weeks preparing to teach the pastors, stepping out of his comfort zone to lead. However, when he arrived, he found someone else already doing the very thing he had prepared for. Upon pivoting and arriving at the project instead, John encountered further issues that were worrisome and outside his control.

John walked into situation after situation where expectations were unmet and things were not done as he was accustomed. The disorganization he faced was unlike his previous mission trips. While he could have asserted himself and insisted on doing things his way, he chose not to. Instead, he let go of his own expectations and followed the leadership in place. Although things might have gone differently or better, John made the choice to trust his Father.

John's ability to follow the Spirit's leading allowed him to adapt when he saw that God was making a change. Without his deep understanding of the training materials, his words wouldn't have had the impact they did. John was able to look beyond the circumstances and trust that things were unfolding as they should. He recognized that dignity was his to uphold, and he relied on his Father to help him see through the eyes of Christ. A strong spiritual foundation strengthened not only his own composure but also that of the team, reinforcing the belief that God is in control regardless of the situation.

> "A ministry of presence and healthy connection is the foundation for everything else. Teams that are distracted, or sleep deprived, or too connected to their phones, or infighting, or cold to one another are distracted from their purpose."
> —Brian Becker, Point Loma Nazarene University

John approached each challenge with grace, not only due to his Christlike character but also because of his ongoing relationship with Jesus. He did not arrive as a hero bringing Jesus with him;

instead, his posture was to meet Jesus where he already was. At each juncture, John was willing to learn, listen to Christ, and gain a new perspective on the vastness of God. He returned home with a deeply personal gift from Christ: a peace that surpasses all understanding.

Rooted in Purpose: Kingdom Building

If you've served in short-term missions long enough, you've likely heard questions like, "Why not just send the money?" or, "Can't the local people handle it themselves?" It's true that sending money might save costs associated with sending a team and meeting their needs. We also recognize that the local people are often capable of managing projects, many times even more effectively than the unskilled labor that teams might provide. Some might argue that teams can be disruptive, diverting time and attention away from ongoing ministries. From a strategic standpoint, this perspective has merit—more money, greater efficiency, and fewer distractions seem logical. However, kingdom work requires us to use a different set of plans.

Building the kingdom sometimes calls for a shift in priorities. Jesus moves our focus from merely completing tasks to caring for the hearts of his people. While concerns about strategy and funding will always be present, short-term missions engage us in a higher calling. We are his kingdom builders. A holistic approach to ministry emphasizes God's perspective, which centers on uniting his church and shifting our focus to the people behind the tasks, helping them see his handiwork from a new vantage point. Addressing physical needs, fostering relationships, and connecting on a heart level are things that soften souls and pave the way for spiritual growth—a truly worthy goal. At the heart of every missions project, we find God seeking the hearts of his people, and this connection should be a priority for us as well.

Teams come to serve, but the mission does not belong to them, nor does it belong to us; it always belongs to God. It was his idea first, and it will remain his after everyone returns home. The mission is far greater than we are and has existed long before our arrival. God's mission is reconciliation. He calls us, his creation, to reconcile with him. Kingdom building unites us through our relationship with Christ. As part of God's church, we are drawn into his mission of reconciling creation to himself. The church exists because of God's mission. The church doesn't have a mission; the mission has a church. We are the church, and our role is to align with God's mission of reconciliation.

A Time of Revival

Revival services are a tradition deeply rooted in our Christian heritage. Church members set aside their regular routines to attend revival services, aiming to renew their devotion and connection to the Lord. An evangelist, dedicated to proclaiming the goodness of God, speaks night after night at camp meetings or under giant tents set up in the middle of town, bringing the good news with the hope of igniting a spark that could lead to a revival among the people.

To experience revival is to encounter the goodness of God—to see him, feel his presence, and be reminded of our relationship with him and one another. Revival represents a return to something that was fading, a rekindling of what was once known. It begins as a spark in a person's heart, leading to a renewed commitment in their walk with the Lord. This spark can grow into a transformative experience for individuals, churches, communities, towns, and even nations.

Today, while we may not see as many old-fashioned tent revivals coming through town as we did in the past, we should remember that revival is still very much alive. People joining short-term missions teams step away from their routines to find themselves experiencing the goodness of God firsthand. They encounter the same Holy Spirit sparking revival in their hearts as the one found in traditional revival services.

We can trust that God is at work on short-term mission trips, often bringing about revival. Some may find the spark leading to sanctification, others may experience salvation and baptism, and some might be called into ministry. Those returning home often carry the inspiration to ignite something extraordinary in their local churches and communities, while those who remain witness the ongoing impact of the project. It's not far-fetched to say that short-term missions very well stand on equal footing with traditional tent revivals or camp meetings steeped in Christian tradition.

Revival certainly occurs during short-term missions projects—the Spirit moves, and it is up to us to fan the flame. Leaders must be intentional in fostering the spiritual impact on the teams they oversee.

Insider Perspective
Let's Tithe a Church!

In the summer of 1987, the small building of South Salem Church of the Nazarene was showing signs of age. Despite the sweltering temperatures and lack of air-conditioning, the joyful spirit of the congregation made each Sunday morning a vibrant occasion. These were exciting days for the church, inspired by the uplifting messages of their beloved pastor, Ralph Marchbanks. The pews were often filled to capacity, and the congregation was quickly outgrowing their building.

Pastor Ralph and the church board decided it was time to build a new facility. The project was ambitious, but the congregation was enthusiastic and believed the Lord was guiding them. Before the planning progressed too far, Pastor Ralph proposed that they tithe the project funds. Referencing Proverbs 3:9–10, which speaks of honoring the Lord with one's wealth, he instructed the church board to allocate a portion of the project funds to a worthy cause.

The board learned about a grassroots ministry emerging in Nazarene churches worldwide. Led by Dr. Paul Gammersfelter, an ophthalmologist from Columbus, Ohio, this ministry aimed to address the urgent need for church buildings on the mission field. Dr. Paul and his team of skilled, faith-driven volunteers traveled to Panama to build churches not as professional missionaries but as ordinary people using their talents to support the mission work. The young ministry soon gained its name, "Work & Witness," opening doors for laypeople to use their skills in unconventional ways for Christ's work on the mission field. Hearing about this, Pastor Ralph and the board decided that tithing their building project funds would involve contributing to this ministry. They assembled their first Work & Witness team and sent them to Cali, Colombia, to work with missionaries and Pastor Adalberto Herrera. The team built re-

Principle 7: Spirituality

lationships while constructing a church, marking the beginning of a new chapter.

Upon returning, construction on the new building at South Salem Nazarene Church began. The project exceeded expectations, finishing on time and under budget. The blessings of the tithe didn't stop there; the church sent another team to Cali to complete their work while South Salem continued to grow. Within a few years, the church added on to the new building and, astonishingly, was debt free by the time the addition was finished. The tithe had blessed both churches, leading to the establishment of a thriving congregation in Cali.

By 1989, after the Cali church had been completed, Colombian missionaries had to evacuate due to unrest, closing the doors to missionaries and Work & Witness teams. Despite this development, the Cali church flourished, growing into the largest Nazarene church in the world, with an average of twenty-five thousand worshipers each weekend. It became a beacon of growth and revival, planting more than twenty-five churches since the arrival of the first Work & Witness team.

The decision to tithe a church before building their own set South Salem on a transformative path. They developed a passion for missions that has continued to flourish. Over the years, they have sent Work & Witness teams globally, served nationally, and supported sister churches within their district. Several missionaries were sent from their own congregation to serve in various countries, including Ecuador, Guatemala, Indonesia, Kenya, Mexico, the Philippines, Saipan, Poland, and Tanzania. Remarkably, three of the missionaries sent from South Salem had parents who were part of that first team to Colombia.

More than three decades later, Colombia reopened its doors to missionaries. In 2024, South Salem eagerly sent a missions team back to Colombia, marking one of the first teams to be received in thirty-five years. The team leader was the son of one of the original team members, and two others from the initial team joined as well, totaling thirteen people working in Montenegro. They reconnected with Pastor Herrera, who is still pastoring the church in Cali, now called The House of Prayer. The joyful reunion was a testament to the lasting impact of their earlier mission.

The trip was a blessing, strengthening existing relationships and forming new ones. Baptisms of team members occurred both in Colombia and at home, with several team members joining South Salem Church. The team implemented what they learned into their outreach programs, igniting a spark that continues to spread today.

Walking into South Salem Church feels like coming home to a place where hearts have always been set on something bigger than themselves. The building is still beautifully cared for, and the warm smiles that greet you are as welcoming as ever. But what really stands out is the church's unwavering focus on sharing God's love beyond their walls. Their mission of reconciliation, both at home and around the world, has stayed strong. You can feel it in the way they continue to seek God's heart, pouring their time and energy into reaching others with his grace. It's clear that their legacy of faithfulness goes far beyond constructing buildings but is about making a lasting impact on the world in the precious name of Jesus Christ.

Questions to Consider
Let's Tithe a Church!

1. Why did the church board decide to tithe a church?

2. What was the immediate outcome?

3. How did the trajectory of both churches (Cali & South Salem) change?

4. What is most surprising about this story?

5. How might this story speak into the desired outcomes of your next missions project?

Principle 7: Spirituality

Discussion
Let's Tithe a Church!

The South Salem Church chose to tithe a church because they believed it was the biblical way to do things. They sought to honor the Lord with their firstfruits, driven not by personal gain but by obedience to God's leading. They trusted him and found him to be more than trustworthy.

The blessings of their decision were evident almost immediately. Their church grew, and they were able to build a new facility debt free. Moreover, their tithe contributed to the construction of another church. This act set in motion a trajectory of change that unfolded over years, revealing a ripple effect of God's goodness that continues to impact countless lives even today.

Revival often happens on short-term mission trips. The journey not only renews the spirit of those who participate but also spreads the goodness of God to all they encounter. This transformative impact, both immediate and long term, showcases God's glory and warms hearts for generations to come. If we remain attentive, we can witness the flame of revival lighting the world, demonstrating the enduring power and goodness of God.

Let's remember that the outcome of all we do belongs to God. Our role is to faithfully serve, love others, and give our best, but the results are always in his hands. This truth brings peace, knowing that it's not about the size of our efforts or the immediate impact we see but about trusting God to work through us in ways beyond our understanding. In his timing and in his way, he takes what we offer and multiplies it for his glory. Let's continue to walk forward with open hearts, knowing that he holds the outcomes. In that, we find rest.

Firsthand Faith: Called to Witness God's Goodness

The story of Ruth in the Old Testament gives us a great example of the importance of witnesses. When Boaz bought land from Naomi's family, he made sure to call witnesses because having people who saw the transaction firsthand was essential in case there were future disagreements about the land. Their presence added credibility, just like we still rely on witnesses today for important things like weddings, court testimonies, and document signing.

A witness is simply someone who has experienced something firsthand. Because they've seen it with their own eyes, they can speak with confidence about what happened. *Bearing* witness is different; it means sharing that personal experience with others. Let's say you've never tasted a mango before. You might hear friends rave about how delicious it is and trust their description. But once you take a bite yourself, you know for sure what it tastes like.

Think about Jesus's first miracle at the wedding in Cana, when he turned water into wine. The servants who were just following instructions ended up seeing a miracle—water turning into wine before their very eyes (see John 2:5–9). They knew exactly what had happened. Imagine them in heaven today, still reminiscing about that incredible moment. But why didn't Jesus just make the wine appear in the jars from the start? Why ask the servants to fill them up? Jesus cares more about dignity and participation than flashy displays. He wanted the servants to be part of the miracle, to witness it firsthand. By doing so, he created a deeper connection between them and his work.

This idea is woven all throughout the Bible. God desires a community of witnesses, people who experience him personally and then share their experience with others. Today, those who are called to serve are like the servants at Cana. Jesus invites us into his story, letting us witness his goodness and experience his presence as we serve. This not only deepens our relationship with him but also brings us closer to one another.

Leaders don't have to be evangelists to help their teams encounter God. Site coordinators and team leaders have the joy of guiding their teams to witness Jesus at work. They can share stories, encourage participation, and create Christ-centered spaces where teams can experience God's goodness firsthand.

Cross-cultural teams often need help understanding the deeper meaning behind their experiences. Site coordinators and leaders play a key role in helping teams reflect on what they're witnessing. Group devotions are a special opportunity to process these moments, interpreting them through the lens of both culture and Scripture, while sharing stories with warmth and dignity.

Seeing God at work firsthand changes everything. Old ways of thinking give way to new understandings, and team members begin to align their lives more closely with Christ's purpose. Leaders, site coordinators, and hosts have the unique privilege of showing their teams where God is moving, inviting them to witness his goodness and be transformed by it.

Luke 22:27 (NLT)

Who is more important, the one who sits at the table or the one who serves? The one who sits at the table, of course. But not here! For I am among you as one who serves.

Witnessing Poverty: An Ethnocentric View

When visiting some world areas, teams may be exposed to living conditions that are in extreme contrast to anything they have ever experienced before, a situation that often brings up questions and concerns that aren't easy to understand, let alone explain. When trying to explain extreme poverty to visitors encountering it for the first time, it's important to emphasize that poverty goes beyond a lack of money or material possessions. It affects many aspects of life, creating hurdles and closing doors that others take for granted. It often means living without basic needs being met, facing uncertainty and hardship daily in an environment where solutions aren't simple and material possessions aren't usually the answer.

It's crucial for site coordinators, hosts, and leaders to highlight the resilience, dignity, and strength that people living in severe circumstances often display. While their surroundings may seem harsh, many individuals and communities find ways to thrive in other aspects, like maintaining strong family bonds, deep faith, or vibrant cultural traditions. Understanding poverty requires seeing both the challenges and the humanity of those who live in it. Encourage visitors to approach these communities with empathy, avoiding pity and instead recognizing how people navigate their circumstances with courage and creativity.

The beauty of poverty can be found in the resilience, simplicity, and deep-rooted sense of community among its people. In places where material wealth is scarce, the richness of human connection, creativity, and faith often flourishes in remarkable ways. Families and neighbors lean on one another, sharing not only resources but also joys and sorrows. The focus on relationships over possessions creates a tapestry of life where love, solidarity, and gratitude are woven into the fabric of everyday existence. This beauty is not in the lack itself but in the profound human spirit that thrives in the face of adversity.

Visiting team members might mistakenly view poverty through a lens that emphasizes what is lacking rather than noticing and affirming what is present. They may assume that the absence of material wealth equates to a lack of happiness, fulfillment, or dignity. This perspective can lead to a narrow and superficial understanding of the lives and values of those living with limited material resources. The assumption that having more material goods or comforts automatically leads to a better life overlooks the intrinsic worth and wisdom found in simpler, more sustainable ways of living.

Visitors may also underestimate the agency and resilience of those living in poverty, mistakenly believing that their interventions or donations alone can bring about change. While well intentioned, these efforts sometimes overlook the existing strengths within communities—strengths that have sustained them for generations. True understanding comes not from pity or charity but from recognizing and respecting the cultural richness, ingenuity, and strength of those who navigate life with fewer resources. The beauty of poverty lies not in romanticizing hardship but in acknowledging the dignity, creativity, and deep human connection that can flourish even when material wealth is absent.

For many short-term missions team members, witnessing the stark contrast between their own material resources and the realities of those with less can bring up feelings of discomfort, struggle,

Principle 7: Spirituality

or even guilt. Understanding these emotions takes time, but they don't have to create distance. Instead, they can become a path toward deeper understanding and compassion. Whether we come from places of abundance or scarcity, we all have something to offer and something to learn. The discomfort invites us to reflect with humility, considering how we might channel our generosity more purposefully, reflect on our shared humanity, and see Christ in new places. It's not about feeling guilty for what we have or don't have but about allowing these experiences to open our hearts to one another. By embracing that tension and letting it shape us, we can continue to grow, building relationships that honor the dignity of every person, regardless of their circumstances. In doing so, we join in building God's kingdom and become part of a shared journey of hope, generosity, and transformation.

As Christians, it's important to recognize that transformation through Jesus Christ has a profound impact on individuals and communities. When people in poverty encounter Christ, they often find the strength and guidance to make life-altering changes. By quitting harmful habits like drinking, gambling, or other self-indulgences, they become able to hold down jobs, care for their families, secure housing, and pay for their children's education. This transformation not only fosters a stable and safe family environment but also offers a pathway out of the cycle of poverty. Empowering people with faith and practical support is key to breaking the chains of poverty and restoring dignity to them, their families, and their communities.

We must not forget that those with means also face their own unique forms of poverty, although these may not be immediately recognized as such. One significant issue is the poverty of relationship. Wealth can create barriers to genuine connection if people hide their vulnerability or struggle to relate to those with different backgrounds and experiences, leading to feelings of isolation and loneliness despite material abundance. The constant pressure to maintain and care for possessions can foster anxiety and stress because it takes a substantial amount of time, distracting from relationships, spiritual matters, and self-care. Coming from circumstances where the focus is on material goods brings with it the potential to distract from spiritual growth and inner peace. Those who have never experienced need may experience a disconnect from the struggles and realities of others, making it a challenge to understand or relate to the experiences of those who live with less. This challenge can result in a diminished capacity for compassion and a skewed perspective on what truly matters in life. Christians can learn from brothers and sisters in Christ living with less. This learning calls us to recognize that true richness lies in the depth of our connections, the integrity of our values, and the pursuit of a life that serves something greater than ourselves.

True wealth is found in our Christian journey, stemming from our relationship with Jesus, rather than in material riches. This wealth is found in the peace, joy, and love that come from knowing Christ and being rooted in his promises. It's the deep contentment that persists despite life's challenges, the assurance of God's presence in every circumstance, and the hope of eternal life. This spiritual richness enables us to live with purpose, extending grace and compassion to others. As Proverbs 3:5–6 remind us, "Trust in the Lord with all your heart and lean not on your own understanding; in all your ways submit to him, and he will make your paths straight." This trust in God cultivates a wealth that transcends earthly possessions, enriching our souls and shaping our lives in profound ways.

Insider Perspective
The Heart of the Hijab

Fatima's journey toward Christ began the day she and her family were uprooted from their homeland. Her home and belongings were scattered among the rubble left on the fractured streets of her neighborhood. The remnants of war were all that remained of Aleppo, her hometown. Aleppo was the hardest-hit city in the Syrian war, and it was in shambles. They had no choice but to leave, joining an exodos of biblical proportions.

Fatima's fate merged with the millions of Syrians whose only hope for survival was to choose the humiliating path of losing everything in order to secure the ominous status of "refugee." Fatima felt hot tears run down her cheeks as she blended in with the river

Principle 7: Spirituality

of people trying to get out. Determination fueled by fear was the only thing strong enough to propel her feet forward, step by step, into the dreadful unknown. She walked, clinging to her only possessions, the only things that ever mattered—her husband, Ishmael, her six-year-old daughter, Manal, and the hijab she clutched tightly around her hair.

The impact of the Syrian refugee crisis on neighboring countries was overwhelming. Lebanon received nearly 35 percent of the six and a half million refugees who were soon to make up more than a quarter of the Lebanese population. They arrived emptyhanded, without supplies, and with no way to care for themselves or their families. The sheer numbers took their toll on the limited resources of the government. The refugees were vulnerable, and the Lebanese people became more and more exhausted by the demand of caring for them.

Fatima's family arrived in Lebanon no differently than the rest. Ishmael's hands were as empty as his pockets. They had no crumbs left to feed Manal, and there were no beds. They were hungry and exhausted. In the warm climate of the Middle East, where hospitality is an anticipated part of the culture, it would be expected for them to have family to meet them and provide for their basic needs until they could stand on their own. With everything and everyone left behind, there was no one to meet and care for them in this new place.

They soon found themselves waiting in lines, uncertain and unsure of what was to come. There was always something more that was needed, and they waited behind hundreds and thousands of others whose needs were just as vital. What everyone needed first and foremost was a warm meal and a place to rest. Those helping were overwhelmed and tired as they shuffled people around from one place to another. The social workers and refugees were in a world of hurt, the resources were limited, and there was never enough to go around. A deep sense of unease overcame Fatima and her husband as their vulnerabilities lay open and exposed by the cruelties of war.

God cared deeply for Fatima and her family. He had a plan and was at work in the hearts of his people. A young Lebanese couple from a Christ-centered church in Beirut had been praying for the refugees arriving in their city. Their church had opened its doors to help many of the new arrivals, but they felt God was asking them to do something more. The couple met Fatima, Manal, and Ishmael at the weekly dinner their church held to welcome their new neighbors. Not unlike others, Ishmael had a long beard and wore the traditional clothing indicating the religious beliefs of his family. The couple from the church couldn't ignore the many hardships that Fatima and Ishmael faced as they tried to care for their young daughter. They felt the Lord's prompting to open their home to the young family.

They welcomed the refugee family into their home in the Christian spirit of hospitality. They didn't have an agenda other than to share the love of Christ as they attended to their needs and offered the comforts of home, including meals and a safe place to rest their weary heads. As they learned about their guests, they discovered their heartfelt needs and offered further support. They helped Ishmael find a job and a suitable school for Manal. A real and true friendship formed in the holy space of hospitality.

Relationships in the Middle East center around honor and shame. The Christian couple knew they couldn't verbally share Christ with Ishmael and Fatima because of the power imbalances involved. The shame of being vulnerable and dependent would obligate the Syrian refugee family to accept Christ in order to show respect to those hosting them. It wouldn't be genuine. It would be to express honor because of the relationship dynamic at hand and not in the truth of understanding who Christ truly is. The Syrians were in a weaker position, prone to feelings of shame, and what they needed was something far more than words alone. They needed real Christian love in the form of action and friendship.

A few people from church—a team of prayerful individuals with the same heart and intention of this young couple, and who could be trusted to simply show the love of Christ and foster a sense of belonging—were invited to come alongside Fatima's vulnerable family. Soon, Ishmael took a job in Turkey while Fatima and Manal were left in the care of her new friends. The women invited Fatima into their homes and encouraged their children to make

Principle 7: Spirituality

friends with Manal. They helped Fatima find medical care and other much-needed resources, and this process made them all genuine friends. Anytime Fatima had a need, she knew she could depend on these friends to help her. Fatima and Manal felt honored, accepted, and loved in the family of Christian believers. She was finding a place where she belonged.

It wasn't at all what she had expected. The people outside the church weren't as kind as she had hoped, and the people inside were so different than what she'd previously thought. She had heard rumors about Christians and their freedom to dress in short skirts and drink alcohol, and she wanted no part of it. But what she found in the church was entirely different. She asked her new friends, "Why are you so kind? We haven't found everyone here in Lebanon to be so kind, but you are very kind to us." Fatima felt the warmth coming from her new church family as they reflected the light of Christ.

As a beautiful woman, Fatima wore a hijab as a symbol of her modesty and a reminder that she belonged to something bigger than herself. She was part her family and her religion, part of a community. Her covering showed that she was honorable while also extending honor to all the men and women in her company. In the collective culture of Fatima's family, laying down her hijab wasn't something that could be done lightly.

Fatima experienced unconditional love from her Christian friends that brought with it a true sense of belonging. She was surprised by the modesty of the women she met at church. Their heads may not be covered, but it was clearly revealed by their character and their actions. She understood that they valued modesty as much as she did. There wasn't a hidden strategy to win her to the Lord, and she was never made to feel that their way was right while hers was wrong. The women never once asked her to remove her hijab or give up her faith in exchange for theirs. They simply offered sincere friendship through a household of faith in a way that she would find truly hospitable. Fatima and Manal had a place where they belonged, and they felt it.

As Fatima experienced the light of Christ shining through her Christian friends, she found true freedom. Now that she has learned another way, she has discovered the freedom to love God as her good Father. In finding this freedom, of her own accord she was able to lay down her hijab and move from her works-based convictions to a more powerful, love-based faith in the community of those who love Jesus. She gladly stepped into the warm embrace of God and let him hold her as his dearly beloved daughter. She now models modesty in her community in the way of her Christian sisters—through her character and her actions.

Ishmael continues to reside in Turkey. When visiting Beirut, he always takes time to make connections with his Christian friends at the church. Fatima's mother, a devout Muslim, also visits from time to time, and she too loves the church. She is always sure to thank everyone for loving her precious daughter and granddaughter so well. Fatima now works with an international Christian youth ministry, restoring other young women to Christ through loving and caring relationships.

Questions to Consider
The Heart of the Hijab

1. Where is the thread of dignity revealed in this story?

2. How did the church witness to Fatima?

3. Why didn't they simply tell her about Jesus?

4. How do you think the Christians felt about Fatima wearing a hijab?

5. What stands out to you as a significant factor in Fatima's journey to Christ?

6. How does this story impact the way you think about short-term missions?

Discussion
The Heart of the Hijab

We can follow the thread of dignity throughout Fatima's story, seeing where it began to unravel and recognizing how it became the path that led her family to experience the love of Christ. The Christians who reached out to Fatima's family offered their kindness with no strings attached—no obligations, no hidden expectations. The love they shared was pure, given freely and unconditionally.

This family of believers truly lived out the heart of hospitality. They didn't just welcome strangers into their home; they embraced the differences that made Fatima's family unique. They took the time to understand the challenges the family faced, and they likely made personal sacrifices to meet their needs. In doing so, they built a trust that blossomed into friendship. Most importantly, they didn't demand anything in return. There was no pressure for Fatima's family to attend church, to change how they looked, or to alter their beliefs. The church simply loved them, treating them with the dignity of Christ.

Sometimes we think witnessing is just about preaching or sharing the gospel directly. But it's so much more than that. First Peter 3:15 reminds us to "always be prepared to give an answer to everyone who asks you to give the reason for the hope that you have," but it starts with how we live our lives. Our actions, our love, and how we treat others reflect the heart of Christ. When people see his love in us, they naturally begin to wonder, *What makes you different? What is the source of this kindness I'm experiencing?* The church witnessed to Fatima and her family by how they lived, not just with words but through genuine love. They understood that dignity is the universal language of the heart, and they let it guide their every step. They honored the family's culture, took time to truly know them, and built a relationship grounded in trust. There were no unrealistic expectations or demands—only the steady, quiet reflection of God's goodness in their actions. Dignity was the thread that led the way.

Fatima's decision to follow Christ didn't happen overnight, and it's important to recognize that the church's goal may never have been to convert her. Their first priority was to trust Jesus, and he showed them the way—to simply open their homes and hearts without expectation.

And then there's Ishmael. Though he hasn't yet called himself a Christian, he also feels the deep, enduring love of the church, and he knows it is genuine. If the relationship had been transactional—if he had been made to feel like he needed to be saved in exchange for their kindness—he probably would have walked away, and might still be searching for a place where he could rest his heart. But because their love was so sincere, so free of expectations, Ishmael still finds joy in these relationships and goes out of his way to visit his Christian friends whenever he's in town.

"Our focus on the project and the relationship should never be viewed as a means to an end. We should maintain our integrity as we reach out to others in the name of Christ, never befriending someone in exchange for their salvation. Ulterior motives are the very opposite of dignity."
—Greg Taylor, Nazarene Missionary

Anchoring Faith and Unity

Group devotions during a cross-cultural mission trip are like a warm and steady anchor, keeping everyone grounded in faith amidst all the newness and unfamiliarity. It's easy to feel overwhelmed when stepping into a different culture, and it can be dif-

Principle 7: Spirituality

ficult to stay focused. Those moments of gathering together for devotions offer a peaceful pause. They help the team refocus on what truly matters: serving others through the love and guidance of their shared faith.

Daily devotions also create a sense of togetherness that's important in a cross-cultural setting. There's something powerful about coming together to pray, read Scripture, and worship as a team. These shared experiences deepen the bonds among team members, building unity that becomes a source of strength when challenges inevitably arise. By leaning on each other and their collective faith, team members are better equipped to meet these challenges with patience, compassion, and understanding. This unity helps prevent misunderstandings or conflicts by keeping everyone connected to the same mission and spiritual values guiding their actions.

As the team embraces the local culture, they're likely to encounter moments that stretch their comfort zones or challenge their assumptions. Devotional time gives them the chance to process these experiences together, turning to God for wisdom and guidance. This reflection helps ensure that the team's actions remain respectful, sensitive, and aligned with both their own faith and the values of the community they are there to serve. Through devotions, the team continually realigns with their purpose, ensuring their mission is not only impactful but spiritually meaningful and culturally respectful.

Group devotions also have a profound impact on each individual team member. These quiet moments of reflection allow team members to pause, connect with God, and gain clearer perspective on their own role in the mission. As they reflect on Scripture and pray, they often find new insight into their personal journey, whether about their own faith, the people they're serving, or the broader purpose of the work. Devotions help shift focus from personal discomforts to the bigger picture, reminding each person that they are part of something greater than themselves. For many, this time of reflection brings a renewed sense of purpose, deeper empathy, and an openness to seeing the world through the eyes of those they serve. Team members often experience personal growth and transformation in these moments, returning home with a fresh perspective on both their faith and the world around them.

> "Listen to the voice of the Lord during this time when you are outside your comfort zone. He will speak and transform your vision if you let him."
> —Robin Radi, Missionary, South America

Insider Perspective
Light for the Path

G'day, Brother,

It's been a while since we have been in contact directly. I hope you and your family are well and enjoying God's presence of grace and peace each day. I have noticed a lot of exciting things happening for Waverly Church of the Nazarene and the city. I am grateful for your and God's faithfulness to that community over so many years.

I am writing to you to let you know what a transformational impact your short-term missions devotional guide, *Light for the Path,* had on our recent NMT trip to Vanuatu. I was the team pastor. Pauline Sheppard was the coordinator for the trip and the one who discovered your book last year at General Assembly. We had fourteen people, consisting of men and women from seven nationalities, aged fourteen to late seventies, from six different churches, across three time zones, from the two districts that cover all of Australia. Several of us had not met some of the others on the team.

We started meeting around three months prior to the trip to go through the six pre-trip devotions. We met fortnightly via Zoom and spent an hour each time, gathering to reflect and discuss the devotion. Each gathering was challenging and transformational for the team. And, with each gathering, we learned a little more about

Principle 7: Spirituality

one another as we wrestled with God together with the shared goal of surrendering ourselves to God's work in ourselves to prepare us for participating in God's work in Vanuatu. I created the space relationally, and you gave us the inspired material that invited us to be formed by the Holy Spirit in that space. I witnessed the team being moulded and shaped through that time. It was challenging for some, liberating for some, and transforming for us all.

Before the trip started, I prayerfully assigned each team member to a particular during-the-trip devotion. Throughout the two weeks, each member had a turn leading one of the devotions. And the team in turn had an opportunity to hear God's heart through many different voices as they each put some of themselves (culture, experiences, struggles, strengths) into the devotion they led. It was beautifully fulfilling. We experienced the fullness of the kingdom of God through those two weeks. Just as the pre-trip devotions challenged and shaped us, these continued to do so as well. They guided us and held us accountable to staying surrendered, self-emptying, others-centered followers of Jesus seeking to allow God to teach and love us through our hosts even more so than what we were offering them.

I took the liberty of combining the final five post-trip devotions into two. Again, it was wonderful to hear everyone share about the impact and transformation God had made in their lives and how that can further equip and empower our missional presence in our local communities. Many of the team had already shared with their local churches of their experiences, with a focus on honouring the Vanuatu people and culture and preserving their dignity.

The trip was tough in many ways: physically, spiritually, emotionally, mentally, and relationally. There were times when we rubbed each other the wrong way. There were hurts, frustrations, anger, worries, discontentment, etc. All of what you would expect in a diverse team from all over the country putting themselves in a place of serving and sacrificing to a level most had not experienced before. But God was with us. We made it through. We had tough discussions, and we were vulnerable, confessional, gracious, and forgiving. A bond formed and continued to grow closer and stronger throughout the joys and the struggles. That bond was started and strengthened by sitting and seeking together God's light for the path on which we journeyed. The devotions were an essential piece in the successful shaping of the bond we needed to hold onto God and each other through the good times and the tough times.

I have focused my thoughts mainly on the intra-team relationships and growth. But I must also share that through the devotional thoughts, God continued to compel us toward helpful and humble relationships with the local people we worked and shared life with over the course of the mission in Vanuatu. We all left changed because of our willingness to see the dignity and value of our sisters and brothers in Vanuatu; to see, and be ministered to by, the Jesus in our hosts. We were all challenged by the beauty of their culture and the love in their hearts that they shared so readily with us. We learned so much from them. We made genuine friendships. Many have been keeping in contact in the weeks since the trip.

Thanks so much! Know that God is with you, loving you, working in and through you to bring others closer to God and each other, building right relationships of holy love on mission with God, turning strangers into neighbours through Christ's love.

—Pastor Emman T Chapman
Dianella Church of the Nazarene
Perth, Australia

Questions to Consider
Light for the Path

1. Why do you suppose the team leader assigned someone else to be the spiritual leader for the team?

2. What characteristics make a good spiritual leader for a missions team?

3. What did the pastor consider to be instrumental to the overall success of the trip?

Principle 7: Spirituality

4. What was a surprising impact that the devotional book had on their relationships with their brothers and sisters in Vanuatu?

5. What elements of this story would you implement into your ministry?

Discussion
Light for the Path

Pastor Chapman prayerfully led the team's devotional times. He wasn't the team leader. He served as the spiritual leader, focusing on helping the team witness the goodness of God throughout their trip. While the leader and site coordinator managed the logistical details, including times and places for devotions, Pastor Chapman's sole focus on spiritual matters proved invaluable. He took his role seriously, and his dedication made a significant difference in the team's overall experience.

Several months before departure, the team met for pre-trip devotionals, setting the tone for the entire journey well before boarding their flight to Vanuatu. The team leader chose the book *Light for the Path*, which focuses on the same seven principles as *Following Dignity*. After arriving onsite, Pastor Chapman encouraged each team member to lead a devotion themselves, allowing them to share their unique perspectives. These devotional times were intimate, creating a space for God to work through their vulnerabilities and fostering a deeper bond with him and one another.

The team quickly recognized that God was already present in Vanuatu; they came with eyes to witness his goodness. They took the time to seek him, discuss his work, and learn what he was already doing in the community. The people of Vanuatu shared and showed Jesus to them, allowing everyone to experience his goodness together. This profound encounter left them all changed in ways they will never forget.

ⵄⵄⵄ

Isaiah 60:1 (NKJV)

Arise, shine;
For your light has come!
And the glory of the LORD is risen upon you.

Sustaining the Mission

Leading a mission trip comes with its share of pressures—managing logistics, supporting the team, and keeping the project on track. But to sustain the mission long term, holistic self-care is crucial. Taking care of your whole self—physically, emotionally, mentally, and spiritually—will not only help you as a leader but will also benefit the team and the ministry as a whole.

Holistic self-care means recognizing your limits and prioritizing rest before exhaustion sets in. This isn't just about spiritual renewal, though that's important. It's also about getting enough sleep, taking time to exercise, eating well, and incorporating your specific needs that help you recharge. Taking brief breaks throughout the day or stepping away for a moment of quiet can help maintain clarity and focus. A well-rested leader—one who isn't running on empty—is more effective and more able to lead with compassion, clarity, and wisdom.

Sustaining the mission also means balancing your personal life with ministry. Long hours, back-to-back teams, and prolonged time away from family can take a toll on relationships and well-being. It's important to establish healthy boundaries—taking time off between trips to rest and reconnect with loved ones. By doing so, you ensure that your own health and relationships remain strong, which ultimately enhances your ability to serve others.

Building resilience in your team is just as important. Mission trips are often demanding, and many team members are giving up their paid time off work and stepping away from their daily routines to serve. As leaders, we need to incorporate time for rest into the trip schedule, giving balance, focus, and rhythm to the experience. Whether it's taking a few hours to explore the local culture or simply allowing downtime, giving team members space to recharge is essential. These moments of rest not only help them perform better but also allow them to reflect on their experiences and return home with lasting, positive memories.

At the same time, engaging with the local culture provides a unique opportunity for the team to witness the beauty and richness of the community they're serving. For many, this may be a once-in-a-lifetime experience, and embracing it fully—through meaningful connections with the people, their traditions, and their landscape—can be just as nourishing as the work itself. Simultaneously, it allows the hosting community to proudly showcase the beauty of where they live. It would be a shame for visitors to leave having only experienced a small view of the area. By encouraging this exchange, both the visiting team and the local hosts deepen their connection, fostering mutual appreciation and understanding.

> "Short-term missions experiences are much more than accomplishing a service project. They're chapters in our lifelong journey. Each lesson we learn reshapes our understanding of the world, magnifying our spiritual connection and guiding us toward ethical engagement with those who differ from us."
> —Dr. David Wesley,
> Nazarene Theological Seminary

Ultimately, sustaining the mission is about more than completing projects. It's about ensuring that everyone participating, including those leading, comes away feeling fulfilled and inspired to continue serving long after the trip is over. By prioritizing holistic self-care—balancing rest with work, nurturing relationships, and embracing the cultural experience—you create a sustainable rhythm for mission work that is beneficial to everyone involved.

Staying on Mission

In ministry, our hearts are often tugged to address every need that comes our way. With needs being both genuine and ever present, it can be incredibly tough to say no. But our most important responsibility is to love the Lord and stay connected to our own spiritual journey—both for ourselves and for our team members. If we're running on empty, it can really impact our ability to serve those whom God has called us to help.

As leaders, we have a huge role in shaping the spiritual atmosphere of our teams. Our actions set the tone and serve as a powerful example for others. Leaders understand that their personal walk with the Lord is crucial, not just as a model for others but out of a sincere desire to live in truth and light. They make time for spiritual connection, knowing how vital it is for their own journey. Through their guidance, leaders help their team members experience the Lord's presence and activity—in their lives, within their relationships, through their projects, and across the world.

Every short-term mission is at its core a spiritual journey. Teams that walk in the light should expect to grow in their relationship with the Lord. Once the ministry project is complete, team members should be encouraged to weave the lessons they've learned into their ongoing Christian journey. This way, they can share their newfound insights and spread the light they've experienced with others.

Mark 6:30

The apostles gathered around Jesus and reported to him all they had done and taught. Then, because so many people were coming and going that they did not even have a chance to eat, he said to them, "Come with me by yourselves to a quiet place and get some rest."

Principle 7: Spirituality

Bearing Witness

English writer John Ruskin believes the greatest thing the human soul ever does in this world is when we see something and then tell what we saw in a plain, understandable way. He goes on to say that this is the heart of poetry, prophecy, and religion all in one.[1] Sharing stories from mission trips is a powerful way to inspire others and reflect on the impact of service. Bearing witness is our powerful testimony to the goodness of God.

When we share our experiences from mission trips, it's crucial to approach it with respect and honor for the people and cultures we encountered. As we talk about our stories, we're really sharing the goodness of God. It's important to highlight not just the needs but also the strengths and beauty of the communities we served. By acknowledging their resilience, resourcefulness, and unique qualities, we show respect for their dignity and for the work God is doing among them.

When sharing their stories, let's encourage our team members to shine a light on the strengths of the local ministries and partnering teams they're working alongside. It's important to focus on stories that don't make the mission team the sole hero but instead show the beauty of everyone coming together under the guidance of the Holy Spirit. By emphasizing how we accomplish more together than we ever could alone, we celebrate the creativity and dedication of the entire experience. This approach helps strengthen the bond between teams and reminds us that we all grow and are enriched when we work together. In this way, we honor the shared journey and the incredible ways God is at work through every hand involved, highlighting the true spirit of partnership.

When stories are shared with dignity, we open the door to real conversations and connections. This approach helps people engage more deeply, fostering a greater appreciation for the cultures and individuals we've worked with. By focusing on the strengths and beauty of those we serve, rather than viewing them as only needing help, we move past the us-them mindset. This builds trust

---

1. John Ruskin, *Modern Painters, Volume III* (Oakland, CA: University of California, 1856).

and shows respect for everyone involved, making sure we protect the dignity of those who are vulnerable and reducing the chances of misunderstandings or hurt feelings.

Sharing our experiences in this way also highlights the amazing work of God in both our lives and the lives of those we've served. It's not just about recounting what happened; it's about showing how faith and service can truly transform lives. By being authentic and respectful in our storytelling, we not only inspire others to get involved but also celebrate God's presence and work in every part of our journey. Our stories become a beautiful reflection of his love, grace, and hope, inviting others to see and experience how God is moving in their own lives and in the world.

Love in Action

An experience with Christ during a mission trip can profoundly transform a person's life—their future behavior, their thoughts, actions, and overall outlook on life. One of the most significant changes is a shift in priorities. Team members come home and often reevaluate what matters most, often placing greater emphasis on their spiritual journey, on relationships, and on finding new joy in serving others. This shift leads to a more purposeful life where decisions and actions are guided to align with their new insights.

Team members returning home from their trip having genuinely encountered Christ find a deepened sense of compassion and love for others. This is often expressed in a greater desire to serve and help those in need, igniting a renewed sense of purpose and calling. This newfound clarity can influence major life decisions, such as career choices and how they spend their free time, as well as how they engage in relationships. Some may feel led to participate in ministry, missions work, or other forms of service that reflect their commitment to Christ.

Leaders have a key role in helping missions team members make the most of their new insights and experiences. They can offer guidance, support, and opportunities for reflection. One great way to help integrate these experiences is by organizing debriefing sessions after the trip, encouraging group discussion, journaling, or one-on-one chats where team members can think about what they've learned and how it fits into their ongoing journey. By encouraging them to share their insights, leaders help team members solidify these lessons and gain a deeper understanding of their journey.

Ongoing support and accountability are also key to integrating missional insights. Leaders can maintain regular contact with team members after the trip, providing ongoing support through follow-up meetings and offering needed resources supporting their call. Encouraging team members to share their progress, challenges, and continued reflections helps them stay accountable to the commitments they made during the trip, reinforcing their new insights and behaviors.

Creating opportunities for service and involvement is a wonderful way to help team members continue applying what they've learned from their mission trip. Leaders can connect them with local community or church projects where they can practice the lessons from the mission field in their everyday lives. Whether it's volunteering, leading a small group, or joining outreach programs, these activities help make the missions experience a lasting part of their daily routine.

Leaders can also show team members how to weave missions experiences into everyday life by sharing their own stories about how these experiences have shaped their journey. By leading with their own examples, they provide a real-life illustration of how missions insights can influence one's life and decisions. This not only inspires team members to integrate their missions experiences but also ensures that the impact of the trip continues to enrich their lives in meaningful and lasting ways.

Insider Perspective
The Cracked Pots[2]

In 2012, after returning from a mission trip to Guatemala with a team from our home church, the idea of starting something closer to home began to take root. The trip had been a fulfilling experi-

---

2. Written by Debbie Hancock.

ence, and everyone had a desire to keep the spirit of service alive after returning home. My husband, Bill, was not keen on joining a traditional small group but was open to something different, so the idea for a smaller-scale version of Work & Witness at home was born. Word quickly spread about our new service group, and soon enough, a diverse mix of people joined—a lawyer, a teacher, a cook, even an ex-con. The group was affectionately called Cracked Pots, a name that seemed to fit perfectly. We met one or two Saturdays a month, working on various projects around the community—lawn work, roofing, and everything in between. Every session wrapped up with lunch, an essential part of the fellowship.

As time went on, Cracked Pots became more than just a service group; it became a family. The camaraderie, shared experiences, and joy of serving others bonded the group together in a way that no classroom setting ever could. Many members of Cracked Pots went on to join Work & Witness teams, inspired by the sense of purpose they found in serving others. Danaka and Ken were among those who found their way to Cracked Pots. With three kids in tow, they signed up for a mission trip to Masaya, Nicaragua, in 2015. The project, humorously dubbed the "dig a trench, fill a trench" mission, was challenging, but it sparked something in Danaka. She realized she could see herself as a missionary. Upon returning home, she started the process of getting her local minister's license and taking the necessary classes toward ordination. Ken wasn't as quick to embrace the call, but Danaka kept praying.

Their journey continued with another mission trip in 2016 to Tapachula, Chiapas, Mexico, with Stephen and Anne Sickel. This trip was unforgettable, not just for the scorching heat but also for the incredible work they did alongside the local church families. An eye clinic they helped facilitate drew people from all over who were eager for the chance to receive eyeglasses. Each step of the way, it was clear that God was working in their lives.

In July 2018, they joined the Sickels once more, this time at their home in Mexico. By then, Danaka and Ken had begun taking on more leadership roles. Their growth in faith and service was evident to all who knew them. Back home, Danaka joined the staff at their church, first as a bookkeeper and later as an associate pastor.

Principle 7: Spirituality

But her heart felt a tug in another direction. She sensed God calling her to start Sparrow, a house church that provided a much-needed space for worship and community. As her district's Work & Witness coordinator, she also led a team to Tobago, further spreading the message of service and faith.

As their children grew and pursued their own paths, Danaka continued to pray for Ken. Her prayers were answered in 2023 at General Assembly. After attending EXPLORE, Ken felt a profound calling to make a change—not just in his job but in his life. With God's guidance and the support of those around them, Danaka and Ken accepted an assignment to become sponsored missionaries to Thailand.

The story of missions is one of transformation—of how simple acts of service can ignite a lifelong passion for service. It's a testament to the power of community, faith, and the belief that everyone, no matter their background, has something valuable to contribute. As Danaka and Ken live out their next chapter in Thailand, the legacy of Cracked Pots lives on, reminding us all of the importance of serving after the mission trip is over.

Questions to Consider
The Cracked Pots

1. How did Debbie and Bill keep the spirit of serving alive after returning home from their mission trip?

2. What impact did Cracked Pots have on the community?

3. Why do you think Bill preferred serving to small group studies?

4. What was the long-term impact of Cracked Pots?

5. What lessons from Cracked Pots can you implement into your own ministry context?

Discussion
The Cracked Pots

Instead of letting the energy and passion from the mission trip fade, Debbie and Bill created a service group and channeled their energy into ongoing projects in their community. By continuing to serve together, they maintained the sense of purpose and camaraderie that they experienced during the mission trip. This local initiative allowed them to stay connected to the mission mindset, reinforcing their commitment to helping others even after returning home.

The group took on various projects from lawn work to roofing, helping those in need in their local area. Their work not only provided practical assistance to people in the community but also fostered a sense of unity and mutual support. The presence of a diverse group of individuals demonstrated that anyone could make a difference. This service also created a ripple effect, inspiring others to get involved in missions and community service, thereby strengthening the community's overall fabric.

Serving allows God's people to be the hands and feet of Christ, providing a dynamic and practical way to live out our faith. For some, the physical act of serving provides heartfelt connections as opposed to more traditional small group activities where one might be expected to read aloud, answer questions, or pray in front of others. Serving gives a sense of purpose and achievement, creating an entry point to the church body that some personalities are more comfortable with.

The long-term impact of Cracked Pots was profound. The group not only sustained the spirit of service among its members but also became a catalyst for deeper involvement in missions. Many members of Cracked Pots went on to join Work & Witness teams, expanding their influence beyond the local community. The group's sense of family and shared mission created lasting bonds, and their work inspired others to consider how they could serve in meaningful ways. In the case of Danaka and Ken, their involvement with Cracked Pots led them to a life of missionary service, culminating in their acceptance of an assignment to Thailand. The legacy of Cracked Pots is one of transformation and inspiration, demonstrating the lasting impact that consistent service and community can have on individuals and the broader mission of the church.

Spirituality Action Plan

1. Aligning with God's Mission
How can you ensure that the team understands that the mission projects belong to God? What practical steps will you take to reflect this truth in your planning and execution?

2. Prioritizing Heart-Level Connections
How will you guide the team to shift their focus from completing tasks to building meaningful, relational, and spiritual connections with the community?

3. Cultivating a Spiritual Atmosphere
What strategies can you implement to foster an environment of spiritual openness, renewal, and revival among the team during the trip?

4. Witnessing God's Work
How will you help team members actively witness and experience God's work firsthand during the mission, rather than remaining passive observers?

5. Engaging in Group Devotions
Where and when will group devotions take place, and how will these moments create space for reflection, unity, and spiritual growth?

6. Leading with Humility and Openness
How can you prepare the team to approach the mission with humility, valuing the spiritual leadership and expertise of the local church and community?

7. Acknowledging Spiritual Poverty and Beauty
How will you help the team recognize and reflect on the beauty, resilience, and spiritual strength of those they serve, even in the midst of material poverty?

8. Integrating Worship and Learning
What opportunities will there be for combined worship or devotions with the local church? How can this experience enrich the faith and understanding of all?

9. Encouraging Spiritual Reflection
How will you facilitate moments for team members to process their experiences through Scripture, prayer, and discussions, both individually and as a group?

10. Balancing Strategy and Spiritual Goals
How will you intentionally balance the logistical, strategic, and spiritual goals of the trip to ensure that God's work remains at the center of the mission?

11. Carrying the Impact Home
How will you encourage the team to take the spiritual lessons, renewal, and revival they experience on the mission field back to their local communities?

Conclusion: Following the Call to Dignity

Following the call to dignity in our lives brings us closer to Christ and reminds us that every person is created in the image of God. This truth helps us see and experience his love reflected in everyone we meet. Embracing this perspective means approaching others with a heart of a learner, engaging with them in the spirit of hospitality, and seeking to understand their cultures, backgrounds, and worldviews with genuine curiosity. By letting God shape our expectations, we focus on our spiritual purpose, aligning our hearts with the call in Romans 12 to offer ourselves as living sacrifices, holy and pleasing to God. This act of worship transforms us, renewing our minds and helping us discern God's will for our lives—good, pleasing, and perfect.

As we journey through life, let's hold fast to the powerful truth that Paul shares in Romans: we are one body with many members, each uniquely gifted and united in Christ. Whether our calling is to preach, serve, teach, encourage, give, lead, or show mercy, every role is essential. By embracing our gifts with grace and humility, we not only enrich the body of Christ but also help fulfill God's purpose in our communities and around the globe.

Living out these principles means letting love lead the way. Christ calls us to a love that clings to what is good, honors others above ourselves, maintains our spiritual fervor, and remains joyful in hope, patient in affliction, and faithful in prayer. We are to share with those in need and practice hospitality, reflecting his love in a world yearning for grace and truth.

In a world that craves authenticity and compassion, the dignity we uphold in our missions work shines brightly as a beacon of hope.

It bridges cultural gaps, addresses global challenges, and spreads the message of Christ's love. As we return from our missions, the principles of dignity we embrace inspire others and contribute to a broader movement of love and justice, advancing God's kingdom on earth.

In the grand tapestry of our journey, embracing dignity is the thread that brings us closer to Christ. By honoring each person we encounter and reflecting the deep love and respect Jesus shows, we transform not only our own hearts but also the world around us. Our dedication to treating others with grace, learning from diverse cultures, and building authentic relationships aligns us with God's will and strengthens our connection to his purpose. Let's move forward with the spirit of dignity and compassion, serving with renewed passion and sharing the boundless love of Christ in everything we do.

Defining Terms

General Terms

This section defines various words and phrases that are found throughout the book. Having a common understanding of what is meant by the words used will help us become more unified in our shared goal to build God's kingdom wherever we find ourselves on the mission field.

Accountability: Responsibility taken for actions and following through with commitments. Recognizing when it's necessary to apologize and committing to change hurtful behaviors.

Bear Witness: A witness shares their experience or firsthand knowledge as a testimony. In the Christian sense, they share the goodness of God as they have witnessed it.

Biblical Hospitality: To welcome, love, protect, and care for travelers or foreigners in need. Treating the stranger with brotherly love.

Briefings: Preparing others by giving them needed instructions for a plan or event.

Call: A deep knowing felt in the soul of a person when they are invited to join God's work in a particular way. A call is accompanied by faith and compels movement or direction.

Cold-Climate Culture: Cultures that view tasks as priority. Usually experienced in world areas where traditionally the climate has dictated getting things done in order to survive winter. Cold-climate cultures are conscientious of time and efficiency, direct in their communication, and prefer to be appreciated as independent individuals.

Context: The interrelated conditions around words and actions that bring meaning to the circumstances at hand. What happens prior to, after, the time, place, and setting in which circumstances occur is considered context, all having the ability to create or change meaning of what's being said or done.

Cultural Competence: Having knowledge of other cultures, including their holidays, histories, currencies, and politics. Cultural competence gives someone the ability to navigate another culture well and get things done.

Cultural Hospitality: Rules, roles, and expectations of hospitality are determined by culture. Hospitality is practiced worldwide, yet the expectations for guests and hosts varies greatly depending on culture.

Cultural Humility: Cultural humility goes a step further than cultural competence. It takes the posture from "I know all about this culture" to a more dynamic stance of "I am willing to learn about the intricacies of subcultures, relationships, and the hearts of people."

Culture: The observable social practices of a people group. These practices are often unspoken but are understood by everyone in the group. They are born out of an agreed-upon set of values. While these values may be less visible to the outsider, they are intuitive to the members of the group.

Culture Shock: When a person becomes acutely aware of the differences and/or conflicts in values, customs, and traditions between their home culture and the new culture they are in.

Debriefing: The process of talking through events after a task is complete. The task can be a mission, a project, or simply the activities of the day. Information is shared in order to unpack, learn, and process what happened. It places events in context and brings the broader scope of the overall mission into perspective.

Dependency Syndrome: Individuals or communities relying on assistance and depending on others for donations and outside help rather than creatively seeking sustainable solutions to reach their goals in their own context.

Defining Terms

Dignity: The innate worth of a person, place, or culture. It goes deeper than respect. It is the unearned yet priceless value that each person carries simply by being a child of God.

Discipleship: A journey that Christians make with other people as they go from no faith, to new faith, to mature faith, walking alongside others with evangelistic intent until they repent and believe. The journey continues until they are fully devoted, sanctified disciple makers.

Dominant Culture: The group that is most powerful in terms of wealth, prestige, status, and influence. They readily assume the role of leadership and move forward without understanding the full impact they have on others.

Ethnocentric: The belief that one's own culture, ethnicity, or way of life is superior to others. People with an ethnocentric perspective tend to evaluate other cultures based on the standards and values of their own.

Expectations: The strong belief that something will happen in the future. Planning that someone will or should achieve something.

Fairness: Treating people justly, with equality, according to practices and policies that are agreed on by those participating and those observing.

Fear-Power Worldview: The heartfelt needs of those living with this worldview strive to rid themselves of fear by gaining power over unseen spiritual forces. Fear-power cultures are often found in tribal settings.

Flexibility: A person or object having the ability to change or be changed easily according to the situation.

Guest: The one who visits, the stranger, or the one who is away from home. They have been invited. Their role is to graciously accept everything that comes with the welcome. The visiting team sets aside their way of doing things in order to learn the intricacies of their role as guests in the culture.

Guilt-Innocence Worldview: The heartfelt needs of the people with this worldview strive to remain innocent and free from guilt. Western cultures are often described as guilt-innocence cultures.

High-Context Culture: Communication is often indirect, and much is conveyed through nonverbal cues such as body language, facial expressions, and tone of voice. People may assume a shared understanding based on their shared cultural context.

Hijab: Generally refers to various head coverings conventionally worn by Muslim women. Although a hijab can come in different forms, it often specifically refers to a headscarf that covers the hair, neck, and ears while leaving the face visible.

Honor-Shame Worldview: Found in much of the world, especially including Asia and the Middle East, those who view the world through the honor and shame lens find value in honoring relationships, people, and societal status. They gain honor by being esteemed in the social community. They avoid shame at all costs, which comes when they do something that the social community disapproves of.

Host: Those who have permanent ownership of the project. They live there, they manage the project, and they will care for it after their guests leave. They anticipate and provide for the hospitality needs of their visitors in the spirit of brotherly love.

Hosting Team: The hosting team lives in the location where a short-term missions project will be taking place. The vision for the project originates *from* the hosting team, not from the missions team. The hosting team members are the rightful owners of the project. The hosts have been there long before the missions team arrives, and they will be responsible for the outcome and ongoing maintenance of the project after the team leaves. The voice of the hosting team carries the most weight; it should be trusted and heard above everyone else's.

Impact: The lasting, transformative change that is present long after an event takes place.

Incarnation: God became flesh and lived among us. God became human in the form of Jesus Christ, the Son of God, and second Person of the Trinity.

Defining Terms

Inclusion: The practice of providing equal access and a sense of belonging for everyone—those participating in the project, their families, the supporting churches, and the community at large.

Interpreter: A person who orally translates language through speech, such as a sermon given from a guest speaking another language during a church service.

Koinonia: A Greek word used frequently in the New Testament to describe the bond and heartfelt joy that are created through deep fellowship within the body of Christ. *Koinonia* is experienced when hospitality and the prayerful hearts of a body of believers come together in unity, creating something together that has eternal value for the kingdom of God.

Leader: Effective leaders prioritize the well-being and success of their team members by enabling them to accomplish tasks with dignity and foster a sense of trust and collaboration.

Light for the Path: A devotional book for short-term missions presented by the Church of the Nazarene, designed to guide the team to approach their mission with a focus on dignity.

Low-Context Culture: Communication tends to be more direct, and people may rely on verbal expressions rather than nonverbal cues. The emphasis is on clarity and precision in conveying the message.

Missions Team: A group of people, visiting from elsewhere, who contribute to an identified project initiated by the hosting team. Missions teams help by bringing resources. All team members should come with the posture of a learner.

Partnership: Two or more people, or groups of people, coming together to accomplish a goal. Together they bring the necessary and often different resources and skills to complete a project. Healthy partnerships always view each other as having equal value. All parties have something to give, and all have something to receive.

Per Diem: The daily allowance for each person's expected expenses while working on the project, including meals, lodging, and incidentals.

Poverty: A multifaceted condition characterized by lack of essential resources and opportunities necessary for individuals to lead a basic and dignified life, regardless of the prevailing level of wealth in their society.

Power Dynamics: The balance of power between two or more people. There is a distinction between those with power and those without; those with power have an advantage.

Prevenient Grace: The divine influence that precedes and enables human response, offering grace that draws us deeper into our relationship with God. It is grace that goes before us, preparing both missionaries and those they serve by fostering openness, understanding, and readiness for transformation.

Project: A defined activity that will assist in accomplishing a goal set by the hosting team to develop and expand the ministry of the Church of the Nazarene.

Resources: The people, expertise, labor, funds, equipment, and materials that contribute to the completion of a project.

Roles: There are many roles in a project. Each role is filled by a person who will accomplish tasks and duties specific to their assigned role. The roles align harmoniously to complete the overall project.

Saving Face: Refers to the act of preserving one's reputation, dignity, or honor in social interactions, particularly in situations that could potentially cause embarrassment, shame, or loss of respect. Saving face involves maintaining a positive self-image and avoiding situations or actions that may diminish one's standing in the eyes of others.

Service: The action of helping or doing work for someone else's benefit.

Short-Term Missions: The umbrella term for any team gathered from a local church or district going to minister alongside Christian brothers and sisters in another context for a short period of time. A short-term mission trip can last anywhere from seven days up to three months.

Site Coordinator: The person who facilitates the project on the ground. The site coordinator is appointed by the district or field and is approved by the region. The role of site coordinator can be filled by any approved field ministry coordinator who receives a visiting team. The main objective of the site coordinator is to be the point person between the hosting team and their culture, and that of the missions team. The presence of the site coordinator is significant. The hosting team needs to be heard and appreciated by the missions team. The site coordinator plays a key role in assuring this will happen.

Social Capital: Credit earned through resources and/or social influences. The social capital brought by short-term missions teams can be leveraged through local networks, bringing the ability to increase public esteem in leaders at the forefront of local ministries.

Spirituality: Christian spirituality consists primarily of living in the Spirit. When you turn to God and receive salvation, God's Holy Spirit comes to live within you. Your spirit comes alive, and you have a spiritual relationship with God that you could not have had otherwise.

Structural Dignity: The guidelines, policies, and regulations set in place to ensure that dignity is maintained for everyone who is impacted by the structure of the system.

Subculture: A smaller group within a larger group having a distinct culture differing from the larger one. For example, a Christian population residing within the mainly Buddhist country of Myanmar would be considered a subculture of that larger community.

Team Leader: Works directly with both the site coordinator and the missions team. The team leader will gain understanding of the entire scope of the project through detailed communication with the site coordinator, and will guide the missions team as they work to complete the project.

Transactional Relationship: A relationship where both (or all) parties are interested in what they have to gain. Partners do things for each other with the expectation of reciprocation. Transactional relationships serve a clear purpose, and when that purpose has been fulfilled, the relationship ends.

Translator: A person who translates written material from one language to another.

Vulnerable: People who can easily be physically or mentally hurt, influenced, or attacked. They are compromised already, and more harm can easily fall on them. They are dependent, exposed, and in need.

Warm-Climate Culture: In these cultures, relationships are highly valued. Usually experienced in climates where the temperatures are warm but this culture can be found in rural or tribal settings in cooler climates as well. Warm-climate cultures are event oriented, focused on relationships, indirect in their communication style, and value obligations to the collective group above personal wants and desires.

White Elephant: A possession or gift that is more of a burden than a benefit because it's expensive to maintain, impractical, or unwanted.

Work & Witness: A construction ministry in the Church of the Nazarene. Teams from one church or district come alongside another church or district locally or globally to help their brothers and sisters in Christ build physical structures that will serve them in ministry.

Witness: To observe, experience, or have firsthand knowledge of. To be a witness is to have information gained from personal observation or experience.

Worldview: The lens through which a person views the world. The subjective perspective of an individual based on their own values creates the paradigm by which they make sense of the world.

Project-Specific Terms

This list will define in detail the different types of short-term missions projects that might be found within the official missions structure of the Church of the Nazarene.

Approved Projects: Projects that are affirmed by the district, the field, the region, and the global church. When the project is affirmed and approved, it will be eligible to receive designated funds through the Global Missions office.

Community Projects: These projects fall under the responsibility of the local church. Leaders should encourage and support the church as they reach out to their communities. Funds brought in through donors and teams customarily go specifically to Nazarene properties. Exceptions at times may be necessary. It's important to have clear objectives for such funds, and working through the field strategy coordinator in these instances is essential.

District Projects: The district provides leadership development to the pastors and the churches on their district. The site coordinator listens to and works alongside district leadership to find projects that support the vision of the district, such as training pastors, updating district properties, or developing new ministries.

Field Projects: In world areas where there is a field structure in place, the site coordinator will work directly with the field strategy coordinator. The field office, seminary, or university may have several projects they dream of accomplishing. These can be great opportunities for an outside team to come alongside to help with a project. The team can bring funds, labor, and/or expertise.

Local Church Projects: The local church is at the heart of short-term missions. When two or more churches come alongside each other to complete a project, they encourage and learn from each other in significant ways. Local churches are on the front lines of building and expanding God's kingdom. They have a direct relationship with people who need to hear the gospel. Projects that support their ministries are essential.

Global and Regional Initiatives: At times, a region or the office of Global Missions will work within a field or district to accomplish a specific project.

Project: A defined activity that will assist in accomplishing a goal set by the hosting team to develop and expand the ministry of the Church of the Nazarene.

Terms Specific to the Church of the Nazarene

Today there are 30,000 Nazarene churches in more than 160 world areas. While the language, music, and cultural settings vary greatly, the Church of the Nazarene is connected as one through the structure of what we call the **global church**. This beautiful structure allows all Nazarenes to serve God together as a family in one accord. This list defines some of the structural and organizational terms and entities that allow the Church of the Nazarene to function globally as one segment of the body of Christ.

Board of General Superintendents: The Church of the Nazarene has six elected elders who constitute the Board of General Superintendents. This is the highest office in the denomination, and it is charged with the responsibility of administering the global work of the Church of the Nazarene. The general superintendents are elected by the global church during General Assembly. Each year one of the six general superintendents is appointed over one of the six world regions and will preside over all of their district assemblies and perform the ordination of ministers on the region.

District: Each field is divided up into districts that are led by district superintendents. The district superintendent works closely with field leaders, pastors, and churches on the district. They are the experts in their culture and context. The global church relies heavily on the district superintendent to develop the best strategies for church development on their district.

District Assembly: Every year each district in the Church of the Nazarene gathers to celebrate and conduct the business of the church. One of the general superintendents presides over the event, hearing pastors report on their ministries and ordaining new pastors.

Field: Each region is divided into fields. The field is led by the field strategy coordinator, who is selected and appointed by the global church. The field strategy coordinator works closely with the district superintendents and missionaries on their field. They understand

Defining Terms

the cultural context of the field and work together set the strategies for developing the Church of the Nazarene in their context.

Field Ministry Coordinator: The person who leads a ministry within the field structure. They work under the field strategy coordinator to help facilitate one or more ministries on the districts in their field.

General Assembly: Once every four years, more than twenty thousand Nazarenes and delegates of the global Church of the Nazarene gather to conduct the business of the church and celebrate what God is doing around the world.

Global Ministries: Through global ministries, the Church of the Nazarene makes an impact for Christ around the world. These ministries include: Nazarene Compassionate Ministries (NCM), Nazarene Missions International (NMI), Nazarene Discipleship International (NDI), Nazarene Youth International (NYI), Jesus Film Harvest Partners, Global Nazarene Publications, Work & Witness, and World Mission Broadcast. These global ministries have coordinators at each level of the global church (global, regional, field, district, and local church).

Global Ministry Center: The global headquarters for the Church of the Nazarene, located in Lenexa, Kansas, USA. The offices for the Board of General Superintendents, the general Secretary for the Church of the Nazarene, and each of the global ministries, including the Global Missions office, are located at the Global Ministry Center (or GMC).

Global Missions: The missions department of the Church of the Nazarene is led by the Global Missions director. The Global Missions office is located in the Global Ministry Center. They support the mission of the church by working with regional and field leaders. They work to expand the church globally through Nazarene ministries. An important role of Global Missions is to appoint and place Nazarene missionaries in strategic locations to the benefit of the global church.

Nazarene Compassionate Ministries (NCM): A global ministry of the Church of the Nazarene. NCM partners with local Nazarene congregations around the world to clothe, shelter, feed, heal, educate, and live in solidarity with those who suffer under oppression, injustice, violence, poverty, hunger, and disease. NCM exists in and through the Church of the Nazarene to proclaim the gospel to all people in word and deed.

NCM's Child Sponsorship Program: NCM's child sponsorship program is based on a holistic child development model that seeks to simultaneously address key aspects of a child's life—spiritual, physical, intellectual, emotional, and relational—through learning opportunities and developmental interventions. Through this model, children are encouraged to grow into the people God created them to be.

Nazarene Discipleship International: A global ministry of the Church of the Nazarene whose mission is to carry out the Great Commission to children, youth, and adults in preparation for a lifelong journey of being and making Christlike disciples in the nations.

Nazarene Missions International (NMI): The organization for mobilizing the local church in missions in the Church of the Nazarene. NMI is also the denomination's representative for missions on the district and in the local church.

Region: The Church of the Nazarene is divided into six major world areas, which are referred to as regions. The six regions are Africa, Asia-Pacific, Eurasia, Mesoamerica, South America, and USA/Canada. Each region is led by a regional director. On each of the six regions there is a regional office with missionaries and staff to assist with strategy, missionary placement, and the ministries of the fields in that particular world region.

About the Authors

Terri Taylor and her husband, Greg, are originally from Oregon. Their journey in missions began in 1997 when they volunteered with the Church of the Nazarene in Guatemala. Later that year, they moved to the Philippines to serve as global missionaries on the Asia-Pacific Region, coordinating Work & Witness. During their years overseas, they raised their two children and built lasting relationships as they were deeply shaped by the people they came to serve. Their time in the Philippines transformed their understanding of ministry, teaching them to walk humbly and with compassion in every cross-cultural setting. In 2011, the Taylors relocated to Lenexa, Kansas, to serve at the Global Ministry Center. Terri joined the Global Missions team, walking alongside missionary candidates as they discern their call and prepare for service around the world. Now back in Oregon, Greg and Terri serve missionally in their local community. Terri continues her service in Global Missions, encouraging, equipping, and supporting those stepping into missions with clarity, dignity, and the heart of Christ.

Stephen Sickel and his wife, Anne, met at and graduated from MidAmerica Nazarene University, where Stephen studied international business. United by a shared call to missions, they stepped into missionary service with the Church of the Nazarene in 2009 as Work & Witness coordinators in Costa Rica. Their journey led them to serve across Central America, eventually moving to southern Mexico. In 2019, they transitioned to the Global Ministry Center in Lenexa, Kansas, where Stephen now coordinates Nazarene Missions Teams, Projects, and Partnerships, formerly known as Work & Witness. Stephen and Anne are passionate about mobilizing the global church to participate in God's mission. They are the proud parents of three children who have grown up with a deep love for the global church and its mission.

www.ingramcontent.com/pod-product-compliance
Lightning Source LLC
Chambersburg PA
CBHW050855160426
43194CB00011B/2167